Ray & Me

by
Marci Soto

MONOGRAPH
PUBLISHING

Ray & Me

by
Marci Soto

Published by:
Monograph Publishing, LLC
1 Putt Lane
Eureka, Missouri   63025
636-938-1100

Library of congress number: Cataloging in publication date: On file

ISBN # 978-0-9799482-7-5
1 2 3 4 5 14 13 12 11

Printed in the United States of America by Multi-Ad printing

Book and dust cover design by Ellie Jones, MathisJones
        Communications, LLC
Cover design by William E. Mathis, MathisJones
        Communications LLC

Cover Photo of Marci and Ray by Don Eaker.
Photo, inside front flap, is the image that Marci sent Ray's manager when she called to talk to Ray for the first time.
Photo, inside back flap taken by Mitzi (Soto) Foster.
Picture on page vi is Marci's self portrait in charcoal.
Picture on page 7 is Marci's charcoal portrait of Ray.

Dedicated to Lisa and Mitzi
my beautiful daughters.
Thank you for your
love and support
now and throughout
our Ray Charles years.
I will love you
forever.

Acknowledgements

It has taken six years of writing to finally get to the completion of this book. I couldn't have done it without the help and encouragement of several very special individuals. I would like to acknowledge and thank, from the bottom of my heart, Lisa Soto O'Brien and Mitzi Soto Foster, my daughters, for their undying support and pride in their mom. To my best friend in the world, Mary Ann Cavaioli, I am grateful for her believing in me no matter what I endeavor to do and for listening patiently while I read every chapter of my book to her. Writing this book has been therapeutic, but at times so stressful I couldn't continue. I'm grateful to Mary Ann for gently nudging me on.

Special thanks goes to Don and Colleen Eaker for sharing so much of their lives with Ray and me, and sometimes with just Ray, when they made special trips to Dallas to visit him while he performed there. I truly appreciate Don taking all the wonderful photographs of Ray and me. I think the one on the cover especially captures the love that Ray and I shared.

I am grateful to Ellie Jones, my editor, for transitioning and polishing my factual writing so that it flows like a stream. She also did the design of this book and, the best part of all, has become a good friend through the process.

Thank you to Bill Mathis for taking my own charcoal sketches of Ray and me and blending them with Don's photo, then adding the musical notes "I Can't Stop Loving You" to ultimately design a beautiful and unique cover for my book.

Last, but by far, not least, thank you to Sharon Carmickle-Smith for transcribing the recorded conversations between Ray and me, and for somehow deciphering my illegible longhand, written in pencil with numerous eraser smudges. She pieced all my inserts into the story like a puzzle, which could not have been easy. I appreciate her family sharing her with me these past six years.

Henry

As I was writing this book, several people told me that they wanted to hear more about my ex-husband, Henry. Since my book is about my life with Ray, I didn't think it was that important to talk about Henry. But since there seems to be a real curiosity about him, I decided to add this section.

My life with Henry was a true roller coaster. There were many times during our years together that he was fun, exciting and very loving. We went places, laughed a lot, and had very special family times. But there was a mean and secretive side to him, especially after he had been drinking, and at those times I was terrified of him. It wasn't until years later, after he died, that I began to learn about his true character. I was so naive back then. There were things that he did that I did not understand, but when I questioned him, he would brush me off or tell me it was none of my business. Eventually I quit asking. I didn't want to know.

I found out later, for instance, that when we first met, Henry wanted to make me a prostitute. He thought I would make him rich. He said when he saw me, dollar signs were clicking in his head. That didn't happen. Instead, we got together and I became pregnant with Lisa, and eventually married him. After we divorced, he married Darlene, a girl he cheated on me with. They stayed together for several years.

One time during the Darlene years, Lisa and Mitzi remember swimming in their dad's pool when plain-clothed police raided Henry's apartment complex with shotguns. Everyone was terrified not knowing who the gunmen were or who they were going to shoot. The landlord hustled everyone from the pool as the gunmen rushed through. Mitzi and Lisa were shocked and frightened as they stood there and watched the police bust the door down and take their daddy away in handcuffs. Mitzi and Lisa had to wait for Henry's mother to come, by taxi, to pick them up. The girls remember clearly to this day how the "big men with guns came to take their daddy away."

Henry never stayed in a local jail for long–someone always bailed him out immediately. He was arrested many times and served time in some notorious prisons. Ironically, he was never in prison when he was with me, although he did time before and after our marriage.

Oddly enough, I came to like Darlene. She took excellent care of my girls when they went to visit their dad, and they still think of her. She divorced Henry when he was in prison, and we lost touch with her for awhile. Some time later we got a phone call from her and she told us she didn't want Henry to know where she was. He later married another woman, Sandra, and adopted her son, Mando. My girls and Sandra's kids have merged into what we consider one big, happy family.

I learned a lot about Henry from Sandra. Through her, I found out that Henry had owned many houses of ill repute, one of which was located on the first floor of the same building that housed the most infamous madam in New Orleans, Norma Wallace.

I learned that Henry also owned a bar, "Funky Butts" where many under-the-table "business deals" were conducted.

The most shocking information Sandra shared was Henry told her that, at one time, he was a hit man for the underworld. (Henry would *never* have told me that.)

She also told me that Henry and his "characters" had a judge in their pocket, and a physician "friend" who checked the "working girls" to make sure they were clean.

Henry took credit for the success of a young attorney in New Orleans, straight out of school, according to Sandra. Henry sent him so many "characters," that finally the mafia began using him. He has had a long-lasting career. (I did know this attorney.)

Sandra and Henry eventually separated, and during this time there was a woman who was crazy about him. Henry nick-named her "the Animal." Women just seemed to love him. This woman wanted Henry to leave Sandra, and when he wouldn't, she hung posters around town with Henry's picture and phone number on them stating, "I'm gay. Call me." Henry was furious and the fight began between the two of them. Shortly thereafter, Henry was jumped, severely beaten, and robbed of what they thought was his Rolex watch. Earlier, assuming that something was going to happen, Sandra told him to replace his Rolex watch with a cheap Quartz watch, and *that* was what was stolen.

The beating made Sandra and Mando angry, and they were accused of "drive-by shooting" her duplex. (Henry lived in the other side of the duplex.) Henry said he hit the floor as bullets flew through the windows. Sandra was questioned about the shooting, but she denied it and was never charged. Mando was arrested two days later and charged, but because of lack of evidence, was released.

Henry moved back in with Sandra and remained sober for awhile. Then he was diagnosed with throat cancer and had to have a tracheotomy. Lisa and Mitzi wanted to visit them, so they flew to New Orleans with a layover in Dallas. They called their dad from Dallas, and they could tell he had been drinking. He showed up at the airport drunk, so Mando drove them to their dad's house. Then Sandra put him out of her house for good.

By this time, Henry was very sick, so he went back to the woman who had done the posters and who had wanted him so badly. Sandra divorced him, even though she loved him (and still does).

The cancer spread quickly throughout his body. None of us saw him during this time. We thought he was living with a "Kathy Bates-type" character in the movie *Misery,* so everyone stayed clear. We called him during his illness, but because of his tracheotomy, he was extremely hard to understand.

Henry had a miserable death. He had gotten hooked up with a quack doctor who shot clorox and vitamins in his veins, so his death was very agonizing. The quack was paid with Henry's one-of-a-kind Rolex watch. There was a law suit against this "doctor," and Mando, Lisa and Mitzi each received a substantial settlement. It certainly did not compensate for the suffering she had put their dad through.

Henry did some pretty awful things to me when I was his wife, and I know it was largely because he always feared my leaving him. But, he came to my rescue many times. He had connections and could stop situations from happening, or at the very least, if they did happen, he could make someone sorry they were living.

The once-notorious Henry Soto is laid to rest in a crypt in Lake Lawn Cemetary in New Orleans Louisiana. The girls and I still miss him, especially when we go to New Orleans. Henry loved New Orleans with a passion. He was "Mr. New Orleans" to us.

Although I did not really want to talk about Henry in this book, I realize that he was an integral part of my life, and probably the main reason I became involved with Ray. All I ever really wanted was to be a wife and mother, living in a nice house, taking care of a loving husband and family. I always sought that normalcy, that tranquility in my life. I have found that peace now, but it was a long, long journey getting here.

and Ray...

I can't stop loving you.

Prelude

My 1966 white Mustang chugged lamely into the Baton Rouge truck stop spewing, sputtering and steaming like an old-time locomotive.

Oh God! Car trouble, and we weren't even out of Louisiana. The engine was running hot from a damaged radiator. If I had known, I would have had it fixed before we left.

I knew that my husband, Henry, had wrecked the car, but I didn't know how badly. I had no idea where he was. He could have been hot on my trail. I just didn't know, and I was plenty scared. My heart pounded and my mind was racing. I had to have a police escort to get me out of New Orleans and "safely" on the highway...but I still didn't feel safe.

All I wanted to do was get out of New Orleans alive. I was making progress until I had this unfortunate bit of bad luck. It was a major obstacle, but it wasn't about to stop me!

My two little girls, with their beautiful dark hair and olive skin, were snuggled comfortably in the back seat. We were leaving my abusive husband, their dad, for St. Louis, Missouri to my folks first, and then on to our final destination, Los Angeles, California–to the man who I had loved for eons but had only met in real life the year before–Ray Charles. Yes, *that* Ray Charles. That great musical genius.

So how did a neglected, abused housewife from New Orleans ever meet Ray Charles?

This is my story.

1
Ray and Me
∾∾

It was just another uneventful night at 1919 Cooper Road in Gretna, Louisiana, a quiet, peaceful suburb of New Orleans located just across the Mississippi River. The kids and I were alone, as we always were in the evening (alone, that is, unless my ex-husband "dropped in" unexpectedly as he often did). They were playing quietly while I cleaned and listened to *The Tonight Show* in the background. Suddenly, I heard Johnny Carson say, "Ladies and Gentlemen, the great Mr. Ray Charles."

I dropped my dust cloth and flew into the family room where I sat mesmerized for the next hour listening as Ray sang, *"I Can't Stop Loving You," "Georgia," "I Got a Woman,"* and more. I was hypnotized. I knew he was going to be on the Carson show because my friend Ann had called earlier so I wouldn't miss him. She knew I was mesmerized by Ray.

As I watched, Ray began talking about the plight of the black man, saying "The only thing the black man ever had was his music and his woman." What would it be like to be "his woman" I fantasized?

Listening to his voice, I had an overwhelming desire to touch him. I could feel him and smell his aroma even though I had never met him. I wanted desperately to be "his woman," but of course, I knew how impossible that was. Since the late fifties when I first heard his music, I had been, and still was, hopelessly in love with Ray Charles. The interview with Johnny Carson fueled my imagination, and the daydreams began swirling around in my head like a New Orleans hurricane. I was absolutely and completely obsessed with this soulful man.

I brought myself back to reality as I realized it was bedtime for my little girls, ages two and four. I tucked them cozily in bed and they listened intently to the story I was telling them as I bounced the bed and scratched their backs. That was part of our nightly routine (which also included singing their favorite bedtime song that I made up about the cows chewing bubble gum and the horses eating jellybeans). When they had finally fallen asleep, I looked at their sweet little faces, kissed them goodnight and tiptoed quietly out of the room.

Now I had private time, and I found myself desperately trying to remember everything that Ray and Johnny had talked about. I remembered that Ray had mentioned that he was currently playing at the Coconut Grove in Los Angeles, and would be there for the next few days. This could be my chance!

Never before had I known how to reach him, but *now* I did. I was going to act on that bit of information–at least I was going to try–but first I had to work up the courage. That meant calling my three girl friends, Ann, Linda and Mary Ann for reinforcement. I was about to do the most daring thing I had ever done in my life–call Ray Charles!

Ann and Linda were my two best friends in New Orleans. Ann and I had known each other since we were in high school in my hometown in Southeast Missouri. Linda was a more recent acquaintance from uptown New Orleans, where I had lived before moving to Cooper Road.

Mary Ann was, and still is, more like a sister to me than a best friend. I have known her since my late teens and there isn't anything that Mary Ann doesn't know about me. She occasionally reminds me of things that I have long since forgotten, some of which I wish she would forget!

Needless to say, I got very little sleep that warm night in July as I planned my strategy, going over and over in my head what I was going to say if I really reached Ray. Common sense told me I would never get through to him, but I was a nervous wreck anyway, just thinking about it. The other thing I was thinking was *how am I going to call the love of my life when my husband might pop in at any moment?*

2
Calling the Coconut Grove

ೋ

My husband, Enrique Lorrenzo Soto, a.k.a. Henry, and I were separated. Even though *he* was living with another woman, he was still very present in my life and very much in control of me, or so he thought. I was deathly afraid of him and had to consider every move I made because even little things made him angry.

The first thing I did that next morning after hearing Ray on *The Tonight Show* was wake up my little girls, watch them stretch and yawn sleepily and listen to them tell me about their dreams. This was our usual routine and this sunny morning in July of 1968 was no exception. We went into the kitchen for breakfast, usually a freshly picked plantain from our tree on the patio and oatmeal or French toast. They always watched cartoons while they ate, and that gave me a chance to call Ann and Linda. Mary Ann lived in Kansas City, so I only made that long-distance call when it was something really important. Even though I couldn't afford to call often, we wrote lots and lots of letters. I missed her.

When Ann had called the night before to tell me that Ray was going to be on Johnny Carson, she made me promise to call her the next morning. I was dying to talk to her and tell her of my plan to call the Coconut Grove. My mind was spinning. *How crazy can you be, Marci? You can't just pick up the phone and call Ray Charles!*

When I told Ann my plan, she surprised me when she said, "Go ahead. What do you have to lose? You might be able to talk to him, and then at least part of your dream will be fulfilled. You'll hear his voice on the phone with you."

"Oh my God, Ann! I don't know what I'd do if I actually spoke with Ray Charles on the phone."

"Well," she said. "You have all day to think about it."

"Yes, I know. He probably won't be there until 7:00 or 8:00 tonight and that's about 9:00 or 10:00 our time."

What if Henry walks in?? I'll have to hang up on Ray Charles! Oh, God!!!

When I talked to Linda, she said the same thing that Ann had said. "Marci, go ahead and call him."

I still wanted to talk to Mary Ann before I made my final decision. I figured this call qualified as "important," so I called her. She had also seen Ray on *The Tonight Show* and told me to go for it. She said, "You're so unhappy. Maybe you'll really get to talk to him. It's worth a try."

That did it. With Mary Ann's final encouragement, my mind was made up, and the day was looking longer and longer.

I busied myself doing the usual morning chores; making beds, picking up toys, doing laundry, washing the breakfast dishes, etc. The kids wanted to play in their little pool, which was beyond a wall of sliding glass doors on the newly built patio. The patio was concrete, inlaid with beautiful geometrically cut slabs of maroon and cobalt blue marble, and secluded by a red-wood privacy fence. (The fence has a story of its own...but I'll get to that later on). Soon it was lunchtime, then naptime, and then more private time for me. Would this afternoon *ever* end? I had to keep busy or I was going to go crazy.

To calm myself down, I decided to draw. I set up my easel and began sketching a charcoal portrait of Ray. I was copying his portrait from one of his album covers, and I was listening to his music as I sketched. I was obsessed. By evening, I had his face outlined and his features in place, and I was beginning to add the shading. I had never done a charcoal drawing before in my life!

When Henry came in, he said, "Damn, baby. That's very hip. I didn't know you could do that. I always knew you were artistic–you know, the way you decorate and the caricature you

painted of me on "the throne," but I damn sure didn't know you could do a real portrait."

"I didn't either," I responded.

After he scrutinized the portrait, he ate dinner with the kids, made some phone calls (he was *always* on the phone), and then he left. I couldn't wait for him to leave, even though his compliment about my drawing made me feel very confident. I sketched six portraits of Ray that year.

Finally, it was evening, and I was scurrying around, bathing the kids and getting them ready for bed. I was in a frenzy, anticipating that crucial moment when I would actually pick up the phone and dial the number for the Coconut Grove. Oh, God!!

Both Linda and Ann called to see if I was really going to do it, or if I had lost my nerve. I honestly wasn't sure. They began coaching me on.

It was seconds before 9:30, 7:30 p.m. Los Angeles time, and I was sinking fast. They kept saying, "Do it!" So when I hung up with them, I took a deep breath and called the Coconut Grove, person to person, for Mr. Ray Charles. Holy Shit!! Was I really doing this? Yes I was, and the phone was ringing!

A man with a melodious voice said, "Hello?"

The operator said, "I have a person to person call for Ray Charles."

The man said, "I'll take it, operator."

I could barely speak, but squeaked out a little "Hello."

He said, "May I ask who's calling?"

I said, "My name is Marci. I've been in love with Ray Charles for years, and I would love just to be able to talk to him."

"Well, I'm Joe Adams, Ray's manager. Will I do?"

"No, I'm sorry. You sound very nice but there are no substitutes for Ray."

Joe said, "Well, dear, in that case why don't you write a note and send a full length photograph of yourself to 2107 W. Washington Blvd., Los Angeles, California."

Then he said, "Ray isn't here right now and we'll be in San Francisco for the next couple of weeks, but when we return, you will hear from him."

I was gushing, "Really? Are you sure?"

"Yes, I can assure you that you will."

"Oh, thank you Mr. Adams."

"Joe will do just fine," he said.

I thanked him again and said goodbye.

I couldn't believe my good fortune–I actually spoke to Ray Charles' personal manager. I was ecstatic...I was euphoric. It didn't seem real, but it was. I really *had* talked to Joe Adams, just about the closest person to Ray Charles that I could imagine.

Now all I had to do was find the most flattering picture of me, one that Joe Adams would find attractive. Obviously, he was going to act as Ray's eyes and would be the one describing me to Ray, so I wanted that description to be appealing enough to make Ray Charles want to talk to me...and possibly meet me...*Oh my God Marci! Are you crazy? You've gone way beyond reality this time!*

Needless to say, the rest of that night was spent in a daze as I relived my conversation with Joe Adams. *Am I really going to hear from Ray Charles? Of course not, Marci. Don't be ridiculous.*

The first thing I did was call Ann, Linda, and of course Mary Ann. Ann wanted to know how I could be sure that Joe Adams really was who he claimed to be.

"I don't know, but I believe him," I said. "I thought there was a certain air of authority in his voice."

Linda was excited too, and Mary Ann said, "Marci, I knew you could do it. And when he gets your picture, and Joe tells him how beautiful you are, he will want to call you."

She made me feel better, but I still had two weeks to wait, and I still had that letter to write.

Days later, after much contemplation, I set about trying to

write it. I made myself a pot of strong, black coffee and situated myself at the breakfast table. I watched the feathery fronds of the weeping willow tree sway in the breeze, and that helped to quiet me so that I could think. But nothing came to me. I had no idea what to say to this man who I so adored, yet knew absolutely nothing about…

Actually, I did know something. About ten years ago I read about Ray's drug bust in *Life Magazine*, but I had heard him say on television later that he was now drug free. I probably would never have tried to contact him had he not freed himself of heroin, especially after what I had heard Henry say about some of his underworld associates who were addicts.

Personally, I've never done drugs and my tolerance for people who do is very low. As much as I loved Ray, I would never have had the respect for him that I came to have.

I had to stop daydreaming and get back to writing the letter. I had already whiled away a few days trying to think of what to write, but the words just wouldn't come. I really wanted my letter to be there when Ray returned from San Francisco, so after considerable thought, I just wrote simply:

> "Hi Ray.
> I've loved your music ever since I first heard it.
> I fell in love with your picture and I desperately
> want to meet you. I'm five foot three inches tall
> and weigh one hundred and five pounds. I have
> dark hair and hazel eyes. I hope my picture
> pleases you, and you decide to call me."

I enclosed a full-length photo taken by professional St. Louis photographer Peter Patrick who had shot pictures of me for a local magazine. I still had my portfolio, thank God!

I signed my short note, wrote down my phone number, and crossed my fingers. Now I had to get it in the mail without Henry finding out. Even though he was living with another woman, I was not allowed much freedom, and certainly not to be with another man. Finding my letter would have guaranteed me a vicious beating. I felt so special–as if I had the biggest secret, and everyone would be so shocked if they knew that I, (little ol' me), was mailing a personal letter to Ray Charles. I was in heaven.

My little girls, Lisa and Mitzi, walked with me to the corner and I deposited my letter safely in the mailbox. Watching Lisa skipping along and Mitzi trying to keep up with her was amusing and heartwarming to me. As we returned home from our little stroll, I found myself reflecting on the events of the past few days, reminiscing about the past and what had brought me to this point in my life.

3
Gaslight Square

෨෧

I drifted back to a time when I first began listening to Ray Charles. It was probably about 1958, and I was working at the Park Plaza Hotel barbershop as a manicurist. I was almost twenty years old and had just discovered Gaslight Square.

Gaslight Square was *the* hot spot in the Central West End area of St. Louis in the mid 50's and 60's, and was comparable to Bourbon Street in New Orleans. Many up-and-coming stars got their start there, or at least made their presence known in the bars and nightclubs.

My life was exciting in those days. Gaslight Square was growing at the speed of light. Olive Street, for those few blocks, was lively and charming, with the lovely gaslights giving off a foggy, ethereal glow. The many clubs lining each side of the street were booming – they were busy every night of the week. People of all walks of life were interacting with one another, in and out of the clubs. The sidewalks were as crowded as they are in South Beach today with interesting people everywhere.

I had just met Mary Ann, who, nearly fifty years later, is still my best friend. Her boyfriend, Pat Aluisa, owned a club called "Le Jazz Hot" where a trio performed nightly; Bobby Betz, a blind pianist, Maxine Kent, a vocalist, and Dallas Bartley, the bass player.

Dallas had written a song called "*Early in the Morning*" which was on Ray's album, "*Genius Sings the Blues.*" Boy, was I ever impressed when I heard that song! (I found out later that Dallas made very little money, if any, for writing it). I wanted to hear the song over and over–anything to bring me closer to Ray Charles. It was at that moment that I fell madly and irretrievably in love...with a voice on an album. It was crazy, but it was so real.

Mary Ann and I saw many of the stars that got their start at Gaslight Square. We saw Barbara Streisand sitting on a tall stool at the Crystal Palace, her face powdered chalk white, singing her wonderful songs. Alex Cord and Barry Primus were acting in a play, also at the Crystal Palace. Later, the Smothers Brothers, Lenny Bruce, Woody Allen, and Phyllis Diller, among others, performed there.

Dakota Staton and Nancy Wilson performed up the street at Georgies. Jeanne Trevor, our own local and wonderful jazz singer, worked down the street at the Black Horse. Trio Tres Bien, was on the corner at the Dark Side.

Dixie Land Jazz played at the Golden Eagle and Silver Dollar. There was a piano bar at the Red Carpet (where I wound up working after living in Los Angeles for a couple of years).

The "Roaring Twenties" was showing a shoot-'em-up gangster play, and Steve McQueen was in St. Louis filming "The Great St. Louis Bank Robbery."

One night, just as I had gotten home from a date, my phone rang. It was almost midnight and I couldn't imagine who was calling. It was Pat Aluisa, Mary Ann's beau. He was at his club and told me that Steve McQueen was there at a party and wanted to meet me. Pat frequently threw big, fabulous parties at their carriage house ,located behind"Le Jazz Hot" and any celebrities in town usually made an appearance.

"No thanks," I told him. "Not tonight. It's late and I have to work tomorrow."

I had no idea who Steve McQueen was! He had a hit television series called *Wanted Dead or Alive* , but I had never seen it. At twenty years old, I wasn't watching much television.

Steve got on the phone and said, "Marci, Pat showed me your picture in the *Guzzlers Gazzett,* (a local magazine where I had appeared on the cover), "and I would love to meet you. I'll send a car for you."

I said, "Oh, no thank you. I can't make it tonight–maybe another time."

"Please let me pick you up, just for an hour," Steve persisted.

"Okay, okay, but I'll drive myself," I said.

I thought to myself, "I'm not going to get stuck with someone I don't even know. If I drive myself, at least I can leave when I want to."

Steve was waiting for me and greeted me at the door. He put his arms around me in a warm hug and said, "Hi Marci, I'm Steve, and I'm so glad you came."

He was great. He was so nice and attentive ... and talkative. I liked him. We went to my apartment after socializing for an hour or so, and spent the rest of the night talking. The next morning, I dropped him off at Pat and Mary Ann's carriage house, where he was staying while filming. That night he was back in my apartment, and the next morning, he left for L.A. By the time he returned to St. Louis to wrap his film, I had moved to Los Angeles. Before he left, he had given me the number to Universal Studios where he would be filming and asked me to call him.

4
Moving to L.A.
❧

When I found an apartment and job in Los Angeles, I called Steve McQueen. The studio told me that he was on location filming, but to leave my number and they would make sure he got the message. Shortly thereafter, one of my co-workers came to my desk and said, "Marci, you have a call on hold. He says he's Steve McQueen. Is it the *real* Steve McQueen?"

I laughed and said, "Yes. I have been expecting him to call."

He came to my apartment and I introduced him to my roommate, Jinny. She always seemed to have a chip on her shoulder and was hard to get along with. I asked her if I could borrow a tea bag to make Steve a cup of hot tea, and she said no. He really wanted a cup of tea, so we left in his old, beat-up, wood paneled station wagon and headed to a drive-in where he could get one. He said, "Marci, you have to move. Get away from that crazy bitch. She's nuts and one day she might hurt you."

I had told him other stories about Jinny, and her attitude about the tea bag was the final straw. Steve's warnings scared me, so I acted fast. The very next day, I found a cute little cottage on La Cienega Boulevard in Hollywood and moved. Everything was furnished so all I had to move were my clothes, which I could fit in a cab. (I didn't have a car then).

Steve was an interesting guy–a little quirky sometimes. He bummed cigarettes because he was always trying to quit smoking and rarely carried them. Once when we were out, he ran out of cigarettes so we stopped at a drugstore. He said, "I won't be long unless I get stopped by fans."

I watched him dodging around, holding a magazine in front

of his face as he came out the door. He acted like he was being chased in hot pursuit, but no one had even been looking at him. This happened long before he became a super star and a house-hold name.

Ironically, I never saw or heard from him again. Years later, I read of his illness in the tabloids. He had gone to a hospital in Mexico and the address had been published in the tabloid. Mary Ann and I both wrote to him, but neither of us got a response. We really hadn't expected to, we just hoped our letters reached him.

࿖

I continued living in my cute little cottage in Hollywood, and working as a dealer car trader. Our office was on the corner of the famous Hollywood and Vine. Ironically, Ray's booking agent, Hal Zieger also occupied an office there and had booked Ray at the Hollywood Palladium. (I didn't know any of this until recently, after reading Michael Lydon's "*Ray Charles: Man and Music*"). Had I been aware that Ray's booking agent was right there, I would have begged him for an introduction. (After I learned some of the other things that he had written in his book, however, I might not have been so interested!).

I hadn't actually known that Ray lived in L.A. at the same time I lived there. Those days, he was heavily into heroin, so I'm glad I didn't know that part of Ray's life. It would have made me sad.

࿖

One morning my phone rang at work. I answered, "Dealer Trader" and a very pronounced southern sounding female said, "Haaa ahmm, Jean down here at the Lincoln Mercury Dealer in Downy. Do you have a..." and she described the car that she needed.

I said, "Where are you from Jean?"

"Birmingham, Alabama," she drawled. "And I saw you last night at the car show. Your boss was taking you around introducin' you to the dealers."

We were not supposed to fraternize with the dealers but because of my appearance back then, I made a lot of trades so my boss encouraged me to be friendly with them. I dated a couple of them and they were very nice to me, but I thought they were too old, so I stopped dating them.

Jean wanted to get together and go out. Since I didn't have a car and she had access to a dealer auto, she opted to meet me at my cottage and then stay for the weekend. I panicked at her suggestion–I didn't have curtains or even a bedspread. No dishes, pots, nothing; just clothes, a few washcloths and towels, that's it. How could I have a weekend guest when I had nothing? What was I going to do? I didn't have the money yet to buy all those things and here I was about to have a guest.

I thought, "I'll call Johnny Noga." He was Johnny Mathis' manager who I had met in St. Louis at the Chase Club when I went to the Johnny Mathis show.

He said, "Get ready, I'll pick you up and we'll go to the store."

He was there in no time and we went to the department store just across the street from where I worked. I picked out the things I needed; he paid for them, then took me to lunch, and dropped me back at my cottage. I talked to him occasionally after that but never saw him again. No–I never slept with him–not once–and I even flew to Chicago with him to a Johnny Mathis concert. He was just a very nice man. During that era, men wined and dined a woman and didn't expect anything except her company in return. When I worked at the Chase Park Plaza barbershop as a manicurist, all I had to say was, "I like that dress in the window at Saks" or "Everyone is wearing Joy perfume," and very soon I would have it. I'm not ashamed to say that I got used to that generosity.

Johnny helped me get the items I needed to get my apartment together and ready for my guest. That Saturday morning I heard this heavy southern accent asking my neighbor where my place was. I hurried out to greet her. Jean was cute as a button – blonde curly hair, blue eyes, just adorable. We became good friends.

I eventually quit my job and moved to Downy, California to a huge apartment complex with a pool. Jean became my new roommate. We had such good times together. She would be a very significant person in my life when, in 1969, I moved back to Los Angeles from New Orleans to be with Ray.

So, back to my story...

5
Calling Ray Charles

So there I was, that hot July in 1968, waiting impatiently day after endless day, for the phone to ring, hoping against hope that Ray Charles would be on the other end, but not allowing myself to believe it could really happen. Hoping, wishing, and dreaming, but never actually believing.

I continued my charcoal drawings as if I were willing him to call me. Henry kept telling me, and everyone else he knew, how good my drawings were. If Henry ever found out I was waiting to actually hear from the man in the portraits, I wouldn't have been around for Ray's call–or anything else for that matter.

Henry wasn't worried about Ray Charles, though. How would someone like me ever meet someone like him?

Henry would have just said, "Get your head out of the clouds...stop thinking you're Marilyn Monroe and get back down to earth with the rest of us. Stop acting so high and mighty. You ain't shit."

Being stuck in Gretna, Louisiana with very little freedom, there really wasn't anything for Henry to worry about. He was right. I wasn't shit. I was pretty damned ordinary.

Two weeks came and went and no phone call. I knew that my worst fears had come true. He wasn't going to call. I was right. Who the hell was I to think Ray Charles was going to call *me*? It was just a fluke that I had gotten in touch with his manager in the first place. I told myself how absurd I was to have allowed myself to get so excited over such an impossibility. *Come on Marci, snap out of it.*

On the 15th day I told my friend Ann how miserable I was,

and how disappointed. I said, "I'm gonna call R.P.M. Studios tonight just to see if he's back from the tour."

She said, "Go ahead. Maybe you'll find out something and at least end this anticipation."

End the anticipation? How about end this dream–I just needed to get it over with. I was sick at heart, but that night, around 11:00 p.m., long after I put my kids to bed, I called R.P.M. Studios. It took that long to work up my courage.

With my heart palpitating so hard it was about to pop out of my chest, I dialed the number. The phone was ringing and ringing and ringing. I just knew that no one would be there. Finally someone said, "Hello," in that familiar melodious voice. It startled me to death! "Joe Adams here."

Nervously I said, "Hi Joe, it's Marci from New Orleans. Do you remember me?"

"Yes, indeed I do. I have your picture right here, and my dear, you are beautiful. Are you sure I won't do?" he teased. "And you're in luck. Guess who's here?"

"Ray?" I half whispered. I couldn't breathe. "Oh my gosh."
Joe said, "Here he is."
Then I heard, "Yeaaah," a sweet growling sound.
I said, "Is this really Ray Charles?"
"'Fraid so," he said.

I must have babbled incoherently, I have no idea what I said, but he stopped me by saying, "Listen honey, you sound so sweet, and I would love to talk to you, but Joe and I are kind of busy. Could you call me tomorrow around 2:00 p.m.?"

"Oh yes, yes I can." He gave me a private number, "Yes, yes until tomorrow then."

For nearly thirty years I had the same reaction to his voice that I had that first night–millions of butterflies in my stomach. I didn't sleep that night. I had finally spoken to Ray Charles! I had actually heard his voice talking to *me*! I had never been so elated in my life. My body was trembling. My heart was beating so fast I thought it would burst. I felt weak, faint, and dizzy, all at the same time.

It was too late to call Ann or Linda, but I knew I could always call Mary Ann, any time, day or night (and I still can). She was always the one I needed to confide in the most.

"Mary Ann," I cried. "You're never gonna believe it!"

"What? What?" she said.

"I just talked to Ray Charles and he asked me to call him back tomorrow at 2:00 p.m.!"

"Really!! Oh my gosh!!! Are you all right?"

"No! No! I'm not. I'm a wreck," I said. "I don't know what to say. Oh, God! I'll probably sound ridiculous. I'll be so nervous."

"You'll be okay," she said reassuringly. "Just be yourself. Go sit down, be quiet and think about what you want to say."

"But I can't think. I'm in a daze, and I'm completely blank. I'll just have to be spontaneous."

Mary Ann said, "Well that's how you usually respond."

She was right. I never rehearsed what I was gonna say. I just blurted it out. For the good or the bad of it, that was just me. And believe it or not, that spontaneity and honesty was one of the things Ray loved about me.

I was so very grateful for my friends during this time. I called them my loyal support team. They were always there for me. I don't think I could have accomplished what I set out to do without them encouraging me. I truly needed and appreciated them.

Once again I was playing the waiting game–now I was waiting for 2:00 p.m. the next day. Hour upon endless hour, I was parading through my house, wondering about everything. *Will Henry be here at 2:00 p.m. tomorrow? What will I talk about? Will Ray even be there?* Then back to bed. Sleep continued to elude me. Then up again, sketching on my portrait. This madness continued until the wee hours of the morning. Finally, I became weary and fell into an exhausted sleep just as it was time for my little girls to get up. I had slept almost two hours, and in came Lisa and Mitzi climbing in bed with me. "Mama," the accent was on the second ma as in Ma-ma', New Orleans style.

It was time to get up and start my daily routine. But this day was different; I was calling Ray Charles–and my heart was skipping beats.

I was so excited and nervous...and more than a little scared–not so much of getting caught by Henry, but of the excitement and adventure that had invaded my quiet, uninteresting life. In my wildest dreams, I could never have imagined that I would be preparing my children's breakfast and, at the same time, worrying about what I was gonna say to *Ray Charles* on the phone! There were flashes in my mind saying, *You're crazy. You're dreaming. You're hallucinating. This isn't happening.* But it was definitely happening–and I could only hope I didn't have heart failure before it did. I, "Miss Marci-you-ain't-shit-Soto," had been given Ray Charles' private phone number, by none other than Mr. Ray Charles himself. Yes!!! Yes!!! Yes!!!

After breakfast, I did my morning routine. I was like a robot. I functioned, but my mind was three thousand miles away in Los Angeles, California. I wondered what Ray was doing at that moment? Was he anticipating this phone call too? Was he eagerly waiting for 2:00 p.m.? *Of course not Marci, don't be silly. He hardly knows you exist.*

Time was creeping by at a snail's pace. *God. It's only 11 o'clock. I have three more hours to wait.* I started cleaning my house. I was always neurotic about keeping my house clean. I still am.

At 1:45 p.m. I turned the vacuum off, put Lisa and Mitzi down for a nap, and hoped to God Henry didn't pull in the driveway. At 2:10 my kids were sound asleep, and it was time. I wasn't *right* on time because I didn't want to appear too eager.

"Operator, I'd like to place a person-to-person call to Mr. Ray Charles, please." Then I gave her the number. I felt good inside knowing that number. I felt special. I was also nervous, trembling like a leaf.

The phone was ringing. Then, I heard that sweet, growling sound that I would hear for the next half of my life.

"Yeah," Ray said.

"Person-to-person for Mr. Ray Charles."

"Yeah, all right operator. I'll take it."

I was giddy as a schoolgirl. "Hi Ray. It's Marci."

"Yeah, I thought it might be you. Listen honey, I find this kind of strange. No one has ever just called up and actually gotten me on the phone. Do you have E.S.P. or something? Maybe you're a good witch."

"No, no I'm not. Well...then again, some people might think so."

Ray laughed. "Well, how did you manage to get me?"

He was really curious and seemed a little concerned about it.

"I saw you on the Johnny Carson show. I've always loved your music, and I also like your looks, so I just took a chance and called the Coconut Grove. Your manager, Joe Adams, came to the phone. Didn't he tell you?"

"Yeah, he did, but I must say, I'm astonished by all this. Do you know how rare it is for someone to get through to me?"

"I'm sure it is, but it wasn't for me."

"I know," he laughed. "That's what scares me."

"Well, I'm normal, so don't be scared." (After my nearly thirty-year tenure with Ray, I proved a thousand times over that that statement was certifiably wrong).

"Marci, you sound so sweet. Is there any chance of me meeting you?"

I nearly fell over. *Oh my gosh!! Is there ever!!* But I just said, "Oh, yes, that would be wonderful."

What I didn't tell him was that I was married to the devil him-self–Diablo, Mephistopheles–in the form of one Enrique Lorenzo Soto. I would tell Ray about him later. I certainly didn't want to scare him off and miss the opportunity to finally meet him.

Ray said he would check his itinerary and call me back in a couple of days to let me know his schedule.

I didn't know how I was going to arrange that meeting without getting beaten half to death, but I also knew that noth-ing short of death (or something wrong with one of my kids), could stop me. My mind began working overtime.

In my wildest dreams I never expected anything like this to happen. I couldn't believe I even talked to him, much less heard him say he would like to come all the way to New Orleans just to meet me. True to his word, though, he called two days later. I was listening to *"Drown in My Own Tears,"* a song by Ray that I especially liked.

The phone rang. I picked it up and said, "Hello?"

"Yeah, Marci, this is Ray Charles."

"I know who you are," I flirted.

"Oh yeah? How did you know that?"

"Ray, I could tell your voice anywhere."

"Listen honey, Joe's going to New York next week, and I was wondering if it would be a good time to see you? I'll go to New York with him and we'll just come on down to New Orleans. That way I can kill two birds with one stone."

I hate that saying. I still don't even know what he meant when he said it to me. I guess Joe had business in New York, and Ray had business in New Orleans. I really wanted to meet him in St. Louis, though, because my folks were there and it was a lot safer for me. So I said, "Could we meet in St. Louis since its closer to New York and my folks are there?"

His response was, "St. Louis is not closer to New York."

"It seems like it is to me," I argued.

"No, listen honey, New Orleans is closer. Take my word for it. I travel all over the world, and I know what I'm talking about."

"Okay," I said. I tried to steer him away from New Orleans, but it didn't work.

That was the first of many differences of opinion we had that I lost. Over the next three decades, I found that he was right about almost everything. I remember saying to Bob Taylor, Ray's valet, after I had known him for a while, "Gosh, Ray thinks he knows everything."

Bob's response was, "Yes, but the truth is, he does."

And he did. He really was a wise man. During our relationship, I never ceased to be amazed and awe struck by his intelligence. I truly did listen to every word he said.

He had to call me back a few more times to fine-tune our arrangements, and the next time he called was on the weekend. I was just busy talking away, so intrigued that I didn't hear Henry pull in the driveway. The back door opened and there he was. I slammed the phone down!!! Oh my God! My heart was pounding through my chest.

"Who were you talking to?" he asked.

"What!!!" I said too loudly. "Oh, Linda."

Then he said, "Well, did you hang up on her?"

"No, I almost dropped the phone." I lied.

I was panic stricken that Ray would call back, but he didn't. Thank God.

It seemed like Henry stayed longer this time than he ever did. When he finally left, I called Ray collect. He had told me anytime I wanted to talk to him to call collect and he would always accept the charges. And he did, for nearly thirty years.

"What happened?" he asked when the call was put through.

"My husband came in."

"But Marci, I thought you said…"

I didn't let him finish. "I did say I was separated, and I am, but he still comes every day to see the kids." *And to check on me,* I thought, but I didn't tell Ray that part. I asked him to please hang up if he ever called and Henry answered. He wasn't pleased, but said okay. I could tell he found it disturbing.

Ray seemed concerned that I had a husband still coming around, but it didn't dissuade him. He told me the date he could be in New Orleans was August 28, 1968 and he would call back about the arrival time after he checked with the airline. We talked about irrelevant things, then he asked how my kids were (which he did for three decades, without fail, every time we spoke). That made him very special to me. Then he began telling me how sweet I sounded, how he couldn't wait to meet me in person, and that Joe had told him that I was petite and beautiful. Ray said in his book, *Brother Ray*, that he would probably choose the ugly woman given the choice, but I seriously doubt that he would have called me if Joe had said I was small and ugly!

Ray wantd to know where he should stay when he came to New Orleans. I suggested the Fontainebleau Hotel because it was an upscale hotel at that time. He asked me to make reservations for two rooms. (The extra one was for Joe Adams).

I was worried that someone might find out he was in town. I didn't want to arouse suspicion, so I asked if I could book him under an assumed name. My initial fear was that he would rethink meeting me, given all the secrecy connected with seeing me, but instead he said, "Yeah, book it under James Young."

All these years I thought Ray just pulled that name out of a cloud, but in 2004 I ran across the name in the book, *Ray Charles: Man and Music,* a biography about Ray. He actually knew someone named James Young. He was one of the big boys at the deaf and blind school who controlled the radio, much to Ray's chagrin. After telling one another how we couldn't wait to meet, we reluctantly said goodbye.

Once again, I was waiting for a phone call. The next thing I needed to do was arrange for a babysitter for August 28th, and figure out what I was going to tell Henry.

Ann and I discussed my dilemma and decided I would say we were meeting for lunch at Three Sisters restaurant in the French Quarter, then we were going to Mason Blanche on Canal Street for some shopping. That would give me about four hours, enough time to introduce myself and converse for a bit...or so I thought. (It didn't *exactly* happen that way). Before I went on this "pretend" shopping spree, I had to go shopping for real. I wanted to get Joe Adams a gift to show him my appreciation for being so nice to me.

When I told Ray I wanted to get Joe a gift I asked if he thought a silk handkerchief would be appropriate.

"Well, honey, a silk handkerchief is always good," he assured me.

I decided on a small, gold tie pin and a silk handkerchief, had them gift wrapped, and hid them until it was time to go. I also had one of my portraits framed for Ray. I told him I had done charcoal portraits of him and he said he would like to have one. I gave him what I considered the best one, but I didn't know to spray a fixative on it, having never had an art lesson. I worried that the charcoal would be rubbed off by the time he got to L.A. Later, when I asked him about it he said it was fine, "It must be good, cause folks be tellin' me it looks just like me." I told him to have someone spray it with hairspray to protect it, and he did. He told me in 1988 that he still had that portrait that I did of him twenty years before.

Ray called me on the 25th of August to tell me that he would be checking into the Fontainebleau Hotel, at around 11:00 a.m. My plan to have lunch and shop for four hours was perfect. I would leave home at 10:30 and arrive at the hotel right on time.

When Ray arrived in New York he called again, and I said, "Is this real? Are you really coming to see me? I can't believe it."

"Well, sweetheart, you'd better believe it, 'cause I'm gonna be there."

"Oh My God Ray! I'm so excited I can hardly contain myself."

"Well contain yourself, honey, and I'll see you around 11:00 a.m."

That was our last phone conversation before we met and I was beside myself waiting for tomorrow. I couldn't wait to meet the love of my life for the very first time.

Prepare myself? Was he kidding? I was numb. I couldn't get organized. I was absolutely paralyzed. I needed to make a list of "to-dos;" manicure, pedicure, facial and fix my long, thick hair that took forever. Instead, I just sat there, thoughtless and nearly helpless. I was actually meeting Ray Charles the next day!

Talking frequently to Ray during the past week had made me feel more comfortable. I felt like I knew him. He made an effort to make me feel relaxed, but I was running away with excitement. Madly in love was an understatement. I was deliriously in love.

I couldn't possibly imagine how I would feel tomorrow when I saw him in the flesh and actually touched him.

6
Meeting Ray Charles
ঔৎ৵

Time was slipping away, and I hadn't accomplished anything towards getting myself ready for my big day. My babies were hungry, so I made them dinner, but I couldn't eat! Henry showed up and ate with the kids, and I was glad. Now I could tell him my plans for tomorrow. I was so apprehensive, fearing he would say, "Absolutely not. You're not going anywhere." But he didn't. He just said, "Okay, Baby." Henry called everyone Baby. I breathed a sigh of relief. Anxiety had been bottled up inside me for days, dreading that conversation, and it felt good to get it over with.

He kissed the kids goodnight and left saying he would take the old car and leave me the Mustang. Great!! I didn't even have to ask for that one! I was beginning to have a few little pangs of guilt, but not for long. All I had to do was recall the physical brutality that I had endured for years from the wrath of a drunken Henry. I should have been free of him, but I wasn't free at all. He was living with another woman, and I was still under his thumb.

After I thought about it a minute, I started to become suspicious. Why was he being so nice? Why wasn't he questioning me more? It was unlike Henry not to want to know every little detail of my whereabouts. Now I was paranoid. Maybe he was setting me up. Maybe he was going to let me hang myself–get rid of me so he could keep our children. After all, he had a good lawyer, Sal Panzeca. What did I have? Nothing!

Oh come on Marci, your paranoia is running rampant. Get control of yourself.

I relived every step I had taken after contacting Ray and there was just no way Henry could have found out anything unless he had wire tapped my phone.

☙❧

My phone had actually been tapped before, but Henry didn't do it, the F.B.I did, so that thought wasn't just irrational thinking. It was a definite possibility. There weren't many illegal shenanigans that Henry couldn't do or have done. He knew a lot of New Orleans "characters." They are police "characters" who live their lives in opposition to legal authority.

Our phone had been tapped in mid-1965 after Henry went to jail to visit one of his "character" friends, a Cuban who was under suspicion for a possible connection to the 1963 assassination of President J. F. Kennedy. Thanks to my husband's less-than-desirable associates, I was fearful, angry and uptight for quite some time.

☙❧

I remember distinctly when President Kennedy was shot. November 22, 1963. I had been living on St. Charles Street, in New Orleans, with my friend Cleo. I arrived there a month before, in October. Cleo had a darling apartment uptown, which is my favorite area of New Orleans. We had invited Henry and Duke Dugas (who later became Lisa's Godfather), over for dinner that night, and to everyone's horror, President Kennedy died. That was all we talked about that night, it was so sad. He was the first president I voted for, and I've voted Democrat ever since.

I met Enrique Lorenzo Soto, the very first night I arrived in New Orleans. Cleo and I stopped by the Holliday House, a bar Henry later owned. We sat at the bar and before we could order, Henry was standing beside me, asking if he could buy me a drink.

Cleo warned me adamantly to stay away from Henry Soto, that he was a bad boy. Obviously, I didn't listen–I was really attracted to him. He was so handsome–that black hair and olive skin. Wow. But living with Henry wasn't easy, to say the least. In spite of that, even after all the beatings, all the terror that I felt when he was drunk, I've never been sorry I married him because I have my daughters. They are exactly, precisely, what I wanted and I couldn't have gotten them from anyone else. I love their dark hair and eyes, and their beautiful Latin skin which they inherited from their dad. Luckily, they got their compassion from me. They are perfect.

༄❦

With all these thoughts and doubts running through my head, I knew I would just have to wait and see if Henry knew anything. I convinced myself that he probably was just being nice–he wasn't usually mean unless he drank too much. Once again, it was time to put Lisa and Mitzi to bed and time for me to get the essentials done before bedtime.

Tuesday morning came all too soon. I certainly didn't get much sleep, but I felt great. I was so excited and happy.

The kids and I got in the tub for a nice long bath, had breakfast, and then I started to get ready for Ray. I curled my hair with big, fat, plastic rollers and sat under my old beauty shop hair dryer for an hour, drying my thick hair. The heat made my face red as a beet. *Damn, why didn't I do this last night?* God! It's hard to make a red face look right!

Even though I was absolutely aware, as the whole world was, that Ray Charles was blind, I nonetheless wanted to look my very best for him. I took great care in applying my make-up, and styling my hair. In those days, we teased our hair unmercifully, but I didn't this time. I wanted it to feel loose and smooth.

The suit I chose was light tan, with an off-white brocade overlay. The skirt was straight with a split in back, and the jacket was fitted with lapels and three covered buttons, which I wore with a tear drop diamond necklace, gold hoop earrings, and a chunky, gold link bracelet that I still have. My shoes were plain pumps, covered in the same brocade material.

30

I was ready. Now all I had to do was pick up the babysitter. The kids and I jumped in the car and picked her up, then I called the Fontainebleaue Hotel. Ray hadn't checked in yet. *Oh God! What if he isn't coming?* I was a wreck.

I put my gifts and portrait carefully in the trunk, went back in and called again.

"Has James Young checked in yet?"

"Oh yes ma'am, he just got to his room," the receptionist told me.

"Thank you."

And then I said, Yes! Yes! Yes! Yes! Yes! to myself. "Will you please ring his room?"

"Yeah," that wonderful voice answered.

"Hi Ray, this is Marci. I'll be there in twenty minutes."

"Alright Honey, I'll be waiting."

I picked up Lisa and Mitzi, twirled them around the room, kissed them goodbye, gave the babysitter some last minute instructions, backed the Mustang out, headed for the bridge crossing the Mississippi and was on my way this glorious, sunny day to the Fontainebleaue Hotel, to make my wildest dream come true.

Oh my God, Ray Charles really had come to New Orleans just to meet me!

I pulled in to the front of the Hotel, and had my car valet parked, *Oh God, remember to get rid of that parking ticket.* It was a good feeling walking through the lobby, knowing who I had come here to see. I felt like some sort of magical glow was emanating from me. Everyone would be so impressed, I thought, if they knew that I was on my way to see the great Ray Charles.

More than likely they would have wanted to tar and feather me. After all it was 1968, just three years after blacks were given the practical right to vote. Martin Luther King had just been assassinated a few months earlier. I was a white woman meeting a black man, and this was the deep south.

I made my way through the lobby to the elevator, punched my floor number in, and was getting off on his floor in no time.

31

Walking down the long and dimly lit corridor, I honestly felt like I was floating. The closer I got to the room the more nervous I became. I began desperately trying to gain control of myself to no avail. When I thought of who I had actually come here to meet, I started trembling uncontrollably.

Just stop Marci. Stop and breathe.

As I slowly approached the room, I noticed the door was slightly ajar. I summoned up all the courage inside of me, and lightly knocked. I heard, "Yeah, come in" as the door gently opened. Right there before my very eyes, standing in front of a window, with a black Nehru shirt on, black trousers and black shoes, was the man of my dreams.

I hesitated, nearly reeling with anticipation, and as I gasped for breath, Ray said, "Marci?" Hearing Ray Charles say my name in that sweet growling voice, was a euphony to my ears.

For a moment I couldn't speak. I stood trying to absorb this miracle, and all the time I was thinking, "it can't be real." Finally I whispered breathlessly, as I made my way across the room toward him, "Yes, Ray. I'm Marci."

When I got close enough to touch, he put his hands on my shoulders and ran them the length of my arms to my hands, then he brought them up to my chest, then put his arms around me and held me close. He then turned me around, with my back to him, and walked me toward the bed.

He sat me down on the bed and sat next to me. He began touching my hair, my face and neck, leaning me back on the bed, and bringing his body close to mine. Then he was kissing me and whispering "Don't you think you have on too many clothes?"

I know it happened quickly, but after all, I went there to be as close to him as I could possibly be. And yes, I agreed that I had too many clothes on.

First the jewelry came off: then the jacket, skirt, and bra (no panties as I've never worn them in my life).

Ray was standing, but not taking off his clothes, I turned the covers down and got in bed. Ray sat down on the side, and began stroking my body with feather light touches. Then he told me, "This is how I look at you, baby, and Jesus, honey, you look good."

He continued to caress me, oh, so tenderly, and all the while telling me how lovely I was. I was lost in the ecstasy of Ray Charles, beyond rational thinking or self control. I was completely his. I could no more have pulled myself away from him than I could have willed myself to stop breathing. I belonged, irretrievably, to him.

Our love making was more than amatory. We were bordering on erotic–nothing strange or kinky–just very sensual and romantic. I was burning with a delicious fire that I never wanted to end.

When we decided to take a break from love making, we discovered we were famished. Ray ordered breakfast, cereal, toast, bacon, one egg, and black coffee. I had toast and coffee. I wasn't too interested in food.

As I sat across from Ray at the small table and watched him maneuver his food, I was amazed at how independent he was. He didn't ask me to help him do anything, not fix his coffee, or pour the milk on his cereal, nothing. Ray Charles was a very capable man. Throughout my nearly thirty years with him, I saw him perform some feats that would be difficult for a sighted person.

As we talked over coffee, and a Kool cigarette for Ray, he asked me how long I could stay with him.

"I need to be home by 3:30 p.m.," I said.

He asked me if I would be able to come back.

"I will certainly try," I beamed, so happy he wanted me to.

Ray got back in bed and of course I followed like a puppy dog, never wanting to be apart from him now, not even just across the room.

"Come here baby," he said as I snuggled into his body for two more hours of dreamy, romantic love making. As blissful as it was, I had to prepare to leave him. I pulled the covers back and eased out of bed. Then I showered and got dressed. We clung to one another, not wanting to leave each other.

Ray said, "Marci, do you think you can come back?"

"I don't know," I worried. Inside, I was shouting with joy that he asked me to come back. I told him I would call and let him know.

We walked to the door and he held me, not wanting to let me go, while telling me, "I hope you can come back, baby."

Now when I walked down the corridor I had no apprehension and my heart was singing. As I left the elevator with my heels clicking on the floor of the lobby of the Fontainebleaue Hotel, I had a spring in my stride that I hadn't had in a very long time.

The valet attendant delivered my car, and I drove away under a cloudless sky and a glorious sunshiny day. Driving through the streets of New Orleans, I wanted to shout out my windows, "Hey everybody, I've just spent the last four hours with Ray Charles." But instead I quietly took the bridge across the rolling Mississippi to the little suburb of Gretna.

When I pulled into the driveway, I realized I had forgotten to give Ray the gifts I had so carefully wrapped and placed in the trunk. I had to unload them, and re-hide them under my bed. I thought, "Ray may never get them now." In fact, I may never see him again. I didn't know. But if I didn't, I would always have a wonderful life long memory.

While driving the babysitter home, I was desperately trying to plan my strategy for another few hours away from home, but to no avail. I never did go anywhere and now all of a sudden it would look too suspicious. The kids and I went into the house, and I listened while they told me about their day. Lisa said they played in the back yard, on the swing that hung from a lower limb of the tallest Cypress tree I had ever seen. Then she said they swam and splashed in their little pool on the patio, so it sounded like they had fun.

The phone rang. It was Linda, curious about my meeting with Ray. I told her how wonderful he was, that I was more in love than I thought possible, and that I wanted to go back but couldn't figure out what to tell Henry. I shouldn't have had to tell him a damn thing, but I did.

She told me that she was going to a movie.

"That's it!!!" I was so excited. "I'll say I'm going to the movie with you to see "Gone With the Wind." That movie is four hours long."

"Okay, then I'll really go see it so I can tell you the story," she said.

"Oh Linda, I saw it years ago, so I know the story. I'm just glad its four hours long, and it's currently here in New Orleans. What luck!"

Good! Now I had a plan, and Linda was glad to help me. I knew Henry would be coming soon to exchange cars and see the kids, but I just didn't know when. I didn't know if I would be able to meet Ray again or not, and it made me really anxious.

I spent the rest of the afternoon playing with my kids, making dinner, and sharing lots of telephone conversations with my friends who were eager to hear every detail of my rendezvous with Ray. Of course, I couldn't shut up about it. I pinched myself more than once to make sure I wasn't dreaming.

At about 6:30 p.m. Henry showed up–in a good mood, thank God. I waited until he played with Lisa and Mitzi, and went into the bathroom to read the paper, his usual routine. Then I nervously mentioned that I wanted to go with Linda to a movie. And to my absolute surprise and joy, he offered to stay with the kids. Regardless of our relationship, he really did love his children.

How would I call Ray? And how would I get the portrait to the car with Henry in the house? Damn!!! I always had a crisis. I needed to leave at 7:30 p.m. for the movie at 8:00. Henry said to be home no later than 12:30. That gave me another four hours. Great!!!

Henry went into the family room, turned on the television, got himself comfy in the recliner, and immediately fell asleep. That was my opportunity to put the portrait and gifts back in the trunk. I knew that I didn't dare call Ray with him in the house, though. I hadn't completely lost my mind.

Linda was waiting for me to call and tell her whether or not I could go, so when I called her to verify my plan, I made sure Henry heard me discussing the movie. Time was quickly slipping by and I needed to get going. I hurriedly kissed my little girls, woke their dad and left. Just before I drove onto the highway, I stopped at a pay phone to call Ray. (We didn't have cell phones then).

When I asked the desk clerk to ring Mr. James Young, I got that totally anxious and excited butterfly stomach. *Oh my God I'm ringing Ray Charles' room.* Yes! I was, and then I heard that sweet, "Yeah…"

"Hi Ray, its Marci."

"Yeah, baby."

"If it's still okay, I can come."

"Just come on in, the door will be open."

"Okay. I'll be there in 20 minutes."

This time I wore white pants, a pastel blouse, a light jacket and heels, of course. I wore heels no matter where I went in those days.

Crossing over the Mississippi, the greatest river in the United States, reminded me that the same water I was crossing had rolled all the way from Minnesota through my hometown, St. Louis, Missouri, just hours before, and was emptying where I now lived into the Gulf of Mexico. That wonderful busy river gave me a connection to St. Louis. It made me feel less lonely—and not so far away.

It was the same dreamy feeling I'd have a year later after moving back to St. Louis, sitting on the long set of stairs leading to our apartment and feeling so lonely.

And looking in awe at the infinite, starlit sky, I thought of it as a blanket covering Ray and me, even though he would be in another country. It was my way of dealing with being away from him more than I liked.

Having crossed the bridge, I pulled into the Fontainebleau entrance and valet parked my car for the second time that day. My heels click-clicked on the hard-surfaced floors to the elevator. I was still very excited, but not as nervous as I was the first time. After all, Ray had invited me back, proving to me that he was interested and that I hadn't disappointed him.

The door to his room was slightly open. I gently pushed it, entered, then closed and locked it. He was sitting in his robe, on the side of his bed, smoking a cigarette.

"Hi," I said softly as I walked over to sit beside him.

"Hi, Baby. I'm glad you could come back."

"Me too. I could hardly wait to see you again."

"Me either," he said putting his arm around me and pulling me close.

He asked if I would like to order dinner.

"No thanks, you go ahead. I'll just have a coke." It was past 8:00 p.m. and I had eaten what little I could get down at home. I wasn't able to eat much because I was so excited.

We discussed what his itinerary would be in the near future. He told me he was leaving for Europe as soon as he returned to Los Angeles and would be gone for two months. I was devastated!

"Oh, God! I'll never hear from you again," I moaned.

"What makes you say that, Marci? Of course you will, as soon as I get back."

"I really hope so," I said as I thought to myself, *If I never see you again, you've given me this time, and it's more than I ever dreamed I'd have.*

I needn't have worried. He gave me almost thirty years of *mostly* good memories...mostly.

Snuggling into Ray's body abruptly ended our conversation, as we wove our bodies into each other, gliding like satin over one another. Smooth, liquid movements.

"You fit me to a tee. I can move you any way I want you. You're perfect," he told me.

"Just remember that," I whispered back as I gently nibbled his ear. I covered his face and neck with kisses, murmuring sweet things as I kissed his warm, soft lips.

"Damn Marci, you're sweet, baby," he moaned, as we drifted in and out of oblivion.

It had been months since Henry and I had lived together. To be making love to the one man in the world who I loved so much was exquisite to me. Wishing I could have this forever, but knowing that I couldn't, I threw myself body and soul into the short time I had with him.

While rubbing my shoulders and arms as we cuddled together, he said, "You know Marci, you have the softest skin I've ever touched. Even your feet are soft. If I didn't know better, and you weren't moving the way you are, I'd think I was touching glass…Miss Smooth Skin, that's what I'll call you."

I told him to remember that too, and maybe he'd come back sooner.

"Oh, I'll be back. Nuthin's gonna keep me away from you, Marci." And with that said, he got up and went into the bathroom.

Soon I began smelling marijuana—strong marijuana. I walked over in front of the bathroom door. God!!! The smell just about knocked me over. Not another damned pot head! It brought back unwelcome visions of Henry.

∾∾

Henry had pot stashed all over New Orleans, wrapped in cellophane, and stuck under rocks and in every little culvert. When we went out anywhere, we would have to make at least a half dozen stops before we ever reached our destination just so he could kick rocks over, looking like a damned fool in the beam of the headlights. He always found his stash, much to my chagrin. I didn't like it at all. I especially didn't like that it was illegal and was in the car with me, so I bitched and complained. Depending on his mood he would just do a lot of "awww babies" or slap me around and tell me to "shut the fuck up." On those occasions, I *should* have just shut up, or just asked him to take me home, because when he hit me, it was usually an indication that he had already had too much to drink, and that's when he was dangerous. Instead of just keeping my mouth shut, all too often I would get so mad I'd hit him back, and then things got really heated. He would take me home, all but throw me out, and then he would leave.

This flashback prompted me to wonder if I should tell Ray how abusive Henry could be. But when Ray came out of the bathroom, I looked at him, considered the sweet peaceful expression on his face and made the decision not to tell him anything that would ruin the lovely memories he might have of our time together. I wanted to make an indelible imprint on his soul, because that's what he had done to mine. I did tell him about Henry having marijuana hidden all over New Orleans, though. He laughed and said, "So I take it you don't like reefer."

"No, I don't like it, and I don't do it, but it doesn't bother me if you do." And he did for the nearly thirty years that I spent with him. He made it a point never to do it when my kids were at home, and when it was just the two of us, he would go into the bathroom and close the door, even if we were in a hotel. I don't know if he was showing me respect because I didn't indulge in that sort of thing, or if it was his habit to seek privacy. I didn't ask. I do know that smoking reefer, as I've heard him call it many times, didn't change his personality.

Time was quickly passing by, and we were trying desperately to cram into that last four hour stretch enough togetherness and loving to last for the next two months, until he would be back to see me. Ray walked from the bathroom towards me, where I was sitting on the bed. His step was light as a feather, and his touch soft as a falling snow flake as we touched and snuggled for one last, intoxicating moment. All too quickly, it was time for our sad and sorrowful goodbye.

I had overstayed my time by a half hour, and Ray could sense that I was anxious. He said, "As much as I would love to keep you with me, you had better go. I don't want to cause you any trouble."

"I know…Ray if I never see you again, this is one day in my life that will remain with me forever."

"Marci, I'll be in touch with you as soon as the tour is over. Believe me, honey, you will be on my mind."

"Okay Ray, I hope so." After a lingering kiss, I heard the door softly close. Once again, I found myself in that long corridor, with a feeling of sheer delight mixed with a stab in my heart of deep sadness.

As I relived my wonderful and surprising hours with Ray Charles, I knew that this was one of life's vicissitudes that would be with me throughout eternity. I knew that I was forever changed.

7
Back to Reality
❧❧

Driving the twenty minutes to get home I found myself reliving every moment spent with Ray, but anticipating the wrath of Henry because I was late. I visualized him pacing the floor and eventually working himself into a frenetic rage. I knew there was one thing in my favor, though. He was at home and there was no alcohol in my house, so he at least wouldn't be drunk. As I pulled into the driveway, I saw the back door fly open and Henry standing there yelling, "Where the fuck have you been?"

I have no idea why but I said, "Oh I've been out with Ray Charles."

"Yeah, in your dreams," he said laughing his cynical laugh as he got into the car and backed out with jazz blasting on the radio.

Get the hell out of here, I thought. *I have memories to process and YOU are not in them.*

After checking on my babies, I rushed to the phone and called Ray. "Brother Ray here," he said.

"Hi, Brother Ray. You wanted me to call to let you know I got home safely. So here I am, safe and sound."

"Good, baby…I'm glad to know that."

We chatted for a short while about our breathtaking, whirlwind time together. Then I asked what time he was leaving and he said about five a.m..

"Oh! You'd better get to sleep. You only have about three and a half hours."

"Less than that," he said. "I have to be at the airport at five."

We said goodbye again and I repeated that I hoped I would see him when he returned from Europe.

"You will, Honey," he promised.

❧

By the way, I did give Ray the portrait and the gifts I had bought for Joe Adams. He seemed very appreciative and told me how nice it was of me to think of Joe. I could tell Ray thought a lot of Joe. He seemed to be very close to him and it appeared to me that they shared a mutual respect.

❧

After showering, I put on my signature White Shoulders perfume and finished getting ready for bed. Ray had asked me what kind of perfume I was wearing and said that he liked it, that I had a distinctive, sweet aroma that lingered with him after I left the first time. I hoped it would linger for the next two months–I knew the Cannon Cologne he wore would stay with me. He had left me with a memory that I wished I could press in a book like my first red rose.

Suddenly I was very tired as I turned back the bed covers and slid between the cool sheets, ready to dream of Ray snuggling next to me. Drifting off to sleep, I thought of his gentlemanly charm and sweet easy manner. Yes…this man was etched eternally in my heart.

The next morning I was up early, having had a restless few hours of sleep. I wasn't tired, though. My mind was still spinning from the excitement of the day before.

I went in our small Pullman kitchen and made myself a cup of fisherman's coffee, a warm, fuzzy memory from childhood. My Uncle Leland used to make it. You just put coffee and water in a pot and then boil it. My Aunt Reth, short for Oretha (ironically, Ray's mother's name, too) always said, "If you put a spoon in the pot, it won't boil over." I don't know, I always watched it so that it didn't boil over.

To drink this coffee, it had to be poured through a strainer, and was it ever good. I loved it. Even now I make it, especially when I need to conjure up wonderful memories of Uncle Leland fishing in his hip boots, wading in the river, and Aunt Reth cooking on the camp fire, and my wonderful granny, sitting in a fold up lawn chair, crocheting and moving her mouth with every stitch. The memory was soothing and comforting (except for the poor fish). I never liked fishing then and I still don't.

After enjoying my steaming cup of coffee, I went back to my kid's bedroom. They were just beginning to wake up, rubbing their eyes and stretching their little bodies. "MaMa, MaMa," they squealed as I opened their curtains revealing a bright sunshiny day. I crawled in bed between them and listened while they told me about their evening with their daddy.

The day was Thursday, August 29, 1968 and it was Mitzi's birthday. She was two years old and in five days, on Monday, September 4th, Lisa would be four. On Sunday we were planning a birthday party for the two of them that would include many of their cousins, about fourteen in number, if they all came. My kids had a wonderful large family in New Orleans but as it turned out, this would be their last birthday there.

On this day, though, we were going to have cupcakes with a candle in them and just have a happy little celebration with each other. Mitzi was the birthday queen and she wore a crown and blew out the candles while Lisa and I sang Happy Birthday and watched Mitzi open one small gift. Very soon Mitzi had cake and icing all over her face. (Lisa's little hands were clean. She could never stand messy hands!).

Their main birthday presents would be given to them on Sunday when everyone was here, and we would have a big cake and party. Then on Monday, Lisa would be the queen, wear the crown and open her small gift. Whew! What a busy five days.

On Sunday, cousins, friends, sisters-in-law, and Cuka and Poppy, my mother- and father-in-law, came over for a wonderful, fun birthday party for my little girls. They loved being with their cousins–and do to this day. Despite mine and Henry's issues, we were a close-knit family, and Lisa, Mitzi and I are still close to them.

The party ended and finally, towards evening, everyone had gone. I had two tired, happy little girls and a myriad of new toys to put away.

Henry kissed the kids goodnight, and then he tried to kiss me! Oh God. This was odd. We had been estranged for a few months and now this. I could see that he was trying to rekindle something, and I felt like a zoo animal in a cage. Trapped. I didn't hate my husband. I still cared about him. I had tried everything to make our marriage work, but I just wasn't interested anymore.

୨ৎ

We were doomed from the very beginning, being so different from one another. Going into our marriage, I thought I could make a home for him, cook, clean and take care of him (which, in reality, meant I thought that I could change him). I was willing to sacrifice whatever it took to create a happy home for us.

We had been married in St. Louis in 1964 and I was pregnant with Lisa. Although Henry's home was in New Orleans, he agreed to live in St. Louis. He was still drinking–in fact, when Lisa was born, we had to use my girlfriend's car to get to the hospital because he had drunkenly wrecked my car (right after I made the last payment!). His drinking caused so much heartache for us. Henry was crazy about Lisa, but when she was only four months old, he left us and moved back to New Orleans.

When he started calling and asking me to come to New Orleans, even offering to drive to St. Louis to get Lisa and I, I agreed. I closed my little beauty shop, said good-bye to my folks and left with Henry. Half way to New Orleans the car broke down so we had to get a motel. It was March 1965 and Lisa was six months old. She slept in a play pen that the motel owners were nice enough to lend us. We found out that we couldn't get the car repaired, so we took the train to New Orleans.

Henry left to tow the broken car home, and there I was in New Orleans with his parents, who I had never met. Oh my God! What a mess. We found an apartment quickly but it didn't last long. The owners, an older couple who didn't like us, wanted us to move, so back to his parents we went.

I found a shotgun duplex one block from his folks' house on Camp Street, uptown in New Orleans. When Henry saw it, he was horrified. It needed painting inside and out. It really was pretty awful looking, but I desperately wanted our own place and I was willing to do whatever work it required to make it habitable.

In no time, I had it whipped into shape and Henry thought it looked great. He was so proud of me and bragged to his friends and family that his wife could make a home from nothing. It was while living in New Orleans on Camp Street that I endured Henry at his most brutal. Mostly it was when I would go out with him and he would smack me around in the car on the way home. We lived there from March 1965 until the beginning of 1968 when we moved to Gretna.

About a year before we moved to Gretna, Henry had stopped drinking and we were pretty happy–at least much more so than when he was drinking. I truly was relieved when Henry quit. I finally felt safe. We didn't have these horrible fights anymore and he wasn't as jealous as he was when he was drunk.

Then one night a few months after we moved into our new house in Gretna, I had a sinking, sick feeling that he had started drinking again. I don't know why, I just knew it. Sure enough, one night he called and was drinking, laughing and acting silly. I knew that things could turn sour in a lightening flash–I'd been there so many times. Trembling and shaking, I hurriedly packed a suitcase for the kids and I so that we could leave if things got too bad–that is if he would let me. But he just came in and went to bed, and I knew that hell had come to live with me again.

I remember one particular time when he was hitting me and pulling my hair, I jumped out of the car and ran inside, locking him out. Of course he was sorry, crying and begging me to forgive him the next day. Same old routine. Usually it would take two to three days and then he would come back home. One time when he came home he brought me what he thought was my hair piece, but it was my actual hair that he had pulled out!

Another time he had brought some friends home. I hated it it when he did that. I was never prepared for people late at night, and I always knew there was a good chance things would get ugly. He was sitting in our kitchen and I was sitting beside him–God forbid I'd sit by someone else–he would swear I was flirting with them. He asked me to get him another drink. I was standing in front of the fridge and I told him that I thought he had had enough. He pulled out a pistol and shot at me. He missed me, but put a hole in the refrigerator door.

His friends got the gun and settled him down and I ran into the bedroom. An hour or so later, a chair came flying through the air toward me and it crashed into my knee. It was excruciating. Then he left with his friends and was gone for two or three days.

The next day when my in-laws brought Lisa home, they noticed me limping. When I told them what happened, Poppy immediately got on the phone and called Dr. Shapiro, their family physician, who had me come in for x-rays. Poppy drove me to the doctor while Cuka stayed with Lisa. Sure enough, my bone was chipped, but luckily, it didn't require surgery. The doctor wrapped it and suggested that I stay off of it as much as possible. My in-laws were wonderful. That incident would be only one of many times that they would be summoned to my rescue.

On still another time, we were invited to an outdoor wedding reception. Many of Henry's friends and their families were there. I didn't know anyone well but had met some of them occasionally before, so I was trying to mingle and make small talk. About an hour into the reception, I saw Henry making his way toward me with a scowl on his face. I wracked my brain to think of what I had done to anger him, but it wasn't that. He wanted me to put my sunglasses on.

"Why?" I asked.

"Your eyes are all squinched up," he answered.

"No," I told him. Wrong answer. I should have just put

them on. He shoved me, making me stumble, but I didn't fall.
By then I was so embarrassed I couldn't wait to go to the car,
which was what he ordered me to do.

"Take your ass to the fucking car."

So I went, sobbing and alone to the hot-as-hell car where I
was ordered to sit and wait. I knew Henry well enough to know
that when the Mr. Hyde side of Jekyll and Hyde showed his evil
face, he wasn't going to let it drop. His anger would seethe and
simmer, and I knew that soon he would come to the car and
force me to go back.

Before long, I saw someone come out to the road and get
into his car. I asked him where I could find a pay phone, so he
gave me a ride about a mile up the road to a bar. I thanked
him, went in and called Poppy to come and get me. Then I sat
at the bar, huddled up against the wall as insignificantly as possible, ordered a coke and nervously waited. I don't know how
Henry knew where I was but twenty minutes after I got there
he stormed in the door and came straight to me demanding to
know, "What the fuck do you think you're doing?"

"I called your folks to come get me," I said.

"Get your purse, you're leaving," he shouted.

"No," I exclaimed, and he slapped me.

Then he lit a cigarette and ground it into my left eye, searing
the skin enough that I could hear it sizzle. Someone grabbed
him and threw him out of the bar. I sat there with my hand
cupped over my eye, tears streaming down my face, wondering
what I was going to do. Embarrassed and humiliated, I waited
for Cuka and Poppy to rescue me yet again.   My in-laws
certainly didn't deserve this. They worried about Henry all the
time.

It seemed to me that I was always the cause of Henry's temper flares when he was drunk. It seemed that just looking at
me angered him, but a sober Henry was the most charming
southern gentleman ever. He was delightful and everyone loved
him.

By now we had Mitzi, so I packed the kids up and drove to

St. Louis. Of course Henry would fly up and beg and plead with me to come back and I always forgave him and went home. Until 1969 when I left for good.

8
Henry's Back - and So Is Ray

My life was back to its old redundant routine. Ray was gone on tour and I didn't know if I would ever see him again. Henry began coming to the house more often and staying longer each time. He was trying to reignite feelings in me, but somehow he didn't understand that grabbing me by the throat and slamming me against the wall wasn't the way to do it! The only highlight in my life during that time was Lisa and Mitzi. I loved my little girls so much, and every little thing they did excited me.

Our house in Gretna was on a quiet street with very little traffic so there were always children on the sidewalk–mothers pushing their babies in strollers and walking their dogs, etc. It was a very family-oriented neighborhood. The only thing that livened up our street was when Henry and I would have a major fight, and believe me, that would do it every time.

One day after one of our nasty arguments, Henry hit me and slammed out of the house. As he backed out of the driveway, I ran out, dressed only in a black half slip pulled up over my breast, and hurled a metal trashcan at his car. Classy, huh? I'm not going to white wash myself. I had a horrible temper and I did some horrific things! I just knew I wanted out of this life. I felt so helpless.

One day I was reading the ads in the paper and I saw an I.B.M. class offered, so I signed up for it. Seven weeks later, I hadn't learned a thing. I couldn't type well, and I couldn't read the codes that I did type. Oh! God! What a disaster. Not only was I helpless, I was stupid, too.

And then, out of the blue in mid-October, two good things

49

happened. Henry began spending a lot of time out of town and Ray called.

"Hello," I said.

"Marci?"

"Oh my God! Ray!!!"

"Yeah, baby."

"Oh, I'm so happy you called. I was worried you would forget about me."

"I told you I wouldn't. Listen, Honey, I really want to see you. Is that possible?"

"Yes. Oh, yes. I can't wait!"

"Well, you call and give me a time."

I called him the next morning to see how soon he could come. I told him I could get away for two days. He said he would be in the next morning.

I took my kids to my girlfriend's and headed for the Hyatt Regency, close to the airport. There aren't words to express how happy I was to see him–I just couldn't get close enough to him.

We had two days of absolute bliss, making love, talking, and eating. I felt so comfortable with him. I honestly felt like I was born to be with him and forty years later, I still do.

Ray left for a couple of hours the first night with a New Orleans Radio D.J. (He gave me the number of his radio station so I could call and request a Ray Charles song). While he was gone, I snooped through his things checking for drug paraphernalia, praying I wouldn't find anything. I know it's terrible, but I had to be sure. And much to my relief, I found nothing. The only thing he had was marijuana.

I knew he didn't like being questioned about his drug use. In his autobiography he told someone, "You have your drawers and I have mine. Let's respect each others' privacy." I obviously didn't pay attention to that rule!

I always felt really comfortable when I was with Ray. Once when we were lying in bed talking, I asked him if he had a seeing eye dog? Can you imagine? I'll bet I'm the only nit-wit who ever asked him that. He just said, "No I don't. But I do have a dog."

"What's your dog's name?"

"Duke," he said. "He's a German Shepherd."

We talked about everything, including the murder of Ray's friend, Martin Luther King. Ray said he went to Martin's funeral, and that he was still very sad. Martin was killed in April and it was now October of 1968, only six months later, and the wound was still fresh in Ray's heart.

We ordered room service for dinner, not wanting to get dressed to go out. We only had this night and tomorrow night and I wanted to be with him every second. He always asked if I wanted to go out but I always opted not to, especially in New Orleans. Henry had a lot of "friends," and I didn't want either of us to get shot.

Between August of 1968 and August of 1969, Ray made several trips to New Orleans to see me. He also made one trip to St. Louis, which was the best. I went there to see my family just after Christmas in December of 1968 and was there until after New Year's. When I told Ray I was going to be in St. Louis, he asked if I thought it would be okay if he met me there.

"Oh my God, Yes! That's just what I was hoping for!"

I flew in with my kids (of course), got them settled in at my Mom's and eagerly awaited Ray's phone call telling me when he would be there. My brother Don was nice enough to lend me his car, so I was able to pick up Ray and his valet Bob Taylor (who I had met in New Orleans), from the airport. We stayed at the Holiday Inn on South Lindbergh.

My folks were happy to have their grandchildren, freeing up my time to spend with Ray without any anxieties. It was so nice. We were so happy. Three blissful days and nights together. Heaven couldn't have been any better than that.

When Don needed his car back, I exchanged it for his old truck that had no heater and looked like it had been in a fire. Don's lady of the moment wanted to meet Ray and he didn't want her riding in the old truck, so one evening he brought her to the hotel and we had a short visit. Ray seemed a little un-comfortable and apprehensive. Years later, after he met Don for the second time, he told me that he had worried about meet-ing my brother and that he had been a little scared. But things went well, and I was glad my brother and Ray met and liked each other.

It was during this time together that I began telling Ray bits and pieces of my life. I didn't want to frighten him and take a chance of losing him, but I wanted Ray to know what my life was like. I told him that Henry was abusive at times and that he hit me occasionally. That made Ray really sad, but there was nothing he could do about it.

After our third day together, I drove Ray and Bob to the airport. They were going to Los Angeles and a few days later, I would be heading back to New Orleans. I arrived in New Orleans on January 3, 1969 and in March, Ray was back to see me.

My girlfriend, Ann, had expressed a desire to meet Ray, so on his next visit, I asked if he would mind meeting her.

"Of course not, Honey. I want to meet your friends."

We stopped by her house after I picked him up from the airport. (That was risky–I only picked him up that one time in New Orleans). Ann greeted us warmly, inviting us to have cof-fee and teacakes, which she had made. Ann felt very comfortable with Ray. She said that he seemed down to earth and genuine. He truly was.

While we were sitting there, a Mosquito Hawk flew in her living room. She was going to swat it but Ray said, "Oh! No! No- you never kill a skeeter hawk, they eat mosquitoes." She never got over that. She brought it up over and over.

We were discussing favorite foods and Ray told us what he would consider a fabulous meal. Ann must have been taking mental notes because the next time Ray came to see me, some-time in May, she kept Lisa and Mitzi and shortly after Ray and I got settled in our motel, she called to inform us that she was sending a surprise for Ray by taxi. The driver handed me two large heavy bags. I took them and tipped him. By this time, Ray was standing beside me, smelling the wonderful aroma and wanting to know what it was.

It was everything Ray had told Ann he liked when he visited her a month ago. There were pork chops smothered in gravy, candied sweet potatoes, black-eyed peas, homemade bread and hot apple pie with melted cheese topping, which he said was a favorite. She had made Ray a king's feast! He couldn't get over how nice she was and how much effort she had gone to especially for him.

It smelled so wonderful, we couldn't wait to dig in. I placed the food on the table and then filled Ray's plate. I cut his pork chops, and showed him what everything was by placing his fingers over each serving. Then we dove in, stuffing ourselves, and grazing all night. Ray called Ann the next morning to thank her again and tell her how thrilled he was at her nice gesture and how good the food was.

Each time I was with him, I learned more about how to care for him. When I first met him, I didn't do anything. I didn't know what to do. But as time went on, having become more observant, I learned and wanted to please him.

It seemed like in no time at all, it was time to take him to the airport. I got him to the plane and in his seat–we always boarded first–then I kissed him goodbye and tearfully left the plane.

I drove to Ann's house to pick up my kids and she asked me how my time with Ray was. I said, "It's heaven being with him. It's a whole different world. He's quiet and sweet to me. I love the way he is. He's so easy to talk to. I love touching and being close to him. In fact, Ann, I love everything about him. I wish I never had to leave him."

"How do you think he feels?" she asked.

"I think he likes me. He says he does and he wants to continue being with me. He comes to see me and calls often, and he did meet me in St. Louis. It can't be too easy for him. After all, he has to arrange his schedule around when I can be available. And really, Ann, I don't expect anything. I've already had much more than I ever dreamed I'd have. So if I never see him again, I'll be sad but forever grateful that I've had this experience."

Remember these words because there will come a time when my recalcitrant personality will rear its ugly head and I am no longer that sweet little non-demanding woman. I'm sure that at those times, Ray wished I would have stayed in New Orleans where I was sweet and happy to see him. All good things must come to an end, though, and in any relationship, you must take the bad with the good. There was plenty of both over the next thirty years.

Living my life on this Ray-Henry roller coaster, I was truly an emotional wreck. I felt I should probably confide in Ray, but I just couldn't bring myself to. I was afraid if I told him about my emotional state he might bolt and never see me again, fearing I was some sort of crazy woman. And I probably was.

౼ఞ

Back in 1965, I had a breakdown and signed myself into Touro Infirmary Psyche Ward. I got no relief. My next move was Louisiana State Hospital in Mandeville, Louisiana for what was supposed to be some long-term care. I escaped from there twice with the dubious distinction of being the only patient in the history of their existence at that time to ever do so.

I'm not bragging, believe me.

I was sad–out of control and pitiful, and I was fortunate to have lived to talk about it.

9
Escape From Mandeville
❧

The ground sank and skidded beneath my feet as I ran terrified over a foot or more of rotted leaves through at least a mile of swampy, woodland from the Institution to the highway. I had been told poisonous snakes and wild boar inhabited this swampland, but as scared to death as I was of snakes, I couldn't stand being in that place another second. Navigating through electric barbed wire that could shock me hard enough to knock me down, I ran and ran.

Every time my foot sank into the rotted, soggy leaves my body reacted with molten-liquid fear racing through my veins. I felt like I was gliding through a jungle swamp but I wasn't. I know my feet were hitting the ground fast, and I was running scared, scared, scared–all alone, crazy and terrified.

Two older male patients had seen me begin to walk away from the institution. They stopped, stood statue still and watched me. When they realized I was running away, they warned me of the danger lurking in the woods. I paid no attention and kept right on going. As I cleared the electric fence unscathed, they yelled, "Good luck, you're gonna need it."

I barely heard them. I was running like a hunted, frightened deer through that forest with limbs stinging my cheeks and branches scratching my legs, but nothing was going to slow me down. My heart was pounding and thudding so hard my chest ached but I kept on. Tears were streaming down my face, but my determination overpowered my physical weakness. I kept running until I came to the two-lane highway leading to the bridge that would take me to New Orleans.

Looking back and constantly fearing someone was coming

after me, I flagged down a lone car and thank God he let me get in.

I lied to him about why I was running. I told him I had a fight with my boyfriend, and got out of his car and started walking. He said, "What a jerk." He had no idea that I was an escapee from an Institution for the mentally and emotionally disturbed. He dropped me off and I called a cab from the twenty-five mile bridge crossing Lake Pontchartrain that linked Mandeville to New Orleans. I took the cab to the Holiday House, a bar my husband owned.

Henry was both surprised and happy to see me, but not for long. I was drifting in and out of uncontrollable despondency and couldn't stand the magnified sensations that were overtaking my body and mind. I was rushed back to Touro Infirmary, where I had spent two weeks prior to Mandeville, for knock out shots and then taken back to the Institution via ambulance.

The staff there put me on lockdown, and I wasn't even allowed to be outside on the grounds–I was confined to my quarters. The huge metal doors clanged shut and bolted, and there I was, a prisoner, and I wasn't getting any better.

The doctor put me on a medicine called Thorazine which I thought would help me. I was so desperate, I would go to the nurse's station (they were behind glass), and ask if it was time for my medicine. I said, "I feel like I'm going crazy." She responded, "You already *are* crazy. That's why you're here."

I was either allergic to Thorazine or extremely sensitive to it because I had a terrible reaction to it. I began to feel like the ground was rising. Trees looked as tall as the California Redwoods and the buildings were enormous. Everything was magnified.

Once when Henry was there, (they would let me out when I had a visitor) we were sitting on a picnic table when he suddenly said, "Damn baby, I got to get you inside. You're beet red and swelling. Come on!!"

The nurses stripped me down and put me into a cold shower nearly freezing me to death. All my medication was taken away–I was not even allowed an aspirin for a headache or my nasal spray for a stuffy nose. Nothing. I was suffering from "extreme anxiety." I couldn't sit down. I paced back and forth out of control. I felt so despondent. I felt like there wasn't any help for me. None. I was so scared. I was so petrified that I would be like that for the rest of my life, I contemplated suicide. In fact, when I had traveled in the taxi over Lake Pontchartrain and the waves rushed and broke against the bridge, they had seemed to beckon me–Jump!! Jump!! In my pitiful state, I thought the water would be soothing.

Soon, I was moved to different quarters where I would be more closely observed, but I actually had more freedom there. They tried to teach me to do crafts, but I was unable to concentrate. More than anything, I just wanted to be out of there. I wasn't even allowed phone calls. Once, I wanted to call my mother in St. Louis, Missouri so I walked to the pay phone. The psychiatrist saw me, and in group therapy accused me of sneaking. I was not sneaking. I just wanted to talk to my mother!

When I put my notice in to get released, they told me I would have to wait seven days. There was NO WAY I was going to wait another seven days, so I went under the barbed wire, through the swampy woods and to the highway again, still scared to death but even more determined than the last time.

This time, I got a ride with the driver of an eighteen wheeler who took me to the bridge where I got a taxi across the lake again. I desperately wanted to see my baby. It had been three weeks since I had seen her, and I had never been away from her before. I had only seen her once when Henry dressed her up and brought her to Touro Infirmary, but I could only see her from the fifth story window–and all I could do was wave at her. Children weren't allowed in the psyche ward and I missed her so much!

After getting settled back into our duplex on Camp Street in uptown New Orleans, I began seeing my in-laws' doctor who diagnosed me as having severe panic attacks. He gave me

Valium, which helped to keep me calm, so the attacks subsided and I began to improve. I still had panic attacks but not as frequent and not as severe. Even though they were not as severe, they still gave me the most horrible feeling in the world. It's indescribable.

Within a year, I had another baby, my little Mitzi, August 29, 1966 and a year or so after her birth, we moved to our new home in Gretna. As well as I can remember, I never had an attack when I lived in Gretna, but they returned when I moved back to St. Louis, and occurred randomly for the next fifteen years.

I came to realize later that my panic attacks had actually started in St. Louis, long before I moved to New Orleans or met Henry. The symptoms were not as severe then, but eventually they escalated and finally culminated into me having to be hospitalized.

Recovery Inc. was my ultimate savior. A few meetings and a book called *"Recovery Through Will Training"* by Dr. Abrahms taught me how to control the triggers that brought on the attacks. To this day, though, nearly fifty years later, I still strongly guard my emotions. I've never been the same person that I was before my panic attacks began. They nearly disabled me, stripped my self-confidence, and literally crippled me.

I had to figure out different ways to survive and ultimately earn a living, and eventually I did. I was able to provide for myself and my children by cleaning houses. Cleaning was something I was very good at–I needed no training. I was a natural!

My own house was always spotless. One of my friends jokingly said, "She vacuums the snow" and I was just about that persnickety. Cleaning enabled me to be in a quiet and mostly private environment. I knew I could never function in a public position because I simply wasn't confident enough. Fear and anxiety would bring on a panic attack, so I did what was safe for my health and what was necessary to provide for my little family.

10
More Drama With Henry
❧

Although Henry wasn't the cause of my mental and emotional problems, being married to him certainly didn't help them. My life with him created an ever-present tension–never knowing when he was going to be drunk and abusive to me.

Once, I had just come home from the grocery store and was putting away groceries when the doorbell rang. Two men in suits showed me their badges, said they were F.B.I and asked if they could come in. I asked to see their credentials and, having nothing to hide, I invited them in. They asked questions about Henry, and I answered all I knew. They asked me where he was, and I answered that I really didn't know–he hadn't called or been there for a few days. After fifteen minutes or so they left.

Shortly thereafter, Henry came through the kitchen door, dripping in redwood paint. Remember that redwood fence that I mentioned earlier? Well, he had been painting that fence, and I had no idea he was there. He had no idea the F.B.I had been there. We started laughing. Henry looked so funny with red paint all over him. He didn't tell me why the F.B.I. was looking for him, and I didn't ask. I really didn't care anymore at that point. He usually kept his shady business away from our home, but I guess he had no control of the "Feds" as he called them.

There were times that I fought back when Henry terrorized me. I'll admit, I had a nasty, vicious temper and I could be very brave and vindictive–as long as he was nowhere around. If he couldn't get his hands on me, I could strike back. And some-times, I did.

Once when we were living on Camp Street, Henry slapped me around and then left the house. I snatched all of his clothes from his closet, stuffed them into cardboard boxes and delivered them to the outside of a bar where he was having a good old time. Then I ran in the back door and yelled, "Hey, Henry, your clothes are out here in the pouring rain. Enjoy yourself," and flew back to my car and sped away.

He would stay gone long enough to get sober and get over his anger before he ever tried to come home, so I would be safe. As I mentioned before, he was never mean when he was sober. He was always apologetic and begging me to forgive him after one of those episodes–and I always did.

After his year of sobriety, I had hopes of things remaining good, but it wasn't to be. I discovered through a slip of the tongue from the man who laid our marble patio that Henry had a girlfriend. At this time we were still married, not separated or estranged, and we were supposed to be happy, damn it. We had our new house in Gretna and he wasn't drinking. What went wrong? Everything!

When he started drinking again, I started hearing rumors about him and Darlene. Then I heard he was living with her! Of course, he denied everything, saying, "That ol' girl is nothing but a money maker. I love you. You're my wife."

It was all I could do not to spit in his face. He was drinking heavily and partying again, and then came the last straw. I called one of his friends pretending I knew all about Darlene, and she said, "I know, he had her at the Jazz fest."

Oh my God!!! Now he was flaunting her around in front of people, right under my nose, and I was furious. I took all his suits, shirts, everything to the back yard, set them on fire and cut up his expensive shoes with razor blades. When I told Henry his clothes were a pile of ashes, he laughed and said, "I had six hundred dollars in a suit pocket," and kept on laughing. I was sick. I really needed that money.

Those were some of the reasons why, in mid-1969, I thought that I should be free to do as I pleased, like he did. But I wasn't. I was always under Henry's thumb, and I couldn't escape.

11
Profession of Love

৽৵

Ray came to see me again in April of 1969. This time, he brought me an album, "I'm All Yours Baby," saying all the songs were expressions of his feelings for me. He said that one in particular, "Yours," was exactly how he felt about me, that it was poignant and that he couldn't have written words that described his feelings any better. It was at this point in time that Ray began telling me how dear I was to his heart and that I was special to him. Up until that time, he just said things like, "You're a sweet woman, Marci. Your skin is so smooth. I'm finding I want to be with you more and more."

I couldn't listen to the album until I got home. I asked Ray to tell me the words to "Yours," but he said it would be better if I just heard the song so that I could hear his emotional expression.

It was during this visit in April that I also heard the disturbing news that he was married. What a disappointment. It hadn't occurred to me to ask him, and it had never occurred to me that he had a wife waiting for him at home! Maybe I hadn't wanted to know. At that point, though, I was too deep into him to ever consider giving him up. I was going to be with him any time I could. Even though I didn't like the fact that he was married, and I felt guilty being with him, I just couldn't help myself.

Ray told me, "I'm sorry honey, ain't nuthin' I can do about it— but time can take care of many things."

"What does that mean, Ray?" I asked.

"Just what I said, babe. Time and patience."

He would soon learn that sadly I had plenty of the first, but I had none of the second! Patience was not my virtue.

As I look back, I can see what he meant and wish I would have been more patient. It took until now, after his death and after listening again to our many conversations, that I realize it.

౿ა

I was dying to hear the song on the album. I thought it was so sweet of him to bring it to me and I asked again if he would tell me the words.

"No, Baby. You listen to it and tell me what you think."

I knew what I would think. I was always calling him the genius and giving him lavish accolades. To me, he was the best. There was no one as good, and certainly none better, and I still feel that way all these years later.

Ray asked me what I was going to do about my marriage.

"I don't know," I said. "I don't really have anywhere to go. I don't even have a job." And in my mind I thought, *I don't have the confidence or the qualifications to get one, either.*

"Well, babe, why don't you *try* to find a job?"

"I'm not sure if I can, Ray."

"Honey, you hafta try. Look in the paper and see what's there. Okay?"

We had this night together and then it would be time for him to leave and for me to pick up my kids from my sister-in-law and go back to Gretna.

"I don't want to worry about a job right now, Ray. I just wanna snuggle with you."

"Okay, baby. I wanna snuggle with you too. Come here."

And that's what we did until early morning when it was time to leave. I didn't feel as sad as I usually did because I was eager to go home and listen to the song he had brought me. As soon as I pulled into the driveway and got the kids inside, I put the album on and listened intently to every word.

Oh my God. This was a love song if ever there was one.

I began weeping. I wanted to hold him and tell him how much I loved him. I was very emotional listening to these words:

62

Yours 'till the stars lose their glory
Yours 'till the birds fail to sing
Yours 'till the end of life's story
This pledge to you dear I'll bring.
I'm yours in the gray of December,
here or on far distant shores.
I've never loved anyone the way I love you
How can I when I was born to be just yours.

There were more beautiful love songs that brought me to his mind, he said, but "Yours" said "everything he wanted to tell me." And it certainly said a lot. I couldn't have wished for–or dreamed–that he would say such wonderful things to me.

After listening to the album and hearing all of the other beautiful songs, and then playing and replaying "Yours" over and over until I had memorized the words, I called Ann and Linda and played it for them.

They cried, I cried. We were enchanted and thought it was the most romantic thing any of us had ever heard. I was walking around with my head in the clouds. I had never heard such beautiful words, and to know that they were Ray expressing his feelings for me, I was overcome with love for him.

I couldn't wait to call him, but he wouldn't be in L.A. yet. I made lunch for Lisa, Mitzi and myself, got them settled down playing, poured a cup of chicory coffee that I had recently picked up at the French market in the Quarter, and sat down to reminisce and take stock of my life.

Getting away from Henry was something I knew I had to do eventually. I just couldn't figure out how I was going to do it. Where would I go? What would I do? I had no self-confidence. I had taken that class and wasn't successful. I had no idea how I could take care of my children and myself. To top things off, I was afraid of everything. Going for an interview. Trying to train in front of people. Oh my God, I was so stuck in my small isolated world.

Looking through the classifieds, I noticed an add for the New Orleans Police Department. I had no resume, no experience, no anything, but I forced myself to go and apply.

So here I was, the wife of a man known (*well* known) to the New Orleans police (and not in a good way!) applying for a job at the New Orleans Police Department. Believe it or not, I was actually hired. I was also scared to death. I had false courage because of Ray, but inside I felt like I was coming unwired. I couldn't tell Ray because I didn't want him to know how emotionally unstable I was.

Anxiety flared inside me as I was told to report the next morning for a uniform fitting–a navy blue straight skirt, light blue blouse and two inch black pumps. I dreaded telling Henry. I knew he would explode.

Sure enough he was livid. He said, "No way. You are not working at the goddamned New Orleans Police Station. Everybody will think I'm a snitch. Henry Soto's wife, working for the fucking heat. No way. You can forget that shit," and he stormed out and left.

I kept my appointment anyway, got my uniform and came home to alter it. I was small and everything needed to be altered. In fact, I was an inch too short to qualify for the job, so the lieutenant said to record that I was 5'3 ½". In reality I was only 5'3". I was supposed to be 5'4".

As soon as I knew for sure I had the job, Ray was the first person I called. I was so excited!!!

"Yeah," he said.

"Collect from Marci."

"Okay, operator, I'll take it."

"Ray, guess what? I got a job."

"All right!!! Baby." He was excited too.

"I'm working at the New Orleans Police Department."

"How'd you manage that?"

"I just applied," I answered. Then I told him about the ad in the paper and that I just took a chance and went there.

"Nuthin's impossible, honey," he said.

"I know that Ray–it's the luck of the draw. Remember how I met you?"

"Yeah, I must say, you are different Marci."

We said goodbye and I was faced with the dreaded task of having to tell Henry. When he called, I told him. Of course he threatened me and said he wouldn't help me financially as long as I insisted on working there.

So now I was a "matron" on the New Orleans Police Force. My job was to book female prisoners and escort them to their cells. That was scary. I had to get in an elevator with them and go up to the women's floor.   They were always handcuffed, but still one of them lunged at me once and tried to burn me with her cigarette. I sprayed her with mace, knocked the cigarette on the floor, stepped on it and ground it out. Unfortunately, the mace affected me too.

After that episode, I wouldn't get into the elevator with anyone smoking. The good thing was that after that incident, prisoners were no longer allowed to smoke.

Sometimes I would be put on gate duty–opening the garage gate to let the police cars in and then immediately closing it before the officers took the prisoners out. I saw some things I didn't care for, like when an officer would pull a handcuffed prisoner out of the police car, throw him on the ground and kick him. Not nice. I reported it to my Lieutenant, but it fell through the cracks.

It was a difficult time for me. I didn't earn enough money to support Lisa, Mitzi and I adequately, and true to his word, I got no money from Henry. I really cut corners, but it wouldn't be the last time I would have to do that. Cutting corners would be a life-long way of survival for me. Somehow, I learned how to live very frugally without my kids ever being aware of how bad off we really were. The three of us were always happy.

Henry had sort of disappeared. He didn't come around much, maybe once a week to see Lisa and Mitzi. Now it was common knowledge that he was living with Darlene.

About this time, Ray too seemed to have vanished. There

were no calls, and when I left messages, he didn't respond. This was over a period of about six weeks. I was so disappointed. He had seemed so happy when I told him about my job and now this.

I tried to remember everything I had said to him. What would cause him to just drop me? I couldn't think of anything. I was hurt, but more than that, I was angry.

12
Leaving New Orleans

❧⸙❧

A fellow officer had been asking me out, but because of my relationship with Ray, and because I was afraid of Henry, I declined. Now in my angry frame of mind I thought to hell with them both. Henry had someone else and Ray, I assumed, had lost interest. So I decided to accept a date with the officer. Wrong move! Oh my God!!

It was 10:00 o'clock, and we had just parked the car in the drive after a nice dinner at a quaint, little Italian restaurant with red and white-checkered tablecloths. I was going to show him my house when I heard a loud scratching and banging on the window. I knew who it was! I peeked out, and sure enough it was a furious Henry, cursing, ranting and threatening me. I was scared to death.

I ran in the kitchen and told the officer to draw his gun. At first he wouldn't. "He'll kill us. Get your gun out," I yelled as I ran to my bedroom to get my gun. Now Henry was trying to break the glass slats on the back door.

"Get your gun out!" I demanded again. He did and Henry squealed out of the driveway and left. So did my date. That wasn't the end of this night, though. I went out on the carport where the laundry area was, and on my way back into the house, Henry grabbed me, shoving me into the kitchen where I laid sprawled on the floor. I started scrambling to get up. As soon as I did, he slapped me hard, knocking me reeling across the dining room into the wall. I slid down the wall and fell to the floor. He kicked me, cursing and calling me all kinds of names. Then he just left me lying on the floor with the breath knocked out of me and he walked out the door.

I heard the car start. I feebly made my way to the bedroom, got my gun and stood at the back door. I saw Henry tuning the car radio, and I yelled out "Hey" as loudly as I could. He looked up just as I was pulling the trigger. The bullet grazed the top of the car.

I could see him scurrying to get the car in reverse, back out, and then squeal forward out of sight. He had given me the gun for an occasion such as this. Knowing that I could possibly use it on *him*, how foolish was that?

I called my girlfriend to come and get the gun and she arrived quickly. I thought the police would be surrounding my house any minute, but only one officer came. He took a statement and left. I told him there was no gun. There wasn't anymore.

The next day I was off from work, thank goodness. I needed time to calm myself and regroup. Talk about being in a mess–I was certainly in one...an irate husband, a police officer, and a pistol. What the hell! These things happen in a mystery novel, but it was happening in my life!

My job on the police force was probably over. God!!! I dreaded facing them. It gets worse.

For most of the day, I kept a low profile, too embarrassed to show my face. Towards evening, I ventured out and was immediately approached by my neighbor from across the street.

"Marci, can you come in my house? I want to show you something."

"Sure," I said and followed him into the bedroom where three of his children slept. He showed me where my bullet had entered the front of his house, gone through the bedroom and lodged in the wall just above where his children were sleeping. By this time, I was crying and sick inside, thinking of how tragic this nightmare could have turned out.

"I've never been so ashamed and sorry. The pistol is gone, and I don't want it back," I cried. By now, he had his hands on my shoulders trying to help me get control of myself.

He said, "Listen Marci, I'm not pressing charges. No one

knows this happened. I'm not taking it lightly, but I can understand why you shot at that asshole. I know he hits you."

I was sitting down now to keep from crumpling to the floor. Sobbing and shaking, I should have been begging his forgiveness but instead he was consoling me. I couldn't help but wonder what would have happened if one of the children had sat up or gotten up. I could have killed her.

Crying and miserable, I promised to never bring that gun back into my house, and I didn't (but I did come in contact with it again). Strolling slowly back across the street to my house, my head down and feeling awful, I heard the wall phone ringing. Picking up my pace to a run I got there in time to breathlessly say "Hello," and then I heard, "Yeah, Marci."

"Oh Ray!!! I'm so happy to hear your voice. I thought you forgot me."

"No, baby, I'll never do that. I've been workin' and I've been thinkin' seriously 'bout something–and I needed time."

"What is it, Ray?" I was so curious.

"I'll tell you when I see you," he said.

"When will that be?"

"As soon as you let me. When can you get away?"

"Oh, Ray...tonight, right now, I'm so happy you called. But really, I'll be off next week. Can you come then?"

"Yeah, honey. I'll be there."

When I went to work the next day, my lieutenant called me in his office. I was apprehensive, and with good reason. Henry had been there, filed a complaint against me and told them about the officer. Henry knew because he recognized the police gun. I was politely asked to resign and the officer was put on probation for a few days.

The irony of this whole ordeal is that a known criminal with a seventeen page rap sheet (I know because I read it myself) who supposedly was consistently being pursued by law officials, including the F.B.I., could just walk right into the New Orleans Police Department, file a complaint and ultimately get *me* relieved of my duties.

I was shocked at the severity of my punishment. I really didn't consider that I would be asked to resign. What really happened is they fired me.

My Lieutenant said his hands were tied and I knew they were. He liked me and had actually been in my house himself. He happened to be in my neighborhood one morning (if you can imagine that), and I invited him in for coffee. Imagine how relieved he must have felt that Henry Soto hadn't caught *him* there.

He had to have been aware of Henry's reputation. After all, he had a seventeen-page rap sheet at his fingertips and there was no one on the police force who hadn't heard of Henry Soto. As seems to be the case with many men, it appeared that his attraction to a woman compromised his common sense. Imagine that.

But at least I heard from Ray, although I had no idea what I was going to do. I had no job, no money, and damn near no life.

Driving over the Mississippi River to pick up my girls, I had a heavy heart and a sinking feeling. The only sunshine in my life this day was Lisa and Mitzi. As they came running out to greet me, I knew I would work something out. I just didn't know what.

After driving the babysitter home, I sat at the breakfast table and began sobbing uncontrollably. My poor little girls were trying to consol me, "Don't cry, MaMa. It's okay," when the phone rang.

"Hello?"

"Marci, baby."

"Oh Ray. I'm so glad you called," I started crying again.

"What's wrong, Honey?"

"Oh, everything. Henry beat me up. I lost my job. Oh Ray, just everything. I don't know what to do."

"Marci, calm down baby and listen to me. How would you feel if I get you and the kids a house and you move out here?"

I was stunned. Speechless. I was afraid to even answer him, afraid I hadn't heard correctly.

"What did you say?" I asked.

He repeated what I thought I'd heard.

"Are you serious? You really want me to move to Los Angeles?"

"That's what I said, Marci."

"Oh, Yes! Yes! Yes! I would love it."

I had to call Mary Ann, Linda and Ann immediately to share this exciting news. I was so happy. Oh! My God!! The thrill I was feeling inside. Here was the solution to all my problems. What a relief.

Just think, Marci. Yesterday your life looked absolutely bleak. Hopeless. And now you're moving to Los Angeles to be with the man of your dreams.

Ray could be in New Orleans sooner than we had planned since I no longer had a job commitment. In the meantime, I busied myself contacting and interviewing real estate agents. I needed to sell my house before I left. I was having trouble finding someone to watch Lisa and Mitzi during the time Ray would be here, so he said to get the same babysitter I had when I was working and he would pay her.

I had a restraining order against Henry, so he wasn't supposed to come to our house. He also wasn't aware that I was planning on leaving. Things would get very heated if he thought he was about to lose his family, so of course I didn't tell anyone except my girlfriends.

Ray was waiting for me at The Hyatt Regency. It was always such a thrill to knock on the door and be greeted by Ray. He always seemed so happy to see me–hugging, kissing and telling me how much he missed me.

Still in unbelievable shock and wonder, I asked Ray again, "Are you sure about me moving to Los Angeles?"

"Yes, baby. I told you. We'll get you and the kids a house." He kept saying "a house." (He never did say "an apartment," always a "house").

I asked how much time he would be able to spend with me, given his circumstances.

"Well Babe," he told me. "It's obvious it'll be more than we've got now."

"Don't you have to be home at night?" I asked.

"Long as I don't let the sun catch me" was his answer.

"Why have you made this decision, Ray?"

"It's been a year since we met and I think we'd do better, honey, at least in the same city."

"I love being with you Ray," I said, as I snuggled happily into his body.

"I love you too, Marci" he said. That was the first time he had told me that.

He left and I drove back to Gretna replaying those words over and over, a thousand times in my mind. He had told me that he found me intriguing. Imagine. Me...intriguing. And, because I had actually gotten in touch with him in the first place, he said I was mystifying. What two lovely words! Even though I didn't feel that I especially fit those labels, he certainly made me feel special.

As time went on, he would call me his "Missing Link." It became harder and harder to fit the mold he created for me. Much as I loved him, I would become my own person and remain so throughout our time together. Ray wanted me to be charming, understanding, and silent. Charming, I could be and understanding to a point, but silent wasn't me.

I was also expected to tolerate the loneliness in silence. It didn't happen. At the time of course, I knew little about Ray's expectations. All I knew was that I dearly loved my wonderful "Prince Charming," and that he had come to my rescue. I truly felt like Cinderella–and I was about to put my very life in his hands.

13
Hello Los Angeles...and Goodbye!

Deciding what furniture I should ship and what I would sell was quite frustrating since I had no idea how my new house would look, so I just settled on items that meant something to me. I didn't ship a bed or mattress, assuming that Ray would help me with some of the necessities.

It was early August of 1969, my house was under contract and I was waiting for the buyer's loan to be approved. The house was mine, bought with my own down payment using money from when Henry had demolished my car in St. Louis. The house being in my name only was yet another story...

Henry was a bigamist. Yes that's right, a bigamist, but he didn't know. He thought his previous wife had divorced him. She said she had, but she hadn't. We got the news right before we bought the house, so the house was bought in my name only. Years later, I was grateful for that!

Can you imagine the relief I felt when I heard Henry had another wife? I thought I was finally free, only to discover that "No, I was still considered married." In order to be free, I would have to divorce him.

Sal Panzeca, our attorney, said we should divorce, and then remarry in order to legalize our children. They were considered punitive, whatever the hell that meant. I didn't know and I didn't care. I wasn't having any part of it. I was Mrs. Enrique Lorenzo Soto when both Lisa and Mitzi were born and I had the license to prove it. As far as I was concerned, that was it. Finished.

So the house sold, and I gave away or sold everything I didn't think I would need and then shipped the rest to Los Angeles. Even the refrigerator with the bullet hole in the door sold!

My girlfriends had a little coffee and cake going away party for me. I would miss them so much–I had counted on them so many times and they always came through for me.

Just when I was feeling wonderful and finally free, Henry came back for one more beating. I heard him pull into the carport. I was nervous, but I wanted the kids to be able to see their dad before we left. Henry was shocked when he came in and saw how empty the house was. When he realized that I was leaving him and taking his kids, I could see the disbelief on his face. Then came the anger.

"Where the fuck do you think you're going?"

"Back to St. Louis." I answered.

He lunged at me, throwing me stumbling across the room. My knees buckled under me as I slumped against the living room wall, sobbing, moaning, and begging him to stop. His brows were furrowed menacingly and his lips were curled in a grimacing snarl as he kicked me in the ribs and stomach, knocking the breath from my lungs in a puff.

I was helpless–paralyzed. I couldn't get my breath, couldn't move. He left me lying there. As I lay sprawled on the floor gasping for air, I was grateful when I heard his car start. Eventually, I pulled my bruised body up and, bending nearly double, made my way to the couch, crying and sick inside.

This time Henry hadn't been drinking. He was in a rage. He was losing everything that meant anything to him. As I relive that time, believe it or not, I feel a deep sorrow for him. It's so very sad to watch your whole world as you know it vanish.

I notified the police of what happened, and they stepped up the patrol cars in my neighborhood. My kids were at the neighbor's house playing and luckily didn't see the commotion, but they didn't get to see their dad either.

Right after Henry left, Ray called. When I told him what had happened, he asked if I could leave earlier, like that very night, but I had to wait for the moving van and had to sign the final papers for the house sale. I wouldn't see a cent of that money for two months, not until late September.

By this time, all my in-laws had been informed that we were leaving and they came to say goodbye, including Henry. I was safe with the police patrolling and his relatives there. He was so sad, crying and sorry for everything, but that was part of the cycle–to beat me up then be sorry. This time, however, was the last time. I had somewhere to go, someone who loved and wanted to be with me– someone who was providing a home for my kids and me. I couldn't wait for my new life to begin. I smiled to myself. I felt like singing. I felt wonderful. I was in love. What a wise and comforting man Ray was. And he wanted me.

Later, I would become astutely aware that I should have gotten to know Ray better before making such a drastic change. At the time, however, I was hopeful, excited and very, very much in love. After being with him a year, I trusted and believed in him. That trust gave me the courage and confidence to move my children nearly four thousand miles away from home.

Thinking back, I don't remember whether or not Ray asked me if I needed any financial help to get us there. If he did, I would have said no because I had the money from selling my furniture. My 1966 Mustang was paid for, and I wasn't anticipating any disasters. Further, I was very independent and didn't like asking for help.

The moving van had come and gone and the kids and I were watching as the last pieces of furniture were being removed. I began filling the car trunk with drapes, waste cans full of stuff, bedspreads, sheets and some paintings. One painting was an original African painting brought to me directly from Africa. It was very interesting and I loved it.

My girlfriend pulled into the driveway to deliver my dreaded pistol before I left. I hugged her and took one last look through the house. Each room held such wonderful memories. Looking at our beautiful marble patio, I could visualize my little girls splashing in their little pool and picking plantains off our tree. I could see Henry with redwood paint all over him from painting the fence. I took one last glance at the tall cypress tree in the backyard and saw the kid's swing hanging from it. Finally, I had one last lingering look at the beautiful weeping willow tree, that Lisa and I had spent so many nights watching, sway in the southern breeze as we sang "Willow Weep for Me."

I also couldn't help thinking how relieved my neighbor must feel to have me gone after experiencing the catastrophic event with the bullet going through his walls! The police had been alerted that I was leaving and were there to form a convoy shadowing me out of New Orleans and onto the highway toward Baton Rouge.

Now safely on my way to Los Angeles, California, I was happy but nervous, constantly checking my rear view mirror, making sure I wasn't being followed by a revengeful Henry. After a couple of hours, my girls decided to cuddle up and go to sleep in the backseat. We didn't have seatbelts then and I had made a bed for them with blankets and pillows before we left, so they were snuggled in comfortably.

I felt better now that I had put some distance between New Orleans and me. I was just coming into Baton Rouge when I noticed a blinking light on the dash. What was wrong? Then the car started steaming. Oh! God! What now?

I pulled into a truck stop, my car spewing and steaming. An eighteen-wheeler pulled in behind me and the nice driver came to see if he could help. He said it probably was the radiator leaking, causing the engine to get overheated. I told him I was too tired to deal with it then, and would just get a motel for the night and worry about it in the morning.

Inside the restaurant with my sleepy little girls, I looked through the phone book. The driver, who was familiar with Baton Rouge, helped me find a motel and make arrangements to spend the night.

He told me to follow him since I had no idea where to go and he would make sure I didn't get lost. I appreciated his help, thanked him and got us inside for a night's rest for Lisa and Mitzi. Unfortunately, it was a night of worry for me.

Realizing what a precarious position I had put us in, I thought perhaps I should consider turning back, but to where? My home was gone. I really had no place to go back to. Being so hopeful and in love, I knew that was not an option, so I had to go forward. But having car trouble this soon into my cross-country journey, especially with my two little girls, made me apprehensive.

Having made the trip from St. Louis to Los Angeles once before, I was aware of the great distance and began to rethink my decision to drive. Having the car repaired would cut into my limited budget so I decided to sell it. Ray would just have to help me get a car when I got to LA.

The next morning, I made reservations for the three of us to fly to St. Louis. I also called used car lots and made arrangements to sell my 1966 White Mustang for $300 and a ride to the airport. The dealer got a good deal. My car was only three-years-old and had very low mileage (not too surprising since I was never allowed to go anywhere!). Probably the only thing wrong with the car was the radiator, but I wasn't in any position to bargain. Unfortunately, I lost all of the personal things that were in the trunk, including the original African painting. I assumed it was inexpensive, but it was lovely. There was just no way I could get that and everything else on the plane.

We arrived at the Baton Rouge Airport, then boarded a plane to St. Louis. Everything I had to my name, which was minimal, was on a moving van en route to Los Angeles or in a suitcase on the plane with me. I went from having a house, furniture and an automobile to having practically nothing, but I was still optimistic. It was just one more hurdle on a path that always seemed to be full of hurdles!

When we landed in St. Louis, my brother Don was there to pick us up. We went to my mom's small apartment where I thought we would be spending just a couple of days, but it turned out to be almost a week. Whcn I got to mom's apartment, I called Ray to fill him in on all that had happened, and he told me to stay there until he called me.

After nearly a week with cramped sleeping accommodations and cramping mom's lifestyle (she went to bed at seven o'clock and I knew the kids and I kept her awake even though we were quiet), I felt it was time to move on to my destination. I decided to go ahead and leave, so we boarded a plane bound for Los Angeles and were on our way.

My girlfriend Jean, who had been my roommate when I lived there in 1960, picked us up and drove us to the house she shared with her husband, Don, in San Clemente, about forty-five minutes away. Jean hadn't changed. She was still cute and had that bubbly personality. She opened a beer as we were driving and then tipped a few more. Even though Don complained about her drinking, he brought a six-pack home from work every day and Jean would polish it off. It didn't take long to realize Jean had a problem, which was incidentally the same problem my mother had.

When I called Ray, he was quite surprised to hear that I was in San Clemente. He thought I was still in St. Louis waiting to hear from him. (It was a huge mistake on my part not to have waited to hear from him before we left!).

Three days went by and no word from Ray!! I was getting worried and I was surprised–I thought he wanted me there as soon as possible. After everything we had talked about, I couldn't imagine why he was ignoring me!

We decided to make the best of it and continued to stay with Jean as we waited for Ray to call. There was a wonderful cliff in the back of her house that led to the beach, so Jean, her two kids, Lisa, Mitzi and I ventured down. We had fun playing at the beach, but I was preoccupied wondering what was wrong with Ray.

I spent three days cleaning, doing Jean and Don's laundry and cooking their dinner, trying to do everything to show my

appreciation.   One day I took a cab to the grocery store to buy
at least a weeks worth of groceries for everyone. I hated to feel
like we were freeloading, so I did what I could to pay our way.
I got six or seven grocery bags full, loaded them into the cab
and guess what? I didn't know where to go. I had left and
didn't know Jean's address. Now what the hell was I going to
do? I was so embarrassed. God! How stupid! Finally I remembered the street name, so I just asked the driver to keep driving
until I recognized Jean's house. By now I was in a panic. I
really needed to get back to Jean's soon.

I had contacted an old friend, Cap Capistrani, who I knew
when I lived in LA in 1960, and he was coming to see me. Back
then, there were five or six couples who hung out together. My
boyfriend at the time was Dave Klistoff, a Russian whose folks
moved from Russia to Mexico, then to the United States. Dave
spoke Russian and Spanish fluently and English with a Spanish
accent. He was adorable. I also had a crush on Cap back then,
but I cared deeply for Dave and respected him so nothing ever
happened with Cap. One time he told me, "Marci, I find you
very appealing, but I am my brother's keeper."

Cap and I were still attracted to one another when we met
at Jean's, but this time I was in love with Ray Charles. I'm so
glad I got to see him, though. After our reunion at Jean's house,
I never saw him again.

Finally, on the *fourth* morning, Ray called and asked me to
catch an 8:00 a.m. bus. It was 7:15 a.m. I had forty-five minutes to iron a blouse, find a day care and get to the bus station.
I complained but Ray said, "You can do it."

Luckily Jean's day care accepted Lisa and Mitzi. She drove
me there to register them and then she dropped me off at the
San Clemente bus station. My little Lisa, who was just about
to turn five, was crying. Mitzi, almost three, was okay as long
as she had her big sister. I was the one suffering most, though.
It broke my heart to leave my babies with strangers.

I arrived at the bus station just in the nick of time. The bus
was boarding and the driver was saying, "Last call for Los An-

geles." I asked if he would wait until I could get my ticket. "Yes," he said, "but hurry." I boarded the bus bound for Los Angeles, stressed to the breaking point from rushing so much and worrying that I would miss the bus. But I made it. Ray was right, "It *could* be done." Now all I had to be nervous and excited about was seeing Ray.

I spent that hour wondering why Ray wasn't any more prepared for my arrival than he seemed to be. I had pictured things differently. Why wouldn't he have called the night before, giving me time to make arrangements? And better yet, why didn't he send a car for me?

It didn't take long for me to realize that there wouldn't be any pampering. The bus came to a stop and everyone got off. I stepped down to find Bob Taylor, Ray's valet who I had met in New Orleans, there to greet me. He took me a few steps away to a little Volkswagen Bug and there, sitting in the car, was my sweetheart.

"Oh Ray!! I'm so happy to see you." I was gushing excitedly, oblivious to the people beginning to surround us. By now Ray was out of the car, standing and holding me.

People were saying, "Hey! Ray Charles!!! and Brother Ray!!! and What's happening, Ray?" He bent down and popped the seat up saying, "We better get out of here 'fore all these folks gather 'round us."

I got in the back with Ray in the front and Bob driving. The whole way, I had my head between the two front seats while Ray sat twisted around towards, me holding my hand. He took me to the Ambassador Hotel (where the Coconut Grove is located and where he was playing at the time). The room was lovely and relaxing, and I was with my Ray, thrilled to death and feeling optimistic again.

He asked if I wanted to order breakfast. "No thanks," I said, "I just want to be with you."

For the next two hours, we made love, talked, made more love and he told me how happy he was that I was there, that he just couldn't get enough of me, and that he wanted to spend as much time as possible with me.

We ordered breakfast, then he called Bob to come drive me around to look for an *apartment.* (An apartment?? Not a house??). Ray gave us gas money, lunch money and fifty dollars to hold an apartment. I know it sounds cheap, but honestly it wasn't. Apartments were not very expensive then, nothing like they are today.

Bob drove me all around the area near Ray's studio and I looked at many apartments. Most were unsuitable, and the ones that were suitable didn't accept children. I had to be back at the bus station at 4:00 p.m. to catch my bus back to Jean's, so I never found an apartment that day. Bob dropped me off at the bus station, and that was the last time I saw Ray while I was in Los Angeles!

Going back down the freeway to San Clemente, I wondered why Ray hadn't invited me to his show at the Coconut Grove. I had been there ten years ago when I lived in Los Angeles, but I had never seen Ray perform live. He didn't mention it to me and I hadn't thought to question him.

Jean met me at the bus station and we headed to the day care to pick up our kids. Mine were ecstatic to see their mom. Being so far from home and surrounded by strangers, they really didn't want to be separated from me. They felt very insecure, which I totally understood. They were probably getting vibes from me–I certainly wasn't feeling too secure!

A friend of Don and Jean's came by their house, heard my dilemma and offered to let my kids and I spend the night. He let us borrow his car the next day to look for a place to live. He lived halfway between San Clemente and Los Angeles, so I could get an early start and hopefully find something appropriate.

I reluctantly accepted his offer after questioning Jean like a defense attorney. She assured me that he was harmless, so off we went with yet another stranger, one who repeatedly said, "You're looking for a pie in the sky." I had no idea what he meant then nor do I now unless he meant that he doubted Ray would come through.

I was certainly having doubts, too. Ray's words, "I'll get a house for you and the kids" were ringing in my head, but Ray wasn't mentioning "a house" anymore. In fact, Ray wasn't doing much of anything anymore.

We arrived at Jean's friend's two-bedroom duplex at about 10:00 p.m. He showed us our room, then took us next door to meet his mother who would be babysitting for Lisa and Mitzi the next day. Another stranger for them. God!! This was really getting awful and it was only going to get worse.

The next morning, I left my sad and tearful little girls, with their packed breakfasts and lunches in hand, at the lady's apartment, hoping to God she was as kind as she looked. Then I left for Los Angeles with a hand-drawn map, scribbled directions and a heart full of hope.

Sleep had eluded me the night before. I was afraid to go to sleep for fear I wouldn't be alert enough to protect my kids and me if the man wasn't safe. I did have my loaded gun, but I wasn't looking forward to using that again. I was certainly not as refreshed for my adventure as I would like to have been, but I was determined to keep going.

With my newspaper in hand and apartments check-marked, I set out to find Lisa, Mitzi and me a place to live and to share with Ray. One apartment manager said, "Damn! If Ray Charles brought you all the way out here from New Orleans, you must be sayin' something."

I thought to myself, "Ray didn't bring me here. I've done everything myself. All Ray did was invite my children and I here, and so far it's been a mouthful of unfulfilled promises!"

"Marci, how would you like it if I got you and the kids a house?" That kept resonating in my head.

After persevering for two days, I gave up and the kids and I went back to Jean's, all the way listening to their friend say, "You're looking for a pie in the sky."

It was more like a pie in the face! What the hell was he talking about anyway? Couldn't he see that I was trudging the streets of Los Angeles trying desperately to find my way on my own? I couldn't wait to get away from him. Even though he was nice enough to lend me his car, I couldn't stand the damned fool and just wanted him to shut the hell up.

When Jean heard the news that I didn't find an apartment, she understood how frustrated and disappointed I was and she wasn't surprised when I announced that I felt I should go home to St. Louis. Everything was discouraging. I had applied at the Newport Beach Yacht Club for a waitress job, and at a couple of hotels for a desk clerk position, but to no avail. I was almost at my breaking point.

14

What Happened in Vegas Stayed in Vegas - Until Now!

❧◦❧

Jean really didn't want me to give up. She said, "Marci, wait until the weekend and we'll go to Vegas. I know some club owners and I know someone will give you a job."

She and her husband, Don, had been having trouble, and she wanted to leave him and move with me. We had already looked at one house in Laguna Beach. (It had shag carpet! I had never seen shag carpet before and I loved it). I wasn't able to find a job and Ray certainly wasn't coming through for me. I was definitely in murky water and began thinking how much better off I was living with Henry than with the uncertainty I was living now. A few beatings now and then didn't seem so bad compared to the fear and anxiety I was currently feeling.

I agreed to stay until the weekend and go to Vegas with Jean, but I didn't feel comfortable imposing on her and Don any longer. The kids and I got a motel room in the San Clemente business district. It was modest by all accounts–no television, radio or phone–barely large enough to fit a double bed. It did have a tiny bathroom, thank God! The walls were so thin you could hear the coughing, hacking and wheezing of the neighbors.

I had brought some books, so I entertained my little girls by reading and telling them stories. Very soon, they would fall asleep, so innocent and trusting, depending on their frightened and bewildered mom to take care of them.

The next morning I gathered some sandwiches I had brought with us and we walked to the beach where we spent most of the day. Later we went to a restaurant for an early dinner. My kids got a very nice compliment from an elderly couple who were amazed at how well-behaved and polite they were. They were always well- behaved, but considering the recent turmoil in their young lives, I was even more grateful for their ability to adapt to so many changes. They were absolutely awesome little troopers.

We took a leisurely stroll back to our dark, dreary room, not wanting to be there any more than absolutely necessary. As soon as I put our beach things down, there was a knock on the door. Jean's husband, Don, was there with a message for me to call Ray.

He said Ray told him that he was trying to reach me for some time, but couldn't get an answer. I thanked him and he left. I told my little girls to stay there, that I was going across the street to the phone booth. I closed the door and ran out to call Ray. As soon as I got to the other side of the street, I saw my little girls holding hands, standing at the busy main street. I began hysterically yelling, "Go Back! Go Back!" Thank goodness they waited. I darted through traffic, got them, and we made our way back across the street to the phone.

Ray seemed happy to hear from me. He asked me to come to Los Angeles the next morning at 10:30 a.m. and I said I would. I had no idea how I was going to do it and he didn't offer to help. Thoughts were whirling in my head. *I'll take a cab to the nursery, drop my kids off, then go to the bus station.* Once again, I would have to navigate that busy street with my kids to get to the phone to call a taxi. I was exhausted.

Then, there was another knock on the door. "Marci, it's Jean."

I was so glad to see her. She came to my rescue again by offering to lend me her car. She had sick days coming, so she took off from work and kept all four kids while I chased after Ray Charles, yet again. Lisa and Mitzi liked David and Danielle, Jean's kids, so I was relieved knowing they would be with Jean.

She had come to the motel to see what Ray wanted when he called, and when I told her that he wanted me to come to Los Angeles, she was thrilled. I thought Ray must have found a house or an apartment for us. Now I would be able to stay in Los Angeles.

Jean left and Lisa, Mitzi and I jumped in the awful shower. Then we all piled into our double bed with the see-through sheets. We had snacks in bed and I read stories by a light with a ten watt bulb. Really, the light was so dim I could hardly see.

Lisa finally said, "I don't like it here, do you Mama?"

That was the first time I'd heard even one complaint from my little girls. They never once said they missed their Dad either, but I know they did. I said, "No, Lisa, I don't like it here, but its only for a short time. We aren't staying here forever."

Even at her young age, Lisa could see that we had come down the ladder a couple of rungs. We had left a nice home, modest but nice, in New Orleans for this???? So disappointing. But I had visions of a lovely home in Los Angeles and my sweetheart wanted to see me at 10:30 a.m. Finally, it was going to happen.

Jean picked us up the next morning. Lisa and Mitzi were happy and that made me feel better, much better. Little Mitzi would go anywhere as long as Lisa was going. (She couldn't say Lisa, so she removed the L and it was Eesa for a few years). Lisa couldn't say s or z so Mitzi became Mit the. So cute. Remembering these things still just warms my heart.

Making the journey from San Clemente to Los Angeles normally would have been somewhat daunting, but on this day I felt as if I could tackle any task. I was so happy to be seeing Ray. When I got near West Washington Blvd., I stopped at a service station and called. No answer. It was 10:30 a.m. which was when he said for me to be there. I was on time. I waited a half hour and called again. No answer. I went to a drive-in for coffee, waited another half hour. No answer. This went on until 1:00 p.m. Finally he answered, sounding irritated.

By this time, I had driven back to the service station where I originally called from. Needless to say, I was sick inside and crying.

"Where the hell have you been, Ray? I've been calling since 10:30 a.m.," I said.

"Don't talk to me in that tone of voice. I've got a toothache," he barked. Then he hung up on me. I called again, but he refused to answer. I called his switchboard and was told, "Mr. Charles is unavailable."

When I turned the key to the ignition, the car wouldn't start. There I was heartbroken, crying and the damned car is dead. No sound at all. Nothing. WHAT ELSE COULD HAPPEN???

The service station attendant said I needed a battery. I didn't have enough money with me to pay for it, and no, I didn't have a charge card. I wasn't able to get a credit card until several years later.

Jean came through for me–again. She truly was a God-send. She called a friend who brought me the money to pay for the battery. After waiting what seemed like an eternity for the battery to be installed, I started the long, heartbreaking, embarrassing, humiliating and tearful journey back to San Clemente.

I desperately tried to figure out what happened to make Ray turn on me. Surely what I said wasn't enough to cause him to discard me. Something certainly happened to make him change towards me, but what? I was so stunned by his treatment of me that I couldn't figure anything out. I was absolutely heartbroken and weeping so uncontrollably that I don't even remember driving back to Jean's.

God! Did I ever have regrets. I was definitely paying a price. The memory of that day is just as vivid in my mind, forty years later, as the day it happened. I've never forgotten it. Nor have I ever forgiven Ray, even though he isn't on this earth anymore. I don't dwell on it, in fact I rarely think about it, but when I do, the wound is still fresh in my heart.

The memory still hurts, but more than that, it makes me angry– more angry than when it happened. At the time, I was too hurt to be angry. I was just sick with grief. I knew for sure, after he hung up on me, that my love affair with Ray Charles was over.

My beautiful dream had exploded into a horror film. My Prince Charming had deceived me, pushed me to the limits and thrown me away to sink or swim–and I was sinking fast.

I did, however, discover later why Ray couldn't wait to be rid of me. It was because I had too much baggage–and not my children either. Once again, Henry had reared his ugly, angry head. He had followed me to LA, and I didn't know he was there. More on this a little later.

When I pulled into the driveway, Jean rushed out to greet me with open arms, and I fell into them, sobbing. I told her what happened, between breakdowns of shoulder-shaking crying spells. Now our trip was back on, so I decided to go to our motel and pack for the drive to Las Vegas the next morning. Jean insisted on keeping my kids and me taking her car.

I was grateful for the privacy and solitude of our awful motel room, where I collapsed on the bed and cried until I fell asleep. When I went back to Jean's house to get my kids, she invited us to stay for dinner and spend the night. I declined–I was in no shape for conversation.

Jean said, "Marci, just leave the kids here and you pick all of us up in the morning."

That was good for me since I was still sobbing periodically. Now my kids wouldn't have to see me so sad.

I picked them up the next morning and we headed to Vegas, arriving at Jean's parents house in mid afternoon. I loved Jimmy and Missy Lehner. I knew them from when I shared an apartment with Jean in 1959-1960, but they were strangers to my daughters. So when Jean and I left to go shop for an outfit for me to wear out that night, once again my little girls cried.

All of my dress clothes were in storage. I had shipped everything except the bare necessities, thinking I would be settling in with Ray.

I bought a flamingo two-piece pants and top. It was horrible! I have no idea why I bought that horrendous-looking outfit. It had little teeny tiny pleats all over it, and I felt like a pink elephant in that thing. I didn't look like an elephant at

110 pounds, thank God, more like a gangly flamingo. So, all decked out in my new clothes, I was off to meet my new boss, hopefully. Sure enough, Jean's promise of finding me a job in Vegas had come through and all I needed was to pass the interview.

The casino club was ultra nice–but the conditions weren't so nice–my new "boss" was imposing the casting-couch method of interviewing. I was expected to sleep with this yucky, gross, disgusting man. Being somewhat taken aback by his bluntness, I walked to the bar where Jean sat having a drink while waiting for me. I repeated to Jean what he had said: "Marci, you're a good looking woman. You have the job providing you come to my VIP suite here in Caesar's Palace. After I leave, you and Jean may keep the suite for as long as you're in Vegas."

Ironically, as with the sale of my car, I wasn't in a position to bargain. I needed a job, and I needed one badly. In fact, I was desperate for that casino waitress job. I was reluctantly led through the Casino to the elevator, up to the top floor, and into the beautifully decorated VIP suite, which I couldn't appreciate because of the gruesome task ahead. An hour later, the man was gone, Jean was there and I was in the shower trying to scrub the caustic shame from my body.

After checking on my kids with Jean's mom, and being assured that they were content and having fun, I spoke with them. (At least I had a phone in my room, unlike San Clemente where there was nothing but a bed. Of course, I paid a dear price for this one, literally!). I told Lisa that I would be late, and she was okay. Missy was a wonderful woman who could make anyone feel warm and secure.

Jean and I prepared to go clubbing to celebrate my "great achievement," a job *and* money. My "boss" had left $300 on the dresser with a note saying, "Here's an advance toward your paycheck. Be here for training on Wednesday at 11:30 a.m." Little did I know that I would be in Kansas City, Missouri on Wednesday morning. (Actually, I was there at 4:00 a.m. on Monday, due to an unexpected...and ugly turn of events).

❧

So Jean and I hit the clubs—me in that God awful million pleated flamingo fiasco and Jean in a cute sundress with backless high heels. (In 1960 we called them springalators). We had lots of drinks in different clubs, then went to have something to eat. Some other people were with us, but I don't remember who they were.

Jean and I were seated side-by-side in a booth. Behind us, and back-to-back, was a girl and a cute guy. Suddenly, Jean turned around and said to him in her southern drawl, "Ah wont choo." (I want you). Did she get him? No, his girlfriend got him out of there in a hurry or Jean probably would have gotten him! My money would have definitely been on Jean. She was a compelling force of naivete, innocence and sexuality, which made her very appealing to the opposite sex—and she definitely liked them back.

I was tired and had consumed more to drink than I needed. That VIP suite was becoming more enticing by the second, but Jean wanted to stay out drinking and gambling. I couldn't manage that, so I wove my way to the Caesar's Palace suite and snuggled into the freshly changed sheets, this time to sleep. Thank God!

We stayed in Vegas until Sunday morning, then drove back to San Clemente, where I would be packing our meager belongings for the move to Las Vegas. Lisa, Mitzi and I were going to stay with Jeans folks just until I could find an apartment. Jean was moving to Vegas, too. The drive back to San Clemente was tiring, but I snapped to attention quickly when I got there and found out what was waiting for me.

As soon as we parked, Don bolted out the door, almost hysterically yelling, "Marci, you gotta get out of here. Henry just left and he's coming back."

"What?" I said terrified.

"You gotta go NOW. He's gonna kill you and let the sharks eat the evidence and take his kids to Mexico. And he's furious."

"Oh God! Oh! My God!," I was crying.

I hurriedly packed everything and took a cab to the bus station. Don wouldn't let Jean drive me. He was afraid of Henry and didn't want a big commotion at his house. I couldn't blame him.

Jean and I hugged quickly and I said I didn't know when I would see her again. As it turns out, that was the last time I ever saw her. We did keep in touch for a few years, but then lost contact. I wish I could find her. I tried recently via the computer with no luck. She was such a good friend to me and I still miss her. She would be in her seventies now and probably still just as cute as a bug.

15
Good-bye L.A. - Hello Kansas City

Jean and her children were trying to wave goodbye as Don frantically hovered over them, trying to get them into the house quickly in case Henry reappeared. Lisa, Mitzi and I huddled nervously in the back seat as the taxi sped away toward the bus station. I had no idea how Henry planned to abduct me–whether at gun point or by physically grabbing me and throwing me into his car. Anything was possible with him. Having been choked by him before until I fainted, I knew *that* feeling and it wasn't pleasant. God!!! I was so scared. I had no idea how he found me. I thought I was safe.

Before I let my kids get out of the taxi, I ran into the station entrance and checked to make sure he wasn't there. All was clear, so I grabbed my poor innocent little girls and ran to the entrance. They looked at me and asked, "Where are we going now, Mama?"

"We're taking the big bus to the airplane to see Mary Ann," I said as reassuringly as I could.

I was frightened and nervous as I went to the ticket counter to inquire about the departure time to L.A. Airport and was told it would be boarding in twenty minutes. That gave me a moment of relief. At least I didn't have long to wait.

Scared isn't a strong enough word to describe how I felt. I was terrified. I was looking back over my shoulders constantly. The least little noise sent shivers up my spine, causing me to tremble. "Why are you shaking, Mama?" asked my little Lisa.

I hadn't had a panic attack since before moving to Gretna. Now I was frightened and felt one coming on. It was as if a heavy cloud would start at my head and slowly penetrate my body until it completely engulfed me.

Oh, please, please don't let this happen now. I need to think.

The sudden announcement "Now boarding for L.A. Airport" jolted me back to reality. Thank God!! I scurried my kids onto the bus, took a seat near the back, and tried to be as inconspicuous as possible. Sitting on the edge of my seat, I was dreading the moment when Henry's face might pop up at the front of the bus and he would storm back and drag me through the aisle to God knows where!

I snuggled my kids close to me, trying to hold on to what was real, not allowing myself to drift into this horrible nightmare that had become my life. When the bus door finally clanged shut, I felt a flood of relief. Whew—at least we were safe for the ride to the airport. After that, I had no idea what to expect.

I was so scared my mind began playing tricks on me. If a man got out of his seat, I would think it was Henry, knowing full well it couldn't be. I saw everyone who boarded the bus.

As petrified as I was, though, I couldn't help but contemplate Ray's treatment of me. Still bewildered and in a state of wonderment, all I knew was that I was hurt, grief-stricken and broken-hearted.

"L.A. Airport next stop" the driver announced.

"Oh, gosh. I wonder what awaits me here," I worried.

I only had one suitcase and a carry on so I managed my own luggage. My two little girls followed me to a restroom where I washed us with a cloth from our carry on, changed our clothes (we were dusty from our Vegas trip—didn't get to shower) and hurried to the T.W.A. ticket counter.

"What time is the next flight to Kansas City, Missouri?" I asked.

The ticket agent said, "It leaves in one hour." Then he gave me the gate number. I bought our tickets and waited anxiously at the gate until I heard them announce our flight. As afraid as I was of flying, I wouldn't feel safe until we were airborne. I wanted the hell out of L.A.!

Gratefully, they fed us on planes then, and as awful as airline food was, it tasted good to us. And best of all, we were safe. What a relief. We all slept.

As the plane began the decent to the Kansas City Airport, I began to feel eager and excited. I was about to see a face I dearly loved...Mary Ann's. I had called her from the bus station so she knew we were coming. I told her we would arrive in the wee hours Monday morning. True to form, she was there with her son, Stan, and a friend. I've never been so happy to see a face in my life as I was hers. To me, Mary Ann was milk and cookies–a warm fireplace on a cold winter night. She was my comfort zone. I felt like I had come home from a long, long journey.

Stan and his buddy, Jack, carried my kids. They knew Stan. I just held onto Mary Ann and cried and cried. I was crying from the pain of Ray hurting me so badly, crying from exhaustion and weariness, and finally crying because I felt safe at last.

Mary Ann's two bedroom, two bath townhouse looked like a haven to me. The aroma of delicious cooking filled the air. It was only 5:30 in the morning, yet Mary Ann and Stan had prepared this wonderful food for us. This was so typical of Mary Ann throughout the years. We (or rather she) would cook all day. We would dress up and go clubbing at night, then eat and graze all the next day. (This happened later, after I got settled back in St. Louis, when the kids and I would drive to Kansas City to visit her).

On this morning, however, after feeding her five kids, Stan -19; Toni -10; Barry - 8; Raymond - 4, Maria - 2 1/2 and my two, we lounged in her king sized bed. While sipping our steaming coffee, I relived every heartbreaking detail of my devastating trip. By the time I finished my miserable story, we had gone through two boxes of Kleenex and we both had red, puffy eyes. Needless to say, Mary Ann wasn't too thrilled with Ray Charles. She wanted to call him and give him a piece of her mind, but I didn't want her to. It's strange, because later, her last child, Maria, who was born with Down's Syndrome, didn't seem to like Ray either.

When Ray Charles would appear on television, little Maria would put her hands over her ears, yell and leave the room. When Elvis came on, though, she would smile and watch him. To this day, we have no idea why she behaved so erratically when she saw Ray. Just recently, Mitzi said, "Mom, Maria might have heard you and Mary Ann discussing Ray and understood more than you thought she was capable of."

Maria was the sweetest little thing. Mitzi was reminded that she was the one who made Maria cry for the very first time in her life. We had come to St. Louis from New Orleans for a family visit and to spend time with Mary Ann. We settled the kids down and were getting comfortable ourselves. For some reason, Mary Ann was telling me about Satanic spirits being able to enter your house when suddenly we heard a blood curdling scream emanating from Maria's room. Everyone got up, scurrying frantically to find out what had happened. What could it possibly be? Maria had never cried or screamed. Well…we found little two-year-old Mitzi with her hand stuck between the slats pulling Maria's hair. That was Maria's first encounter with physical pain, and very possibly her only encounter with pain. Mary Ann has always taken such good care of her. When Henry came to get us that day, Mary Ann told him that "the dead would rise from their graves on judgment day." Henry was mortified. "Damn, baby, that's scary." (Henry pronounced it Sca'-Ree!).

I've digressed enough. Back to Kansas City. Mary Ann recalls me being unable to eat, in fact being unable to do much of anything but cry. Two or three days after I got there, I was in the upstairs bathroom when I heard a plop in the commode water, then came profuse bleeding.

"Mary Ann, come quickly," I yelled.

"What's wrong?" she said as she entered the bathroom.

"Look," I pointed.

She told me to sit down while she went to get paper plates and plastic utensils. I could hemorrhage she said. So, scared to death, I sat very still. Retrieving the bloody mass from the commode, she told me I had had a miscarriage.

"Oh my God! Now what?" I whispered. "Do I go to the hospital?"

Mary Ann said, "No, it's no big deal. Go lie down."

Having worked in hospitals as a nurses' assistant and also having had two miscarriages herself, I figured she knew what she was talking about. I trusted her, and did as she said.

I was kind of shocked by this. I had been using a preventative– not the pill, I couldn't take it. Obviously, my preventative didn't work. As I think about it now, I realize how naïve I was then, not to take every precaution. It gives me the cold chills! What if I hadn't left New Orleans? What if I hadn't miscarried? What if? What if? What if? Well, the answer to "what if" is that I would have been in severe trouble.

We stayed with Mary Ann for about a week and a half. Then it was time for me to move on. Mitzi had turned three and Lisa was turning five. I had to get her registered for kindergarten. Besides, that, my brother, Don, had told Henry where I was.

I didn't want him to show up at Mary Ann's. Even though she knew him and wasn't intimidated by him, I certainly didn't want to confront him. I knew how hurt and angry he was at me–leaving him for another man. Knowing him as well as I did, I had good reason to be afraid. Being hurt plus angry, he would be poison.

I didn't have the money to fly to St. Louis, so Mary Ann and Stan drove us to the train station. They waved goodbye as we boarded the train. I hated leaving Mary Ann, but I had to figure out what to do with my life and get started turning things around. I felt overwhelmed and weary, but I couldn't quit. I had two little lives to support and mold into good human beings.

Thankfully, Mary Ann had packed sandwiches for the kids

and me. I only had fourteen cents left to my name. I saved that, just in case I would need to make a phone call. Phone calls were a dime then.

16
St. Louis Woman

❧

Our train rolled into Union Station in downtown St. Louis right on time. I had almost come full circle–New Orleans, St. Louis, Los Angeles, Las Vegas, Kansas City and St. Louis again. Destiny must have meant for me to be in St. Louis because I'm still here, forty years later.

After all that traveling in such a short time, the kids and I had become seasoned travelers. We could be ready to go at a moment's notice. I didn't feel so great about myself, though. Rejection is a hard pill to swallow. My mother had thought it was a bad idea for me to take the kids and go to L.A. in the first place, so I came home with my tail between my legs. I tried to do it as gracefully as I could, but there just isn't a graceful way to handle rejection. It's far too painful.

So we had no choice but to move back into Mom's cramped little apartment, and it truly was an imposition. She had very little money. She barely made ends meet and there was nothing superfluous in her lifestyle.

The kids and I were at the mercy of anyone who would extend a helping hand, and luckily, my family members were most willing to do whatever we needed.

I registered Lisa in Budar kindergarten class. Mitzi and I walked her the few blocks to school every day, and every day she cried, so we would stay an hour and then sneak away. She had been left so often during the past three weeks that she had a difficult time of it. Mitzi and I would just get back to Mom's apartment, and it would be time to go back to get Lisa.

My afternoons were spent combing the newspapers for jobs and calling for interviews. I got no positive responses. It seemed no one needed me for a damn thing. At night, I had dreams of knocking on doors begging for a job, only to be turned away.

I even thought about calling Ray. Not just to ask him to help me, but because I needed answers to questions that were poignant to me. I had a propensity for Ray Charles that didn't fade, no matter what happened between us, and hasn't to this day, but I still had my pride, so I refused to call him.

We had been with my poor mom for about three weeks when an apartment became available next door to my brother, Don. What a break! We moved into our over-the-garage, stand-alone apartment immediately. It had a stove, refrigerator and a huge buffet which the previous tenant had left behind. There were three empty rooms, a small bathroom and a kitchen. We were so happy to finally have a place of our own.

My first purchase was a phone. One day, shortly after we moved in, my friend, Ona, called to inform me that she had a bedroom set for sale. Great! Don picked it up and brought it to the apartment for me. It had been in a fire and cost me $25.00. I sanded and stained it, and believe me, it turned out very nice.

Then Don took me to the Goodwill store where I bought dishes, pots, silverware and bunk beds (which we couldn't use because we had no mattresses). I also bought an old, lumpy mattress for the single bed where the three of us slept until I bought new mattresses for the bunk beds (which was within a week). Ironically, Ray, who could have the best of the best of everything, slept on that lumpy old mattress years later after we moved into our house in Kirkwood, Missouri.

I was moving right along, and was determined to make a home for my kids. We ate our meals sitting on the bed, which was a bit difficult for my little girls.

Then I got a great phone call–my mother called to say "Your check came today." Oh, great, the check from the sale of my house. Now we had lots of money–$2,700.00 to be exact. We had gone from rags to riches, or at least it felt that way to me.

I paid back the money that I had borrowed to get my utilities turned on, pay my rent and get groceries, etc. It felt so good to get everyone paid back.

Next, I called California and had my furniture shipped back. My furniture had gone on a round trip excursion for nothing. What a blatant waste of money–money that I didn't have. My L.A. move had been expensive, both financially and emotionally, and the memory has not dimmed to this day, nor will it ever.

The day our furniture arrived I was soooo happy. Now our apartment was complete and very comfortable, and things were finally falling into place. Lisa was enrolled in Fenton kindergarten. Luckily she had our landlord's son, Timmy Seebold, to walk with her to catch the bus. The first day, Mitzi and I drove behind the bus the two miles or so to Fenton. We were waving and honking the horn. Later Lisa told me she wanted to die. We had embarrassed her! We were feeling less threatened and much more secure, and we were having fun.

Don found an old Chevy and bought it for me, so now I had wheels and could finally do for myself. I was getting more and more independent. Then Dad and Don bought Lisa a pony!

She became quite the rider. She and Smokey, her pony, were inseparable. Once, when Smokey got an eye injury, we brought him to our apartment (we sort of lived in the country), and tied him to a tree on a rope long enough for him to get in Lynn Seebold's shed on piles of straw. Lynn was our friend and landlady. There, we were able to keep a check on Smokey's eye, which, by the way, healed nicely.

One day, I looked out the door and saw the cutest thing. Smokey was lying down and Lisa was propped up against him eating a peanut butter sandwich. She would take a bite, then Smokey would take a bite. It was so cute.

Life was good on the "outskirts of town."

On any given day, we could look out and see Lynn's horse, Hank, grazing in the green pasture, framed by a white, oak

plank, corral-type fence that she built. The pasture ran in front
and on the side of our apartment. On the other side of our
apartment was another acre and a half, where Lynn and Bill's
large house, the lovely pool, (which my kids and I enjoyed), and
my brother's small house were. A long, long driveway, just in
front of our apartment and between the pasture and Lynn's
yard, connected us to the road.

The grounds were park like, just beautiful. There were lots
of large trees and plants. It was peaceful–that is until the mo-
torcycles roared in, or the Seebolds had a big pool party, or Billy
started one of his boats in the garage under our apartment. That
would send me over the edge. Mostly, though, it was a peaceful
atmosphere.

Billy Seebold was a Marine Dealer, but more than that, he
was, and still is, the most famous boat racer in the world. The
parties were great fun with lots of good-looking boat racers. Lynn
fixed all her girlfriends up with boat racers, including me, so I
wasn't twiddling my thumbs waiting for Ray Charles to call.

I finally got a job at the Flaming Pit restaurant. It's probably safe to say that I was the worst waitress in the world. I
wasn't a bad cocktail waitress, but I was a horrible food server.
I couldn't keep anything straight. Orders got screwed up. I
couldn't concentrate. It was awful.

Once, when my car was broken down, I remember having
to drive my brother's old battered pickup truck, with no heater,
to work. I was so cold it would take forever for me to thaw out
and be limber enough to work. Then I would have to battle
the cold going home. At 1:00 in the morning, it seemed even
colder. Driving alone in the wee hours of the morning in the
cold, I was lonely. It was at these times when I most resented
Ray. I thought, "If I hadn't trusted him, my kids and I would
be in a nice warm home in New Orleans." I couldn't help
wondering if he ever thought of me, or ever wondered what
happened to me. I was sure he thought I went back to Henry.

About a year later, when I contacted Jean for the first time
since I left L.A., she told me that Ray had called inquiring about

me. All she could tell him was that I had left L.A. bound for Kansas City. Since Ray hadn't heard much, if anything, about Mary Ann at that time, he would have no idea why I fled to Kansas City.

Two things happened while I was working at the Flaming Pit restaurant. I got offered another job and I got money from Henry via Mary Ann.

As I was picking up an order to serve a customer, I glanced at the door. "Oh God!" I said. "There's my husband and my best friend."

"Your best friend?" my co-worker said in shock. "What the hell's she doin' with your husband?"

"Oh, no," I hurriedly answered, "It isn't like that."

She watched as I served my table and timidly made my way over to where Mary Ann and Henry were sitting. I didn't know if he would grab me and throw me on the floor, so I approached cautiously, ready to bolt at the slightest gesture from Henry. Mary Ann casually got up and walked toward me, hugging me and whispering, "I got you some money, and he promised he wouldn't hurt you." Then she handed me an envelope.

Henry said, "there's $500.00 in the envelope, baby, and can I please see my kids?"

I, of course, was very apprehensive. Here I was facing the man who was going to feed me to the sharks a few months ago. Henry asked if he could come to my apartment the next day, which was Saturday.

"Yes," I agreed, "providing Don's there." He would be my protector if I needed it.

Mary Ann had been visiting in St. Louis, and she had stayed in one of the apartments above "Le Jazz Hot," her ex-husband Pat Aluisa's place. That's where she had run into my ex.

That Saturday, Henry showed up alone in a taxi. The kids were so happy to see their daddy. We all had a nice time. Then he left for the airport and flew back to New Orleans.

He promised that he would send child support, which he did for the next two years. Then he stopped and would send money sporadically. He always sent money for Christmas, birthdays and enough to help me buy their fall and winter school clothes and supplies, though. Mitzi wore Lisa's outgrown clothes, but that was fine because she loved wearing Eesa's clothes.

I quit working at the Flaming Pit and began a job as a coat checker at a club called the Red Onion. The money was a little better, not much, but the job was easier. I loved it when the mob members came in. They were great tippers! I made more money from just one of those guys than I did from all the other customers combined.

The Red Onion was much further away than the Flaming Pit. It was in downtown St. Louis near the water front. I drove there three nights a week in my trusty old Chevy, and made it every time.

I was still stewing over Ray. One day it finally got to me and I couldn't let it go. I wondered what I could do to feel better about what he did to me. I made the decision to send the $50.00 deposit that he had given to me for an apartment back to him.

Not trying to rekindle anything, I got a money order rather than a check, so it would have no return address or phone number on it. I sealed it in an envelope along with a note that I punched out in Braille. It said, "You need this measly $50.00 more than I do. Stick it in your ass," and signed it, "Marci."

My, how things had changed since that wonderful first year in New Orleans when I could never have uttered a hateful word to Ray. Now I couldn't think of anything bad enough to say to the asshole. I am, by nature, a revengeful person, as you will see. Sometimes it takes years, but I'm usually successful!

In order to write Braille, I needed a stylus, slate and Braille paper. I went to the Missouri School for the Blind and the receptionist was nice enough to give me the things I needed. Since I didn't know the Braille alphabet, she also gave me a card with letters from A to Z in raised dots, that I could copy. I still have all of it to this day. I also have another stylus that Ray gave me. It fit my fingers better and he said it would be easier for me to use. It was much easier. It had a bigger point so the raised dots were larger and easier for him to read.

I worked at the Red Onion Wednesday, Thursday and Friday nights, and I left my kids home with a babysitter. Getting home at 2:30 or 3:00 in the morning, then up at 7:00 to get Lisa off to school, then back to sleep with Mitzi 'till 10:00 was our routine. Then Mitzi would eagerly await Lisa's arrival home, asking me over and over, "when is Eesa coming, Mama?"

Soon we would see Lisa's little red plaid coat as she and Timmy, carrying their kindergarten papers, met Mitzi running down the long lane to greet them. Life was good.

17
A Surprise Phone Call

When I sent the money order to Ray, it sort of gave me closure, and I began to accept the fact that I would never see him again. I knew that I could never completely forget him–he was in my heart. I would see him on T.V., hear him on the radio and in stores where I shopped, so there were constant reminders of him. The only way I could not be reminded of him was to stay home with everything turned off.

The kids and I absolutely loved our apartment. We settled in nicely. I worked my three nights a week at the Red Onion and on Sundays we rode horses without fail. Lisa rode her pony and I rode whatever Dad or Don had available, usually a gated Palomino horse named Charlie. He was like sitting in a rocking chair, so easy to ride. Sometimes, I rode Honeycomb, a gated mare. Mitzi always rode behind Grandpa in a little saddle Dad had rigged to fit behind his saddle, and she held onto Dad's belt loops. Thank God they never broke loose–how crazy was that? I can't believe I actually let her do that!

The kids and I had arrived in St. Louis from L.A. in September of 1969. Now fall was approaching and it was terrific riding weather. We rode our horses through the last of November until it became too cold. Then we spent our time preparing for our first Christmas in Sunset Hills. It was so exciting. We decorated a tree that Don cut down and set up in our living room.

All of my family came, including Henry who was there bearing gifts that we had shopped for together. Lisa got a new red and black saddle for Smokey, and the kids got many more dolls and toys and new clothes for winter. All in all it was a

Merry Christmas. Henry was on his best behavior and we got along very well. There was no intimacy between Henry and me though. That never happened between us again.

Don's house was too small for Henry to stay there, so he slept on our couch (actually it was his couch too, since I took it when I left New Orleans). After two or three days, he went back to New Orleans and we resumed our normal, relaxed life style.

Don and I shared groceries for dinner, so he usually ate with us every night. One night we were talking over dinner and he casually said, "Oh, I almost forgot. Ray Charles has been trying to get ahold of you."

"What? What do you mean? How do you know?" I said, completely shocked.

"Well, he called me a couple of days ago and asked if I knew where you were. I said, 'Yes' and he asked for your telephone number. I said, 'Ray I can't give you her number, but I'll tell her you called and she can do whatever she wants.'"

"How did he get your number?" I asked.

He said, "Well, I asked him that and he said he got it when he was here last Christmas."

"Oh, that's right. I gave it to him before I left New Orleans, along with Mom's so he could call me when he got to St. Louis."

I had forgotten all about that. Now all of the progress I had made the past few months toward healing my heart just vanished and I was right back, unquestionably, and as I said when I first met him, irretrievably in love with Ray Charles.

For the next few days, I functioned in a daze. I didn't know whether to call Ray or not. Of course I was dying to, but scared to death and stunned that he was trying to find me after so callously throwing me away just six months ago.

A few nights later, Don said, "Ray Charles has been calling. Are you gonna call him or do you want me to tell him not to bother you anymore?"

"No," I said. "Please don't tell him that!"

I had to muster up the nerve to call him. What if he just wanted to tell me off after that nasty note I sent about the money. I really didn't think I could take any more rejection from Ray. I already had a broken heart, and didn't want it to completely stop beating. And I was still angry with him. If he would have said one wrong thing to me, I would have jumped through the phone at him. So I waited.

I was daydreaming about him constantly and imagining that I talked to him. Finally, I broke down and called him.

"Operator. Collect call to (I gave her the number), Mr. Ray Charles please".

Ray answered, "Yeah."

The operator said, "Collect call from Mar..." Ray interrupted, "I'll take it operator! I'll take it!"

"Hi, Ray," I timidly eeked out, having no idea how he was going to respond to my call.

"Marci, babe, is it really you? I thought I'd lost you forever." Ray couldn't stop. "Baby, don't ever do that again. I don't know what to say. I'm so relieved to hear from you."

I said, "I thought you wanted to be free of me."

"Don't ever say that, Marci. I'll never want that. We're forever, Babe. Honey, when can I see you?"

Within a few days, I picked him and Bob Taylor, his valet, up at the airport in Don's Bonneville and took them to the Holiday Inn. I remember distinctly because Ray really liked Don's Bonneville.

After Bob checked them in, Ray and I went to our room and had "our own little honeymoon" for a couple of days. My imagination paled in comparison to the reality of actually being with Ray.

Questions were resonating in my head. *Why did you discard me Ray? What happened?*

I needed answers, but I didn't get them because I was too afraid to ask. I didn't want to make waves–I just wanted to be with him. I was certain that in time he would tell me what happened and tell me how sorry he was, and he did–eighteen years later! But I pieced it all together myself long before that (which I'll explain later).

After our reunion, there were many phone calls and visits but never enough for me. I gave Ray a lot of grief about that. I put up with it–what else could I do, short of cutting him off completely, and I wasn't ready to do that. That would come later....

We saw each other in motels throughout 1970 and 71. Ray wasn't comfortable coming to my apartment. He knew my Dad didn't approve of his daughter and a black man, although that isn't exactly how Dad phrased it, if you know what I mean.

The kids and I continued riding our horses in parades, trail rides and just around the countryside. Lynn and Billy Seebold had a huge pool party, which I attended–with a date. I went to the boat races and to the big boat racers banquet, and all in all I had fun. But I was still in love with Ray. Even though I wasn't sitting at home, I wasn't actively looking for a different life because Ray was always there, in the back of my mind, tugging and pulling at my heart.

I had been more at peace before I sent the money order because I knew then I wouldn't hear from him. Now, even though I was happy that he was back in my life, I was also uptight and anxious, wondering if every time the phone rang it would be him.

Ray always wanted me to cook something special for him and bring it to the motel when he came. There were certain dishes that he especially liked: neck bones and cabbage; liver smothered in onions; chicken, etc. I took food to him occasionally, but after the kids and I moved into our house in Kirkwood, I cooked more for him because he was there. It was much easier to just serve him at our table than to drag food all over town to a motel.

Ray was fascinated by my family, and he loved hearing my crazy stories about them. Without fail, he would tell me, "Marci, you should write a book about your family. It would be a best seller." I told Ray many stories about my family and me. One of his very favorites, which he would laugh about for years to come, was the one about the Chicken and Dumpling.

I decided to make my Aunt Oretha's splendid recipe for chicken and dumplings for dinner one night. Her chicken and dumplings were to die for–everyone in our family would drive for miles just to eat them. Knowing how my brother loved the dish, I started calling him at work first thing in the morning and continued calling him, teasing him, throughout the day.

I was trying to drive him crazy with anticipation, just to tempt him. I was going to prepare the dumplings and serve them with a couple of vegetables and warm buns, just like Aunt Reth did. Well–mine were not quite like hers!

After work, Don came up the long drive way and backed his pick-up truck into his parking place alongside the corral fence. My kids excitedly ran to greet him as they did every evening. Don was such a good surrogate dad to my little girls. He was always there for them. He picked Lisa and Mitzi up, swung them around and went to his house to shower, yelling up to me "I'll be there in about an hour."

"Good," I yelled back. "I'll put the dumplings in now."

Don said, "Okay, can't wait."

You aren't supposed to stir dumplings, so I just shook the pot as Aunt Reth had said, not removing the lid. When Don came bounding up the stairs, he said, "Boy, this really smells good. I've been waitin' all day for this."

He walked over to the pot, lifted the lid and said, "Oh! What's this? Chicken and.....a dumpling?"

I ran over to look. Oh my God! It was one huge dumpling.

Don and I burst out laughing. "What happened?" he said. "You better call Aunt Reth."

She laughed and said, "Doodie (my nickname) you put too much baking powder in your dough." I took the dumpling out, gave it to Sounder (a neighbor's dog who had adopted us) and we had boiled dry chicken and no dumplings. Don said,

"Don't ever do this to me again."

When I told Ray, hc howled with laughter. Later, as Don was driving Ray and Bob to the airport, Ray mentioned what a good cook I was. Don said, "She is, but don't ever ask her to make you chicken and dumplings."

Ray was laughing so hard. He said, "Yeah, Don. I won't make that mistake. I heard about the big dumpling."

∽∾

During that year (1970), Ray was in St. Louis several times to see me. One of those times, Lisa, my first grader, was in a Christmas program at Rott Elementary School. Ray decided to come anyway. He said he would get a cab to the motel and I could just come after the program when I had Mom and the kids settled in for the night.

Of course, Bob Taylor was always with him during those years. Ray didn't start coming alone until after October of 1971 when I bought my house. Then, I would pick him up at the airport.

So, I got everyone all cozy and snuggled in, then I left for the motel and my sweetheart. As always, I couldn't wait to see him.

I knocked on his door and heard that sweet growl, "Yeah, come on in, babe".

"Hi, Sweetheart," I said as I melted into him. Oh God, I loved that man. I turned into liquid when I was with him. I felt like a cloud that just became enmeshed into his body.

Finally, when I became coherent again, he asked about my kids and the Christmas program.

"Oh, Ray," I answered. "They were so cute. They were not supposed to wave to the parents, only wink. It looked like lights blinking with the whole first grade singing and winking."

"Aww, how cute," Ray said. "I never heard of anyone doing that. It's a cute idea."

"And of course my eyes were glued to Lisa. She was so cute and I'm so proud," I bragged.

110

Ray said, "I know you are, honey. Maybe some day I'll get to meet them."

I said, "Yes, you will, Sweetheart, and soon."

I felt so comfortable with Ray, and he was always so interested in my family. As I mentioned before, he loved to hear my family's stories–he always got a kick out of my escapades!

༄༅

My brother graphically described another incident to Ray which sparked a nickname that stuck with me during our entire time together. Don told Ray, "My sister's a hell cat, Ray."

"Oh, I know that, but tell me what *you* mean." Ray was all ears and laughing.

"Well," Don went on, "one morning, after we all just got in from an all-day and overnight trail ride, I banged on Marci's door and yelled, 'Get up. You gotta go fight Velma.' Velma was Dad's live-in. 'What do you mean?' Marci asked.

'Oh, she's up at the barn rantin' and ravin' about you and Ray Charles.'"

I interrupted, "Don, I can't believe you're telling Ray about that."

He continued, "Dood (Marci) was still groggy and tired from the trail ride and me bustin' in like that. She started putting her tennis shoes on, and I said, 'No, put your cowboy boots on. You're gonna need em.'"

I interrupted again, "So we got in Don's car–my poor little kids crying, 'No Mama, don't fight. Don't fight!!' I told them, "Maybe I can talk to her. I'll be okay. Don't cry.'"

Don explained what had happened to set Velma off as we were on our way to the barn. Velma was mad as hell because when I was in P.N. Hirsh, the store where she worked and where Don's good friend was the manager, she was loudly saying how I should be ashamed of myself going with Ray Charles.

I told her to mind her own business and shut her mouth or I would shut it for her. Ray was laughing.

"Poor Mason, the store manager, didn't know what to do,"

111

I continued. "I left the store mad as hell too. Then all of us, except Velma, went on our weekend trail ride. She had all weekend to stew and rant and rave, and she worked herself into a frenzy.

"When we all got back from our trail ride, Don and Dad took the horses to the barn to unload them and the kids and I went home. We were so tired, we laid down without even showering first.

"Velma started ranting and raving to my brother, and he listened to all of the accusations that he could take. He was really mad at her. That's when he came to get me to shut her up.

"When we pulled into the barnyard, she was ranting and cursing and waving her arms like a wild woman. I got out of the car and here she came, arms spread wide, lunging at me. I grabbed her hair, twisted, and flipped her, rolling her down the barnyard."

Don added, "Like a big tub of lard."

"I let her get up rather than attacking her while she was down. She came running at me again and we both went down, me on top, scraping her shin with my boots. Now I can see why Don told me to wear them. I really did need them!

"My dad kept tugging at me trying to get me to stop fighting her, and Don was pulling him off me. Velma finally gave up. As we were leaving, she started to say something and Don said, 'You'd better shut up or I'll let her out again.'–like he's letting me out of a cage or something.

"My kids said, 'Mama, you're really strong.'"

"What a mess." I said. "I was embarrassed."

After Ray got control of himself from howling with laughter, he started baby talking to me, "Aaww, baby it's all right. Ya gotta do whatcha gotta do."

But I never lived it down. I was Ray's "little hellcat" throughout our relationship.

18
Horses, Ponies and More Stories

Lisa's Christmas program was at the end of 1970; the fight was in mid 1970, and many things happened throughout that year. Mitzi got a tiny pony with a little saddle. She and Porky were quite a team–eventually–but she was a little apprehensive in the beginning. She had a frightening experience riding Lisa's pony, Smokey, and it took her quite awhile to get over it. The horse/pony story was just one more that I related to Ray–he was always so interested in detailed accounts of our lives.

Don was riding his huge Pinto gelding, Comanche, on the lane that went from the back gate to the entrance gate beside the barn. Mitzi was following behind him on Smokey. She was four and a half and it was her first solo ride. Up until then, Mitzi had almost always ridden behind Grandpa, or sometimes in the front of my saddle with me.

My dad was sitting just off the lane in his pickup truck. He was, as usual, telling Don what to do–most likely getting a couple of swigs of Seagram's Seven from his trusty half pint, which he was never without. Dad would always blow on the opening of the bottle, turn it up for a swig, then go "aaaah!" and wipe his mouth with the back of his hand.

Don was riding through the gate with Mitzi and Smokey doing just fine right behind him. Suddenly, a little white fluffy Maltese dog came yipping and yapping up to the fence, at which time Smokey spun around, nearly pitching Mitzi off. She clung to the saddle horn as the pony took off like a bat out of hell.

He was galloping full speed ahead, passing Dad on the left. Dad was sitting in his stationary truck in a frenzy, senselessly twisting the steering wheel left to right yelling, "Get that pony! Don! Get that pony!"

Smokey passed Lisa and me as we were standing on the right, then we ran like hell to catch him. The whole time, Mitzi's saddle was slowing slipping to the side as if in slow motion.

Here came Don, at a full gallop, after Smokey.

Smokey ran to the back gate and stopped dead in his tracks. Mitzi was still hanging on to the saddle like she was glued to it, but the saddle was almost under Smokey's belly. Don and Comanche came to a skidding halt, and Don leapt off like someone in a Wild West show to get Mitzi released from the saddle before Smokey decided to take off again.

Dad was so mad, cursing and storming around, "Who the hell let her get on that pony without tightening the girth?!"

Poor little Mitzi was crying, vowing never to ride by herself again, but of course she did. I have many videos of her riding Smokey in the pasture beside our apartment.

Ray sat on the side of the bed in his nylon shorts and undershirt, smoking his KOOL cigarette, sipping his coffee and listening, fascinated by my Mitzi and Smokey story.

"You say she did ride again?" Ray asked.

"Oh, yeah. She even rode Smokey many more times."

Ray said, "Amazing!" in utter shock.

Believe me, he was amazed by us. It seems like every time I saw Ray I had some crazy story to tell him. He always asked me questions. He was drawn in by my life when I wasn't with him.

⋙⋘

"Okay honey," he'd say. "What have you and the kids been up to since I last talked to you?" I told him about the kids and my trip to the barn in the pouring rain. We made a big mistake. I opened the big gate, drove us in, we fed the horses and I started to turn the Volkswagen around. I immediately slid about twenty-five feet down into the very muddy barnyard. The more I tried to get back onto the road, the further I slid down toward the fence.

Finally, I stopped and got my kids out, walked them through the ankle deep mud, slipping and sliding back up to the road, and told them to stand right there no matter what. I was gonna get that little son-of-a-gun out of there come hell or high water! Well, I had a lot of hell!

I was all over that barnyard. I wound up all the way down by the fence, about a hundred feet from the road where my kids were standing, watching me in disbelief.

Ray said, "Honey, weren't they afraid?"

"Yes they were because they knew their mom, and they knew that no matter what, I would get that car out of there."

"And did you?" he asked.

"Yes, I did. Then I collected my two muddy little girls and we got into our muddy little Volkswagen and safely drove home for a shower, after I hosed off the V.W."

"I just have one thing to tell you, Marci," Ray lectured. "You need to treat your car easier. You know Volkswagens are only four cylinders. Remember? I have one."

"I know Ray, but what was I supposed to do, just sit in the barnyard?"

Ray always taught me things. He told me, for instance, "Never park your car on an incline without using the emergency brake. You don't want it to rest on the transmission." Ironically, ever since he told me that, I just automatically do it.

Once again, Ray left and our lives continued on. The next time I talked to him was when he called, for what he said was the third time before he ever reached me. It would irritate him when he couldn't reach me. He didn't get really mad, but he always let me know how many calls it took for him to finally get me.

"What did you and the kids do today?" he asked.

"Well, first of all I'm sorry it took so long for you to reach me, but I was trying to pull a lawn mower out of a pond."

"You what?" he asked.

"I was trying to help an elderly man, who I don't know but who lives behind me. I was trying to pull his riding mower out of a pond," I answered.

"He flagged me down and asked if I would pull his mower out of his large pond. I told him I would try. I pulled my Volkswagen into his driveway and turned to the right, alongside the pond, which was on the left. There, in the deep pond and down a steep embankment, sat his mower, definitely in the pond, but not completely submerged. As usual, I got my kids out and told them to stand back out of the way.

"He tied a rope on to the front of his mower and to the back bumper of my car and told me to put it in gear and pull.

"I did. Then I heard my kids yelling, 'Stop, Mama! Stop!'

"I did stop, because my little car was sliding down the embankment toward the pond. It wasn't strong enough to pull his mower out.

"That old man tried to convince me to keep trying. He said, 'Come on! Come on! You can do it!,' but I untied the rope, got my kids in the car and left him standing there yelling."

"Honey," Ray said, "Can I give you a suggestion?"

"Sure, what is it sweetheart?" I said.

He laughingly said, "You better stay out of your car for a while!" Then he said he would be here in a few days.

I said, "Oh! Sweetheart! When?"

"In a couple of days," he said. "I'll call you."

When I saw him, as usual I was so excited. He said he could stay for about three days, so we settled in at the Holiday Inn on South Lindbergh. I was captivated all over again. I just couldn't get close enough to this mesmerizing man who I loved so much.

My mother was at my apartment watching Lisa and Mitzi. She mentioned that she would like to meet Ray. She insisted on cooking dinner for him, and of course, Ray agreed. He really did want to meet Mom, having spoken to her on the phone several times. He already liked her.

She called us up at the motel and said, "Come on, dinner's ready." It was about two o'clock Sunday afternoon. Ray wore one of his many three pieced casual suits–jacket, shirt and pants, all matching. This one was a light brown color.

Mom gave Ray and Bob Taylor, his valet, a warm hug and seated them at the table in my small kitchen. Bob sat by the window where he looked out wistfully and told Ray what a lovely view we had. Mom had a sumptuous dinner–Ray and Bob thought so, too. They both stuffed themselves, making Mom feel that her effort was truly appreciated.

I have this visit on video. It's a little faded, but after all, it's over forty years old. It's still clear enough to enjoy, it just isn't sharp. It was taken by an old video camera that had a blinding bright light, and everyone was flinching from it. Well...that is... except for Ray. We had so much fun laughing and talking that day.

Ray finally got to meet Lisa and Mitzi. He seemed to bond with them right away, and they liked him too. Mom and I cleaned up the kitchen while Ray and Bob sipped their coffee. We all moved into the living room, and here came my little girls dripping wet. They had eaten earlier and Lynn had invited them over for a swim. They wrapped their beach towels tightly around their little bodies and sat on the floor next to Ray, who was sitting in our wide chair talking to them. I loved watching that scene.

Every mother loves watching the man she loves giving her children such special attention. That gentleness towards my kids was just one reason, culminating into many more reasons, why I loved him so.

I squeezed myself into the chair with Ray. I always wanted to be as close as I could get to him. Someone, either my mom or Don, took a video of us, starting at our faces, moving down to our feet, and then up our legs, especially mine. (I had on short shorts). Then the camera moved to our faces again. I described this scenario to Ray. We were laughing, wondering why they shot our legs. I still don't know.

While the kids were sitting there, Mitzi was making faces at the camera and staring at Ray. Then Lynn called to ask if she and her friend, Ingrid, from Holland, could come over and meet Ray.

"Just a minute. Let me ask him," I said, "but how did you know he was here?"

"Your kids told me," she said.

When I asked Ray, he said, "Sure, honey. You know I love meeting your friends." He really didn't seem to mind. He was always very gracious about it and he met lots of my friends and relatives throughout the years.

I drove Ray and Bob to the airport on Wednesday. Ray had stayed a long time this visit and I loved it. Anything over a couple of days was heaven to me.

On Thursday, it was time for me to go to work my three nights, and by Sunday, I was tired. I didn't ride with Dad and Don that day, but Lisa and Mitzi did.

Lisa was an avid horse rider, even at the young age of six and seven. She sat on a horse like she was born to ride. Mitzi, on the other hand, bounced like a little rubber ball on Porky. Ponies are hard to guide, so most of the time Porky had a lead rope hooked on to his bridle and someone would pull him along.

One particular day, though, no one was leading Porky. The weather was sweltering as they rode beside a shallow creek. They stopped and rode into the creek for the horses to drink. When the rest of them rode on, Porky was still standing there pawing the water.

Mitzi started crying and Don realized that Porky was going to lie down or worse yet, roll over in the water. That's what horses do when they paw the water. Don rushed and grabbed the rope and led Porky and Mitzi across the creek.

"Oh My God!" Ray gasped, horrified, as I told him the story.

Soon I heard my little girls running up the stairs with Dad and Don right behind them. Mitzi burst in the door yelling, "Mama! Porky tried to drown me. He started to count."

Mitzi thought when Porky pawed the water, he was counting. Everyone cracked up. She was so cute.

Since they had finally met Ray, my kids talked to him when he called. As Mitzi recounted the story the way she saw it, which was Porky counting, Ray said, "Awww, aren't you a lucky little girl to have a pony that can count, Mitz." Always when Ray spoke to Mitzi he called her Mitz, never Mitzi.

I had already told him what really happened, along with another story about Dad's ill-behaved mule.

෨෬

Dad loved little mules and fancy buggies and wagons. Many times, he would drive his mules in parades and on rides. Some of those times, Mitzi would be perched right up there next to her Grandpa. Lisa, of course, always rode Smokey.

Over time, Dad had more than a few pairs of little mules, but this particular pair were named Jinny and Jack. One morning, he stopped by our apartment with Jack in the back of his pick-up truck.

I said, "Dad why are the racks on the pick-up, and where are you taking Jack?"

He said, "That little son-of-a-bitch meets me comin' down the road ever' mornin'. I find where he gets out and fix it, and damned if he's not comin' down the road again the next morning."

I said, "Dad, what are you gonna do? Haul him around with you?"

He said, "Well, by God, it looks like I'm gonna have to!"

So for the next few weeks, everyone would say, "I saw your dad and Jack at the bar," or "Jack and your dad were at the store." You could pass Joe Clarks Restaurant any time and dad would be inside drinking a beer with Jack waiting in the back of his truck.

Jack had another bad habit. He bucked–no one could ride him.

A young kid named Bobby usually rode with us, and one day while we were at the barn, Dad said, "Bobby, you get on Jack. You're little. If he bucks, it won't hurt you much."

Don said, "Well Goddamn, dad. Let's just put Mitzi on him. She's *really* little. It won't hurt her at all!"

Ray would laugh and slap his hands on his legs at these barnyard tales.

I was talking to Ray on the phone once when my dad stopped by looking for my brother. He sat down and drank a beer while Ray continued talking. We had been talking about Quincy Jones. "So you saw him on television, huh?"

"Yeah," I said. "He was directing the orchestra."

Dad interrupted; "Dood, (my nickname) I've got to go."

I said, "You want another beer, daddy? You can take it with you."

"No" he said, and he left.

I said to Ray, "Whew!! I'm glad he's gone."

"Oh shit. You shouldn't say that about your father, honey," he said aggravated.

"Well, I did and I'm not sorry. Just because they're my relatives doesn't mean they can't get on my nerves."

"Yeah, honey but if you're gonna say that, say it in front of him, not behind his back."

I was getting upset with Ray, "I do tell him. Sometimes I don't even let him in. I say, 'Daddy, I'm too nervous.'" Lately I had been having anxiety problems and random panic attacks. Fear of another breakdown was always a dark cloud looming over me. I guarded my emotions with my life.

"Does your dad ask what you're nervous about?" Ray wanted to know.

"No," he just says, "Oh, Goddamn, you and your nerves. You need to get your ass up in the morning and get to work. Then you wouldn't be so damned nervous."

Never mind that I had worked half the night waitressing.

Dad thought everyone should be up at the crack of dawn. If you weren't, he would bang on your door and get you up.

Ray laughed and asked how I was feeling.

I told him I felt okay.

He said, "Well that's good, honey. You sound awfully sweet today."

"Do I sweetheart?" I flirted.

"Yes baby, awfully sweet," he said softly.

I told him I mailed him a letter.

"Oh yeah, should I read it?" he asked.

"Um hmm, I hope you get it. It's kind of cute. You'll like it."

He said, "You know, that's the thing with you. You can be so, so...so...you know? Whatcha would call...you know...how you would take something and condense it, and it becomes...concentrated.

"You can become awfully sweet when you want to. God knows, nobody in the world could be angry with you when you're like that. You know, you have that magnetic .. whatever."

"Oh really? And then what?" I questioned.

"Well...just like you can be concentrated sweet. You can go the other way just as quick." he said sadly.

I said, "I know. That's true."

"I know it's true. You don't have to tell me. I know it," he said, sounding as if he wanted to throw his hands up.

It was during this time that Ray began asking whether or not I was going to get a divorce. I said I hadn't thought about it. He told me that if I did, he would pay for it. This must have been something he wanted badly for him to cough up the money to pay for it.

"I'll think about it," I said and left it at that.

Ray would talk at length to me about everything. My kids were in New Orleans visiting their dad, and I told Ray I was lonely and sad with them gone, but that they would be home in a week.

"Well honey, you only have a week. You'll be all right." He was trying to soothe me.

Suddenly Don, my brother, popped his head in the door asking where Dad was.

Don said, "I guess he got all upset and left."

"I don't know," I said. "He told me how lazy you were. He wants the horse feed unloaded."

"I know," Don replied. "That's what I came over for and now he's gone."

"Well, you took too long for Dad. Do you want to tell Ray hello?"

"Not really," Don said.

"Did you hear that, Ray? He said 'not really.'"

"Well I can dig that," Ray said calmly, but I was irritated as hell.

Don opened the door again, "Do you know where Pop went?"

"No I don't. Go find him yourself. I'm on a phone call!!!"

Then to Ray I said, "Shit on him. I'm not kissing his ass either!"

Ray said, "So I see."

"He's such a snot. I don't blame Daddy sometimes. Don's so damned hateful. He didn't have to say that."

Ray said, "Now wait a minute. If the man told the truth, isn't that better than lying? Honey, my feelings are not hurt."

"Well mine are!" I shouted.

"But they shouldn't be," Ray told me. "Listen baby. Honey, listen. The only reason your feelings should be hurt is if mine were."

"That's not right. Hell! My feelings don't just get hurt when yours are!" Poor Ray was trying to say something to calm me down but couldn't. "Just stop making excuses for him," I snarled.

"It's not a question of making excuses. It's a question of being realistic. Just like I told you a few minutes ago, why be two ways with a person? If you feel a certain way, tell the person how you feel. Who knows? Maybe he's having a bad day. Maybe he's upset about something."

"Who–Don?" I asked.

"Yeah." Ray said, "You know. Just like you get upset, other people can get upset too. I'll say one thing about Don. Aaah...I'm not trying to butter him up or anything, but every time I've ever been around him, he's always nice to me. And every time I've ever called him trying to find you, he's always nice to me. So therefore, I don't think he was…"

I interrupted, "I don't want to waste time talking about him. I get sick enough of him. Let's talk about you."

"Well, ain't nothin' to talk about with me."

"Oh, yes there is. You'll see. I'm gonna interrogate you…" And I did.

19
Conversations with Ray

❦

The phone rang and Lisa picked it up asking "Who is this please?" She stood for a moment, then handed the phone to me and said, "They won't tell me who they are."

"Hello?" I said

"Yeah. Happy Valentine's Day, baby," Ray said sweetly.

"Hi, sweetheart. I'm sorry I sound so bad. I'm hoarse because I have a sore throat. Why wouldn't you tell Lisa who you are?"

"I didn't hear her ask," he answered.

It was February, 1971, and Ray was in Houston, Texas getting ready to go to rehearsal. He was performing with the Houston Symphony and that required a lot of rehearsing.

I asked him if Ann had called. She was my friend who sent his favorite home-cooked food by taxi to our motel in New Orleans.

He remembered, "That's right. She lives here, doesn't she?"

"Yes, she moved there before I left New Orleans."

"Well, if she calls I'll invite her to the concert. How would that be?"

"That's so nice of you, honey," I gushed, so happy with him.

I told him Don went to Mardi Gras.

"Yeah, how do New Orleanans feel about the invasion of all those people into their city?"

"Oh, they love it. It's one big party and they can get drunk in the street."

"Well, if they get drunk, they don't know if they love it or not, do they? Anyway honey, it's 10:00 and you're just waking up."

I told him this was early, that I usually slept until 12:00. I would send Lisa to school, then Mitzi and I went back to sleep. I worked part-time at night and needed rest.

"You do sleep though, don't you?" He worried.

"God, yes. You know I sleep."

He laughed, "Naw, naw, you don't sleep when we're together."

"'Cause you keep me awake," I giggled. "Besides, what would you do if you couldn't wake me? What would you say?"

"Oh," he pondered, "I dunno. I can always think of something when I'm with you."

I asked when he was coming.

"Well, I would like to come around March 6th for a couple of days, if that's okay with you?" Of course, he knew it would be.

Then I said, "Do you love me?"

"Ummm hum," he murmured in a low voice.

"How much?" I flirtingly questioned.

He got upset and began ranting. "I don't know why you always ask me that, as if there's some kind of measuring cup. I never understand why you say that. I really don't, 'cause I..."

I said, "It's just conversation, I guess." (Then I began deliberately teasing him). "I know it's not much," I giggled.

Ray was very irritated. "If you're so sure you know everything, I really shouldn't be answering the question, 'cause you know how much it is and...."

I responded, just as caustic "You're not sweet, you're shitty today. I'm sorry I asked 'cause I really don't give a damn anyway now."

"Do you think you're sweet when you say "Oh, I know you don't love me much?" He was still on a tirade.

I said, "I don't care. Just accept it and go on."

"Okay, I'll do that," he said and was silent for a while. So was I.

That little spat came on fast, and it dissipated just as quickly. We went from spatting to flirting, which often happened with us.

"So, you'll be here the sixth of next month. I guess I'd better get on my birth control pills."

"Yeah, why don't you do that." Then he laughed, a sort of an "I've got a secret" laugh.

"What?" I asked, and we both started giggling and flirting. "What were you giggling about Ray?"

"Oh, really nothin', babe."

I told him to keep his secrets.

"You know, strangely enough, Marci, I don't have any secrets." (I found out later just how many secrets he *did* have–and there were multitudes). At that particular time, I didn't have any secrets from him, but I did accumulate a few along the way. They remained just that–secrets.

Had I known then what I know now about Ray, I might have been a little more liberal with my own life.

As I re-listen to my taped conversations with him, I realize even more why I loved him so. I recognize the wonderful qualities of his character.

I'm aware of the addictions that plagued him throughout his life, but now I'm able to separate that part of his psyche from his genuine character. He was never two-faced, as he reprimanded *me* for being when he told me not to talk about my father behind his back. That's an admirable quality. He also gave folks the benefit of the doubt, as he did my brother when Don refused to say hello to him. That was another great asset, one that I don't have. If someone does that to me, I just think, "Go to hell."

There were some obvious flaws in Ray's character, too, like lying, cheating and frugality. I would venture to say that the last affliction was possibly the worst.

Had I been aware of the lying and cheating and other women in his life, I might have sent him to join Sam Cooke! I didn't find out about them until 2004 when I read, *Man and Music.* I certainly wasn't presumptuous enough to think there wasn't an occasional chippy on the road, but I was shocked at the magnitude of his network of women–and of his cunning ability to keep me completely oblivious to it–for nearly thirty years!

The only other woman who concerned me was his wife. I didn't like him being married, just as he disliked me being married. In fact, he hated it so much he refused to call me "Soto" and referred to me as "Marci Harris," which is my maiden name.

In reality, as I later learned, his wife was my least threat. It was all of the other women in his harem, of which I was an un-witting member, who were my competition. My being unaware of it made me happier–and him safer.

I'm puzzled by where he found the time for all of this amour. No wonder he was so frugal. There were too many of us!

Rather than a harem, as many people referred to Ray's col-lection of women, I tend to think of them as "The Pony Ex-press"–relay women scattered here and there along his route.

Well–enough of me being sarcastic–I digressed and couldn't shut up. I'll get back to my conversations with Ray.

Much to my delight, Ray was able to come to St. Louis earlier than he had planned. I was, as usual, thrilled to death. When we got settled in, we started one of our lengthy conver-sations, this time about, of all things, the Bible. I told him I thought the Bible, was hard to live by. He said he didn't think so. Obviously, he blanked out the "adultery and fornication" parts!

"What about, "Thou Shalt Not Commit Adultery" Ray?

"It definitely does say that. No doubt about it. On the other hand, the Bible says "Thou Shalt Not Kill" too, right? But you find many places where there was war. How the hell you gonna have war if you don't kill," he rationalized.

"Yes, but you don't find many places in the Bible where it says you can go make love to your neighbor if you want to, do you? So stop rationalizing Ray."

"You're not my neighbor," he quickly assured me. That cracked me up and ended our biblical analyzation. Ray had a preternatural way of making anything he wanted to do, socially and morally, acceptable. At least in his mind.

As I cuddled into his body, I said, "I wish we could be together today and every day."

"Babe, if we had that, you might get fed up with me." I assured him I wouldn't, but if he hung round the house too much, I'd tell him to go somewhere.

"Oh, just...just get out, huh? Marci, you're my little hell cat."

"Well, you control my behavior, you know. If you do what you're supposed to do, I'm sweet. If you don't, I'm not. So you do have a choice." He laughed. I'm convinced that he liked my firey personality, even though he complained about my occasional outbursts of temperament.

Lately, I had been cooking things that he said he particularly liked. I told him all of the dishes I had recently made, including neck-bones and cabbage, fried chicken and round steak (that I pounded like he said his Mama did). He said he would love to have some neck-bones and cabbage. I only lived ten minutes from the Holiday Inn, so I went home, warmed some food, and brought it back. He said it was very good and asked me if I knew how to make liver and onions. I said I did, and that was his request for the next time.

My friend, Mary Ann, called me earlier about a problem that she was having, and I brought it up to Ray to see if he could help. She was trying to locate the celebrity father of her eleven year old daughter, who by that time, was aware that Pat Aluisa, Mary Ann's ex-husband and the man who raised her, was not her father. I asked Ray if he knew how we could find her biological father.

He said, "I don't know why she waited so long. That's total destruction, when you wait that long. That's a hell of a thing to hit a cat with. He might not believe her."

"But she looks just like him," I said.

"Don't make no difference, honey. The first thing that crosses a person's mind behind eleven years is, is she mine?"

I kept on. "I think she should try."

Ray was pushing his point. "So what are ya' gonna do. The man has no idea. If you wanna call a spade a spade, the little girl can't have any affection for her father, so really what's the point? The man's gonna think Mary Ann's a kook."

"I don't think so," I persisted. "He was very close to Mary Ann."

Ray was adamant, "You know, honey, that don't mean… you know a man being a man, chances are he might have at least one other girlfriend."

Here was a clue for me, but it went right over my head!! I'm surprised I didn't catch it, but I didn't pay attention to his comment until I transcribed my taped conversations all these years later. If I had caught it and questioned him about it, he would have said, "I was talking about him, not me."

Ray continued on, "I have to tell you, honey, do what you want. But my personal feeling is you're only compounding a wrong. It's bad enough you told the girl. Mary Ann might have to say, 'Well look, I told him and he doesn't want to see you.'"

I said, "Ray if you had a kid, I don't care how old she was, would you feel that way?"

"Yeah," he said, "if I didn't know her. Here's the difference, honey. There's no way in the world…see, that a man can know the child is his. The mother knows it's hers, even if she doesn't know who the father is. But the father really doesn't know. He must believe what the woman tells him."

I said I would take her word for it because I'm honest and would expect others to be.

"Marci, for every person who's like you, I can find twenty that are different. You're a rarity, honey, whether you know it or not." He continued, as if he were talking to Mary Ann, "It took you eleven years to decide to tell me? What happened from one to ten? Now you wanna tell me that? The first thing that's gonna come to my mind is, now I'm gonna get hit for some dollars."

I had wondered about that, too, and shared my concern with Mary Ann. Before I brought it up with Ray, I had talked to my brother, Don, about Mary Ann's dilemma. He agreed with Ray that it would be best left alone. Ray was really pleased that he and Don felt the same way. And even though Ray and I didn't agree, I was glad that I had discussed Mary Ann's situation with him and told him so. His opinion was always very important to me.

Years later, when Toni turned twenty-one, however, Mary Ann found her Dad. I, happily, was able to inform Ray that Toni's father met her and accepted her with open arms...and no one asked him for money. Toni has always been, and still is, the spitting image of her father, Alex Cord, actor, author and horseman.

The ability to discuss things openly with Ray was another character study. No matter what I needed to talk to him about, he would take as long as was necessary to discuss it until he knew I was satisfied or could at least come to a conclusion. When my problem was solved, I would kiss him all over his face, and neck and snuggle into his body, clinging to him like a Koala bear.

❧

"What time of the day were you born, Ray?" I asked, while we were lounging in bed.

"Oh, I guess maybe 10:00 in the morning–seems like I heard that sometime, somewhere along the way. Why?"

"I have this astrology book and I want to know what you are besides a Libra. I know you're on the cusp."

"That's true, I'm a little Virgo, but I think I'm far more Libra."

He liked to be Libra and liked its' symbol. The balanced scales depicted fairness and justice–and that's how he saw himself.

"What are you, other than Taurus, honey?"

"Well, this lady who's an astrologist said I'm Sagittarius. She said that's what she is too, but we're nothing alike."

"Marci, to me, you're not like anybody."

"Is that good or bad, Ray?"

"It's you baby, just you." He said, so sweetly, snuggling me close to him and caressing me softly. Oh! My! God! I loved that man.

We talked and played *Reader's Digest* word games. We did that the whole time we were together, nearly thirty years, then we went to sleep. He was leaving the next day. I heard him come out of the bathroom, unlock the door to our room, and call room service for coffee. Then he sat on the side of the bed, lit his KOOL cigarette, leaned over and gently touched my face, and said, "Babe, it's time to wake up."

"Oh! I love being awakened like this, sweetheart," I said as I kissed his hand and rolled over close to him.

"Better get something on, honey, coffee's on the way."

Soon there was a tap on the door, "Yeah, come in," Ray called, "put it on the table." I added the tip, signed the check, we had our coffee and then left for the airport.

I was always allowed to board the plane with Ray even though Bob Taylor, his valet, was with us. I would hold his hand until the last minute, then go inside and watch the plane take flight and disappear into the clouds. The ride home was always a lonely and tearful journey, but it always made me feel better that Ray called me when he reached his destination. By then, I had been home for three or four hours and was back to the business of life with Lisa and Mitzi.

20
Cheating on Ray

Significant things happened in 1971: I got my wonderful horse, Diablo, I cheated on Ray, got my divorce and moved to my very own house in Kirkwood, Missouri.

Ray was here again. I had told him on the phone that I got a new horse. After I picked him up, we settled in and took care of the "essentials." Then, he asked me about my horse.

I said, "He is a beautiful Appaloosa who I named Diablo. He was a gift from my Dad and Don."

To say that he was spirited would be an understatement. He held his head and tail high, and pranced like a show horse. He was majestic. The one characteristic he had that I had a little problem with was if he didn't want to stop, he would rear on his massive hind legs and paw the air.

"Oh, wow," Ray said as he pensively thought about it.

"We were riding in a parade in downtown St. Louis," I told him, "and I spotted a friend. I reigned Diablo over to speak to my friend and he reared straight up, pawed the air, then pranced and refused to behave. Rather than chance hurting someone in the crowd, I let him catch the other horses. I keep a tight reign on him because he likes to run. He's headstrong."

"Like you," Ray interjected, then asked, "How do you stay on when he rears?"

"I keep my feet in the stirrups, hug his body with my legs and hold onto the saddle horn till he comes down."

Later I had a billy-club and would lightly tap him between his ears; he didn't like that so he stopped rearing.

"Do you run him?" Ray asked. He was very inquisitive

about our horses. I would describe everything to the smallest detail so that he could get a vivid picture in his head.

"Yeah, I do run him. I ease him into a slow cantor, which to me is when he looks his very best. Then I loosen the reigns, and immediately he's in a full blown gallop. I don't let him run too long, though."

"Why?" he asked.

"Because he starts liking it and might decide to keep going," I told him.

He wanted to know if he scared me and how I felt when I ran him. My answer to the first question was "no," and to the second I said, "I feel free and reckless with the wind in my hair, watching Diablo's silver mane blowing and shimmering. I love it."

"You must look pretty riding your horse, baby," Ray said.

Ray could set my blood ablaze and before long, we would be entwined into each others bodies. I loved to feel the sensations of Ray's body pressed close to mine. The poet, Arthur Rimaud, once said to his friend, Paul Verlain, "I found eternity. It's when the sun mingles with the sea."

When I told Ray that, he said, "I've found heaven. It's when my body merges with yours."

My love for him was persistent and overpowering, a constant burning and unrequited desire. When we were together, the world ceased to exist. I was adrift in a sea of undulating delight that would always end too soon. He was only here for one night, then back to the airport–and another sad good-bye. This time he was gone too long.

There were many long phone conversations, but too much time lapsed since I'd seen him, and I wasn't happy.

I said, "Ray I was just gonna tell you not to call me anymore."

"Now why would you tell me something like that?"

I told him I didn't feel that we were seeing enough of each other but I didn't want to discuss it. When I got ready to quit, I would just quit. So we talked about other things.

I had a rash on my legs, and that subject became an hour long discussion trying to figure out what caused it. We finally concluded it was a cheaper brand of baby oil.

He said, "Honey, you do have very sensitive skin–and smooth as glass."

Then he asked me what I had been doing.

I said I had been riding horses with my Dad and Mitzi and had a huge blister on my butt because of tight Levi's and Mitzi being in the saddle with me. I told Daddy I had a blister and he said, "Oh, Goddamn. You're always gripin' about something. Just shut up and keep on ridin'."

Ray was laughing hysterically.

I said, "They don't care what happens to me."

"Yes they do. They love you, honey, just like I do." He was chuckling and saying, "Yeah, you're my sweet girl. I like that."

I said, "Ray, you say you care about me. Do you really?"

"Yes, Marci, don't you think I do?"

"I think you could care more. I am too lonely."

"Marci, honey. Just like I told you before, there's no way I can explain how much I love you–and by the same token, you can't measure love by the amount of days. It's got to go much deeper than that."

I listened, not feeling very reassured. Then I told him the kids and I were driving to Kansas City to see Mary Ann. Ray knew the distance between every city. His mind was like a computer.

He said, "Kansas City is about 250 miles, so it's a five hour drive if you keep driving and don't stop along the way." Then he added, "I just got you in the nick of time. Just think, if I had waited 'till later, after you were gone, and didn't get you until next week, you really woulda' been furious, wouldn't you?"

I said I thought that would be better, then maybe he would be a little more concerned and stop taking me for granted...that he would think, "Ooooh, that woman! If I don't find her...."

He said he would think I had changed my number again.

"Ray, I was so relieved when I changed my number. When

the phone rang, I knew it couldn't be you, so I was no longer living with that anticipation."

"Yeah, but Honey, don't you think that's a terrible thing?" He sounded so sad. "How can you wanna just completely shut me out of your life?"

I said, "I don't want you out of my life, but sometimes it seems easier for me."

Lisa, Mitzi and I left for Kansas City in the evening, and arrived about 1:00 a.m. As usual, Mary Ann and her kids were waiting up to greet us, along with some of her friends. She always had an array of people in and out of her apartment at different intervals throughout the day and evening. Her home was warm and comforting. I felt grounded and loved being there. We spent four or five days with Mary Ann on that visit.

Ray called shortly after we got home and said he would be coming to see me in a few days. Sometime during the week, I went out to a bar with friends, drank too many margaritas, met a guy and he came home with me. You can use your imagination for the rest.

When Ray called, I told him that I had cheated on him. For a moment, he was quiet. Knowing him the way I did, I could visualize the pained look on his face.

Then he said, "I think you're listening to people tell you that I wouldn't give a damn, so much that you began to believe it. See what I mean by what other people tell you?"

"Ray, people find it hard to believe that I don't want to find someone else after all this time." It had been two years.

He had a long response. "Well, honey, I'm not other people. I've lived for forty years and learned quite a bit. I can't expect you to be, act or respond like anybody else. You are you, and that's it. I don't compare you with anybody else or remake you over in my mind. Marci is just Marci, and that's it. Ain't nobody in the world like her, before, and I doubt, ever after—if there is an after. So I don't give a shit what other people think. Let other people think whatever the shit they wanna think 'cause really, it doesn't matter. It's a question of what I think, and what you know. You shouldn't let your emotions care as to what anybody else thinks. If there is a mistake it's that you discuss your private affairs with others. As close as Bob and I are, and you know we're very close, but you know what? We haven't discussed each others' private affairs."

He was talking about Bob Taylor, his valet, and Ray was indeed very close to him. Bob even brought him to his mom's house for an occasional "chittlin" dinner. Bob, a strategic chess player, had a quiet, gentlemanly, aura about him–much like Ray.

I told Ray that my doctor said I should take birth control pills consistently and not stop and start. It was not good for my body, and it was risky. This is what he said in response to that statement.

"I don't think that's a bad idea. God knows it's not a question of my feeling that you're going to be going to bed with anybody. But as far as I'm concerned, my trust in you is that I would feel that maybe...ahhh...you don't need to take them at all. But you see, I could be wrong. Who's to say that you won't be out another night drinking and the same thing will happen?"

"Oh, Ray! It wasn't just the drinks. I've been out lots of nights and it's never happened."

"Well then, how do you explain your cheating on me? Come on, Marci, it had to be something. It's not like you to be doing something like that, and you can't explain it."

"No, I guess I just didn't give a damn, and I was fed up being alone so much."

Ray said he thought I was again listening to other people. He said that's why he stays outside their business and keeps them out of his.

He said, "When folks get to talking it's like a commercial. You hear it so much, until after a while you think there must be some truth in it.

Marci, you gotta get this straight. You know more than anybody else, babe. Who knows more about us than you? Maybe it's just a thing. I..I..I don't know how you could have done anything like that. Since we've gone this far, can I ask when did you do all of this? How long ago?"

I told him a week ago.

"Okay…." Then he was quiet. When he spoke again he said, "Well, I don't know how you could have done that. Especially after I told you I was going to be there in a week." He started talking in a high pitched voice. "Don't make no sense. Everything just don't make sense."

I said I wished I hadn't told him.

"Oh, don't be ridiculous. We won't talk about it anymore. I don't want to make you feel bad. That's not my purpose, babe."

I said, "I've always been straight with you, Ray."

He kept saying, "We won't talk about it any more," but he couldn't stop. "Okay, after I say this, we won't discuss it any more.

I feel like you should go inside yourself and find out what caused you to go against all kinds of grain." He even asked if it would be too hard on my emotions if he came to see me.

I thought that was so sweet, but I wanted him to come. I wanted him with me immediately.

Ray kept on, as if in disbelief. "I'll tell you the truth, Marci. That's not like you. If anybody outside of you would have told me that, I would have called them all kinds of liars. I don't believe even your mother could have made me believe that. I might maybe go along with Don, but even then, I would have a question."

Ray asked, "What does Don think about all this?"

I said, "He's a little protective of me and wouldn't like what I did. But he couldn't care less what people think."

"Well, neither do I," Ray said. "So I guess you think we're a couple of goof-balls. It's because we love you, honey. Of course, our love is from a different way. I think Don's his own man. When it's all said and done, people's opinions don't mean shit. All they're gonna do is talk. They don't feel nothing! To them, it's all sensationalism, or whatever the right word is. But to us it's far more than that, honey. We…we really care."

For some unknown reason, Ray liked it when he and my brother were in agreement. It made him feel like Don accepted my relationship with him, I guess. He told me he was scared and apprehensive about their first meeting.

True to his word, after the initial interrogation about my infidelity, Ray never mentioned it again. He came on Tuesday morning and stayed until Friday. I was a happy woman. I loved him so much and thought he was very sweet about the way he handled my "big mistake."

He said, "I'm very jealous Marci. I don't feel it's an attribute, but I can't help it. Marci, honey, please don't ever do that again." I promised that I wouldn't.

On June 13th, 1971, I was granted my divorce. Ray gave me the money for it. It wasn't very costly since it was a non-contested divorce. Henry didn't even know about it. I said I didn't know where to reach him, and because of that, it was quite a simple procedure. The cost of publishing the notice in local newspapers, the attorney's fee and court costs were the only costs involved. That was it. I was a single woman.

My girlfriends Ona and Karen went with me from court to a restaurant and celebrated.

When Ray heard the news, he said, "I don't have to be afraid now." He said he would be here in about a week. Then he said, "Will you be okay? That'll be a good day, won't it, baby?"

"Oh, yes. It's always a good day when you're here, Ray," I said.

He asked me to call him between 9:00 and 10:00 a.m. Los Angeles time, when I wanted to reach him. That's when he would be in his office, going through what he had to do for the day. It was past mid-1971 and I knew he had been working on a new album, "Volcanic Action of My Soul." I asked if he had finished it.

He said, "Yes. It was released a few months ago."

I asked him to bring it to me.

He said, "I'll handle it right now. Then there won't be any danger of me forgetting it."

He summoned the Manager of Sales to his office and gave him my information. I received Volcanic Action and the album with Booty Butt on it, which I had also requested. They arrived before Ray did.

He told me that Bob and his wife, who he met in Denmark while touring with Ray, had had a baby girl. They named her April.

I didn't see Bob much after I moved to my house in Kirkwood, Missouri because Ray flew to St. Louis by himself. I would get him off the plane, get him through the airport, to my car, and home. I missed seeing Bob. He was my favorite valet.

21
Moving to Kirkwood
❧❧

I began perusing the newspaper for houses to buy. I didn't think I would find anything affordable, but I persistently poured over the "for sale" ads, just in case.

One day, I found three possibilities, all were in Kirkwood and the kids and I looked at each one. We fell in love with a small brick cottage with a nice backyard on a corner lot. I had no credit, so I couldn't get a loan. My brother got the loan, so our house was in his name for a few years. Later, he quitclaim deeded it to me. Don was such a good brother. He was so good to Lisa, Mitzi and me.

In October of 1971, we moved into our adorable little house. Mitzi had just turned five and Lisa turned seven. We set about painting the whole inside an egg shell color. When my girls got older, they didn't want to share a bedroom any more, and since the basement was finished, Lisa took the downstairs bedroom. I added a bathroom with a shower and then she had her own little suite. Mitzi, and I shared the main floor bath.

Our house was modest to say the least– it was very small, but we didn't notice. Thanks again to the Goodwill Store, we were able to decorate it comfortably and, we thought, attractively. Lisa and Mitzi made the transition from one school to the other with no problems. They made new friends and were on their way to a new life in Kirkwood. A lot of other children lived on our deadend street. We were lucky.

My girls had more freedom than my grandchildren do today. It was a safer era and our block was like one big family. All the mothers kept watch, and our life was pretty routine. At dusk, my kids were called in for dinner, then homework, bath, T.V. time, and to bed.

I needed to find a job, so I put ads in the newspapers for house cleaning. Much to my delight, I was in demand, and soon I was working every day. I also learned dog grooming from my friend, Jane Wulle, so I ran ads for that too. Again, I got great response. When I wasn't cleaning houses, I was grooming dogs in the laundry room. I didn't make a fortune, but it certainly helped us survive. And I was really busy.

I was able to buy carpets from Goodwill to cover the ugly brown vinyl tile floors. I tied carpet rolls on top of my Volkswagen and looked like the "Beverly Hillbillies" driving home. My neighbor helped me carry the rugs in and roll them out on the floors. I bought a carpet knife and cut them myself to fit. I placed all the furniture and we were all set.

For years I was "The Little Engine That Could." I guess I still am. I've always been short on patience, so rather than wait for someone to help me, I did everything myself, and I could. I possessed an inner strength, determination, and constitution that I inherited from my mother, "Ruby."

Those character traits enabled me to "not need" Ray. I loved him and wanted him like crazy, but I could survive on my own. I did, on occasion, expect him to contribute, however, and he did so begrudgingly.

My innate independence also gave me the courage to treat him the same way he treated me, even though I wanted him so badly.

I didn't hear from Ray, from mid-September until December. I knew he was touring the U.S. and that he would be touring Europe in October, but I thought he could have at least called me. Okay, I would give him the benefit of the doubt for October since he was out of the country, but he had called me from Europe before, so that wasn't an excuse as far as I was concerned. And what about the whole month of September?

After October, I had moved and changed my phone number so he couldn't reach me. I didn't call him until December 14th and I refused to give him my new number. I called him when *I* wanted to, just like he always called me when *he* wanted to.

When I finally called him, he seemed irritated, especially when I wouldn't give him my new phone number. Every time Ray neglected me for a period of time, I either wouldn't let him come to see me or I would change my number. That was my only means of defense and self respect.

Not only was I angry with Ray for not calling, I was angry and disappointed because I wanted him to share in the excitement of my new house. I really wanted this house to be a place where Ray was comfortable. For three years, we hadn't had a home to be in and now we did...and then I didn't even hear from him! So now he was finding out what it was like to wait and wait for a phone call. And he didn't like it one bit.

Ray said, "You were supposed to call me back, between 10 a.m. and 11 a.m."

I told him I had called for three days and couldn't get him.

"Well, you wanna give me your number?" he asked.

"No, I'll call you back. Do you want me to?" I questioned.

"Well, you can, but you know what that entails. I'm not putting you on. I'm telling you the truth. I try to give you an accurate time, but you can't count on it," he explained.

I said, "That's okay. I understand," in a sweet, sarcastic voice.

His response was an exaggerated "Okay, okay."

"You said you wanted to come here. I thought you might have some idea of when?"

Ray said he thought he had mentioned it would be after Christmas. He said he didn't understand what was so special about Christmas, that everybody gets so hung up on. Even his arranger, Sid Feller, was out. He said, "I don't know man. They go through all that for one day. Next day, they'll look at the bills and they'll be stuck for a whole year." Then he said, "So, Marci, whenever you feel like it. Hopefully, I'll get to hear from you."

I said, "Okay" in a chipper, sarcastic voice.

"When you get the chance, call me," he repeated.

Again, I said, "Okay."

"You will now?" he said again.

"I will," I promised. "Do you love me?"

"Yep," he answered.

"Really?" I asked.

That set him off. "I don't understand why you ask that. Evidently, you don't believe me..."

"No, I don't, but I love to hear it," I said.

"No, Marci. What you're really saying is, 'I'm wasting my time.'"

If I questioned what he said, it would make him upset–and I had a knack for upsetting him, he informed me.

"It isn't wasting your time if I like to hear it, honey," I assured him.

He told me he would never ask me anything if he thought I would lie to him. He said, "If you're gonna lie, it wouldn't be worth it." He went on, "I ask what I wanna know, and I expect the truth."

I said sweetly, "I love you" and I hung up the phone.

I didn't call him back until December 20th. He was still irritable. When I said, "Merry Christmas," his response was, "Merry Christmas and all that jazz."

I said, "You're not being very nice and I was going to sing "Jingle Bells" to you."

"You don't need to," he said, a little cranky.

"Okay, I won't keep you long. Just talk to me a little bit, and I'll hang up."

Ray said, "Go ahead–talk."

"No. You talk to me, Ray. You said no one was in the office so you're able to talk."

"What did you wanna say, Marci? Something important or are you just passing time?"

"No, when I talk to you Ray it's not just to pass the time. It's always 'cause I really want to hear you. Do you want me to shut up?"

"No, I don't. I like listening to you, Marci, no matter what you're talking about."

I told him he sounded happier. He said no, that he was neutral.

I asked if he were ever ecstatic about anything. He said he was when he could have something he wanted but not when he couldn't, and especially not when someone was playing games with him.

"Are you putting me in that category?" I asked.

"That's for you to say," he answered.

I said I couldn't outsmart him if I lived a thousand years.

"You outsmart me, Marci. You do it all the time. You just don't realize it. But then again...maybe you do."

"Keep talking to me, Ray. I like to hear you."

"What good does it do for me to talk? You never listen to me anyway."

I wanted to know when he was coming to see me. He said, he was very busy and didn't see a break soon. That disappointed me so I asked if he thought our love affair was ending, and if it did, whether or not it would bother him.

"Of course it would. How can you ask me that kind of question? Obviously, I wouldn't have any choice in the matter. You hold the key. Don't you?"

"No, I don't hold the key. I know that I can have you anytime I want you, on *your* conditions, as long as everything's the way *you* say. Whenever *you're* able, or *you* can, or *you* want to, no matter what I do. It's not that important to you." I was very upset that he wasn't going to be here sooner.

"What do you mean, it doesn't matter to me?" he said. "Are you gonna go with someone else?"

I said I had thought about it.

"Well, I don't want that. It does matter and you know that. It mattered when you did do it."

I told him I didn't think it made much difference, that he went right on.

He was getting anxious. "Oh come on, Marci, you know

damn well better. You know my situation. You know I don't have a lot of time. And another thing, Marci, I trust you, honey. And you know that, too. You should be glad I feel that way, but you wanna make light of it."

I was listening, but still edgy. "Listen, mister. Let me tell you something. Do you think that coming all the way from New Orleans to L.A. was playing? Do you really think I was making light of it? I guess you're not gonna discuss that! But it's far from playing! I knock myself out making arrangements–trying to spend time with you every time you want to come here, and sometimes it's pretty damned difficult. You're not the only busy person in the world! And do you know what else??? My emotions are involved; my heart, my whole life. I'm hardly playing, Ray!"

He finally got a chance to stop me, and say, "Now calm down, Marci."

"No!" I yelled. "You think I'm a thirteen-year-old child. You even said I was talking immaturely! You think I don't have sense enough to come in out of the rain! I've done pretty damn well on my own!"

"Nobody said you hadn't, Marci. If you love me, why you wanna upset me?"

"I don't," I said.

"You won't even give me your number, Marci."

"That's right. 'Cause whatever the hell I can't do to you anymore, you can't do to me either. Goddamn it!"

Then I switched back to my normal sweet self, and asked him, "When you come, are you gonna stay here with me?"

"No! I'd be a fool to stay there, now wouldn't I? What if your dad or husband comes there, and catches me in your house?"

Ray was referring to the time I moved to L.A., and the truth finally came out why he had treated me the way he did. Furious that I had taken the kids and moved to Los Angeles to be with

Ray Charles, Henry had followed me. He went to the Coconut Grove and sent a note backstage to Ray that said, "I'm Marci's husband and I'm in the audience, Motherfucker." I knew Henry Soto. He didn't go to that show because he was dying to hear Ray Charles. He went to hurt him, and I know that Henry would have killed him had he caught up with him.

So it was clear why Ray didn't want to be associated with me while I was there. Henry had gone to the Coconut Grove the night before I was supposed to meet Ray at 10:00 a.m. in L.A. By now, I had pieced it all together and could see why he distanced himself from me, but he should have called me to explain.

Later, I asked if he got that note and he told me no. I knew better. I had heard from a band member that he did get it, and it had scared him to death.

§

Ray said, "Didn't you say your husband would stop sending you money if he found out I was there?"

"Why don't you pay the bills?" I said, irritated as hell.

"I don't have the bread that everyone thinks I do. Maybe I can't afford it."

"Oh shit!!" I laughed at him. "Ray, you own apartment buildings, airplanes and things that cost a lot of money."

"Well," he answered. "That's exactly why I don't have money to burn."

"You tell me how jealous you are Ray, and you don't want me to be with anyone else. Do you think that's fair? What will I ever have with you? Nothing."

"Marci, you don't know what I go through to be with you," he said.

I retaliated, "You don't know what you put me through either and it's making me more and more bitter. You don't ask if I need anything. All you seem to care about is poking me with a stiff dick periodically, and you think that's enough? You don't help me make decisions. Why the hell don't you leave me alone? I can get screwed anyplace I go, all day and all night! You think I need penis imported here from the West Coast? Well I sure as hell don't!"

Ray was frustrated. "Marci, you upset me talking like that. Honey, if you need something, you should ask me." That put me in a better mood. I didn't need anything, I just wanted to hear him offer.

"Are you going to stay with me?" I asked.

He said, "I don't even have your number."

I told him he didn't need my number to stay at my house, but if I thought he would call on time I'd give him the damn number. I told him that he hangs me up too much and I liked it better this way. I told him I would rather call him and let him sit and wait.

He said, "I don't like it." I knew he didn't like it. He liked to be in control. He was quiet and so was I. Finally he said, "Marci, please give me the number. I'll do whatever you want."

I laughed and said okay. Get your stylus ready. It took him a long time, to punch it out.

He said, "Man, that took some doin'!"

"What, punching out the number?" I asked.

"No–getting it," he said. I giggled at that comment.

Again, I asked if he were staying with me.

His response was, "I don't know if it would be alright with the kids. I think it's important to think about that. They may not like me staying there." I really did love Ray's concern about my kids. That's the part of him that was so endearing to me.

"Ray, the reason I got this house is because I want to share my life with you."

"Marci, you have to think about these things, babe. It's the kid's house too, and I don't want to overstep my boundaries."

I told him I appreciated his concern for my children, but that I didn't want to just give him my body. I wanted him to see how we really lived. His next concern was whether my ex-husband would ever show up unannounced. I assured him that he would not, but that I didn't want to put him under pressure or make him uncomfortable.

His response was, "I don't know...the kids don't know me."

"Well," I asked, "How are you ever going to get to know them unless you try?"

He was very nervous about staying with us. I tried to ease his discomfort by asking questions.

"Do you feel comfortable with me? I know you would be anxious at first, but do you think you ever would be okay?"

"I think so, honey," he answered. Then he said, "Yeah, babe, when we're in a motel I'm comfortable. You know that. But what about work and school? I might interfere with their schedules or something. I don't want to say or do the wrong thing."

My poor baby. He was so unsure about this.

The next thing he said was, "Don't you think we should meet first for dinner, before I just move in?"

I convinced Ray that it would be safe—that I would never let anything happen to him.

"But, I don't want to make trouble," he worried.

I tried to convince him, "No, honey. You won't. More and more I'm realizing how sensitive you are. I really don't mean to hurt you. I love you so much. I want to make you happy, and my only chance is to get you in our house for a length of time so that I can cook your favorite food, etc. I want your robe hanging on the bathroom door. I want part of you with me all the time."

He said, "I understand, babe. That's what I want too."

The kids and I ended up spending a lot of time with Ray Charles in our small house in Kirkwood, on the outskirts of St. Louis, Missouri.

22
Moving In

ᪿᚥᚥ

At long last, Ray finally came to our new house in Kirkwood. He was always sweet and considerate to my kids and me and never overstepped his boundaries. Ray really didn't have boundaries in our house–he was quiet, well-mannered and above all, a gentleman.

His apprehension quickly faded and he was able to relax and get comfortable with Lisa, Mitzi and me. My kids were completely at ease with him, from the first day he arrived at our house in January of 1972 until the last time they were with him in March of 1997.

In a short time, Ray became so laid back that we could leave him home alone. Lisa and Mitzi went to school, I went to work, and Ray was left to fend for himself–and he could. I made coffee and set out his cup and a bowl with dry cereal in it. When he awakened, he got the milk from the fridge, filled his cereal bowl, got his silverware out of the drawer, and poured his coffee. When he finished eating, he always put his dishes in the sink. I didn't ask him to–that was just one more sweet thing about Ray. Then, he would either go back to bed and read or watch television. He liked to watch "The Price is Right," the ballgame, and always the news.

When I was at home, which was most of the time, I would bring Ray's coffee to him in the bedroom. He sat on the side of the bed wearing his nylon boxer shorts and undershirt (which were sometimes dusty pink, faded lavender, other pastel colors or plain white).

Most of the time, he lounged in a jump suit or a robe, either the chocolate brown one I bought him at Neiman Marcus or one that he brought with him.

The first thing he did when he came into the house was unzip his large, heavy, leather garment bag, and hang his coat and clothes in the closet. He then put his shaving kit ("his kit" as he called it), in the tiny space I had cleared for him in the bathroom. His bedroom slippers, (I call them house shoes) went under the bed. Ray didn't take a step, without his slippers on. I wondered why, but forgot to ask. As I reflect on it, I imagine it was so that he wouldn't stub his toe.

We had such good times together–it just seemed so natural to have him here with us. Ray loved White Castle burgers. Most of the time I would already have them when he arrived, but if I hadn't had time to pick them up, he and I would drive to the drive-thru to get them. In a parking lot full of people, no one had a clue that Ray Charles was sitting right next to them in my little blue Volkswagen.

When I became vegetarian and ultimately vegan, there were no more animal products in my house, including White Castle burgers. Years later in 2009, Lisa found a vegan recipe for them. It is so identical I doubt even Ray would have been able to tell the difference.

The girls and I fell into such a comfortable routine with Ray, it seemed like he was just meant to be be there with us. One time when Ray was was napping on the couch, for in-stance, Mitzi and her little neighbor friend came in. I heard Mitzi tell Kelly, "Shhh, shhhh, Ray's sleeping."

That happened regularly. The kids paid no attention to Ray and they didn't seem to bother him either. He didn't even wake up. The kids would go downstairs to their playroom and, kids being kids, soon they would be right back upstairs, going out the front door. Sometimes, I would reprimand them. That would bother Ray more than them running in and out. He would say, "Leave them alone, honey. It's okay." Lisa and Mitzi always treated Ray respectfully.

Sometimes when Ray was here, things got a little too familiar! Once as I was walking from our kitchen toward Ray, who was sitting on the couch at the time, I happened to glance at the window.

"Oh my God, Ray! Someone's peaking in the window!" I screamed.

I'm sure that scared Ray to death. He didn't know who it might be. As it turned out, it was my neighbors and their children! They said they had heard that Ray Charles was here, and they wanted to get a glimpse of him. I asked them to please not do that. Ray walked to the door, greeted them, and they left. I closed the blinds and left them closed.

That kind of invasion of our privacy only happened once. People were usually polite to Ray–usually. On one occasion, however, a woman was quite persistent. We decided to go out to eat during one of Ray's visits and Lisa and Mitzi wanted Chinese food. We dropped their friend, Liz, off at her home and went to a restaurant called Kwan Yin (which is no longer there). Ray, the kids and I were quietly talking and eating when a woman stopped at our table and asked, "Are you Ray Charles?" Ray's answer was always the same, "'Fraid so."

She seemed surprised and said she was happy to meet him. Then she left. Soon she returned with her daughter and became invasive. She asked for Ray's autograph. Ray said, "Obviously, I don't sign my name." Then she looked directly at me and asked, "Who are you all?" That put Ray over the edge. He put his fork down and said, "Our family is just trying to have dinner, lady, if you don't mind."

The proprietor asked her not to bother us anymore and suggested that she leave. Then he expressed his deepest regrets to Ray and me. The woman apologized, and left in a huff.

It was during this time in the early and middle seventies that many of my friends and neighbors came to our house to meet Ray. Mr. and Mrs. Smith, who were teachers and lived behind me, were two of those people. One day they saw Ray and me get out of the car. As soon as we got in the house, the phone rang. It was the Smiths asking if they could, "Quickly run over and meet Ray." I asked him. He scratched his head, furrowed his brow, and answered, "Yeah, I guess so."

When they left, Ray began the process of unpacking while

I busied myself making us snacks, including a glass of milk for Ray. Ray loved milk–it was his favorite drink–and I always had lots of it for him. Personally, I didn't drink milk. I always drank iced tea.

Ray would say, "Babe, you shouldn't drink so much tea. It makes you pee all night. It did, but I drank it anyway. I still do–and it still makes me pee all night!

One thing Ray never, ever, drank was water. He didn't like the taste of it. He liked the taste of the pure water from the springs and wells in the country where he lived as a little boy, but he never was able to acquire a taste for city water.

When I was a little girl, I had the same pure well water that Ray did. I knew why he liked it. It had a soft, light taste.

My grannie drew water in a bucket from a well on our back porch. My mother carried buckets of water from a red pump, that she had to prime with water and pump like hell to get the water to come. Then she carried the bucket as far as a long city block. The water sloshed all over Mom as she struggled to carry the heavy buckets to the house, much like Ray's mother must have struggled to fill those large number four wash tubs she used to earn their meager living.

Ray and I had many similarities. Like Ray's pseudo Mom, Mary Jane, who worked at a saw mill, my Dad also worked at a saw mill–but he owned it. Ray played on a country dirt road as a child and so did I. He hung out in Mr. Pitt's Country Store and I played behind the counters in my grannie's country store. Ray spent much time in church–so did I. My ex-husband Henry's nickname was "Foots," and that was Ray's nickname at the school for the blind. How ironic.

Even though he couldn't see, Ray had an edge of strength about him that made me comfortable. I always felt secure and happy when I was with him. He seemed to love the simplicity of our quiet lifestyle; the warmth and comfort of our cozy little home and the aroma of corn popping, coffee brewing, and at times, bread baking. I loved nothing more than to be cooking and peek into the living room to see Ray napping on the couch, or reading, or watching a game or the news on television. Ray liked "The Price is Right" game show. He got a kick out of the women going all crazy when they won.

One of the cutest things I remember, and I can't forget it because I have a photograph of it, is Ray in my bedroom asleep with Lisa propped up in bed beside him eating a peanut butter sandwich and watching television.

Occasionally Mitzi would sprawl across the foot of the bed, and often Baby, our dog, would make herself comfortable, too. She was a small black Cockapoo and Ray liked her. Ray never flinched. He slept right through everything. He slept like a rock.

Obviously, there was no room for me, but my turn would come later. When the kids were gone or asleep, the little home-maker would magically become a sexy, seductive siren who, according to Ray, "moved mountains and made the earth tremble."

He said, "You can be so, so, so sweet. I think if you asked God he would give you heaven." Then he added, "But there's that other side of you that even the devil would fear."

Ray didn't look at me through a sexual veil, however. He saw the innermost part of me–my heart. He said to me, "I know you, babe, everything about you–inside and out–even your toes."

When Ray sat on the end of the couch, I would lie with my head on a pillow at the other end with my feet on his lap. He felt my toes, one by one, then my feet, calves, knees, thighs and on and on. He had a destination. He definitely knew every-thing about me, and yes, even my toes.

I teasingly said to him, "Do me a favor, honey. Keep that to yourself." We laughed.

Ray and I would sit at our small kitchen table after break-fast, having coffee and talking. We discussed everything: cur-rent affairs, politics, his music and his favorite people, like Martin Luther King. Ray respected Martin because of his pas-sive way of getting his message to the people. I spent many hours with Ray, not only having long discussions, but studying his physiognomy. I studied his face for years, even before I sketched the portraits of him, but there was nothing to compare with sitting across from him and watching his face brim with expression. His character lines and facial movements were hypnotizing, and I was engulfed in them. His brow would furrow and his eyes would strain to open, but couldn't. His mouth was relaxed and soft as he searched for just the right words to answer my question or explain a situation to me.

I've watched him deep in conversation with our friend Don Eaker. I've seen him listen intently to every word, then respond sincerely and thoughtfully. I have studied Ray's face in depth for so many years. I can visualize every character line, every expression, and those expressions are etched eternally in my mind. His sound, even still, resonates through my head–and his aroma permeates the air around me with the familiar fragrance of Cannon Cologne. It is almost insidious the way Ray invaded my heart, pierced it with Cupid's arrow, and moved right on in, and even though he isn't visible anymore, he still resides there.

Ray downplayed his super intelligence and his worldly sophistication by using down-home language, but he could speak eloquently, if he chose to. I was astonished by his knowledge, but also of his extensive vocabulary and command of the English language.

Whenever I asked Ray for advice, or just the answer to a question, he would respond with volumes of conversation, moving along in search of a resolution or an answer. Most times, he would find one, and I would be satisfied that we came to the appropriate conclusion.

Because Ray was gone so much, a large portion of our relationship was carried on over the phone and we would get into some deep, lengthy conversations. Sometimes, he would go on and on and on to the point where I was ready to scream. Once, for example, he asked me if I had gained any weight, stating that I never seemed to gain a pound. I told him I had actually lost a little weight lately and he was concerned. I said I had been having emotional problems and had joined a group therapy class called Recovery, Inc. Ray didn't think therapy was necessary. He thought if you were smart, which he said I was, you didn't need therapy. He asked me why I was doing it.

"Because I don't want to crack up again," I answered.

"Oh! No, no, no–okay. I'm okay with it if you say you have to."

"You don't know because you aren't here enough," I told him.

"Yeah, but Marci, you don't need to do that."

"What do I need to do Ray?" I asked, becoming frustrated with him.

"You oughta pull yourself together, Marci," he said. "You really are a beautiful woman. I'm not just talkin' 'bout your looks now. I'm talkin' about your insides. It's true. You and I argue like hell and we have our disagreements, but when you break it all down, you're a very beautiful person. I don't know why you fight yourself. That's what you do, at least in my mind, but God knows I'm no psychiatrist."

"Ray, maybe you haven't been through what I go through," I answered.

"Well, honey, I think I've been through as much in life as anyone," he said, "and I have problems too, although you don't think I do. You know, with business and worrying about what's gonna happen with this, and trying to project that, and trying to figure this out. I do have problems too.

"I often tell you, honey, if you could somehow understand, you don't know what goes on behind closed doors. Here's an example. You go to somebody's house and you think they're so happy–that's what you see, but come 12 – 1:00 o'clock and you leave. The doors are closed. It's a different thing, 'cause you're not there.

"What I'm tryin to say, honey, is that many times, when we look at a Circus, we don't see what entertainers like myself call, "backstage.""

Oh! My! God!, I thought. He's on a roll and he's completely missed my whole point. I'm talking about my emotional state and he's going on and on about "what goes on behind closed doors."

Finally, I said, "Ray! This has nothing to do with what I'm going through. I can't help myself and you think I should do it without help. I don't want to go back into an institution. I can't stand that!!"

"I wish you would forget that, hon," Ray quietly said to me. "God knows if I could ever get you to forget one thing, it's that. See, if you start talking about that, you may, and I say may, convince yourself sooner or later of that kind of thing again."

Ray couldn't stop. He kept talking....

"You see, you don't need nothing like therapy. There's nothing wrong with you," he continued. "All you need to do is realize you're not the only one with multiple problems."

Ray was mentally and emotionally strong, so obviously he didn't understand what was happening to me. In spite of his advice, I started attending the Recovery, Inc meetings, and I bought the recommended book, *Mental Health Through Will Training* by Dr. Abraham Low. I practiced the progressive steps needed to heal myself.

I did learn a lesson from this experience, however–I learned not to discuss my illness with Ray. He simply didn't understand, nor could he face the fact that I was emotionally fragile. It was my own strength and Dr. Low's book that brought me through to recovery, but it certainly wasn't easy–it took years.

To distract me from my emotional state during our lengthy discussion, Ray changed the subject. He said, "You know something that might make you laugh a bit? I just thought about the most funniest thing in the world."

"What is it, Ray?" I questioned (but I already knew the answer. It was that fight that I had in the barnyard). Ray could never forget that. We re-enacted the whole scene with Ray mimicking my brother, and then me, all the time laughing hysterically. Ultimately, he reminded me that that's how he found out I was a hellcat and, after that incident, he could personally vouch that it was indeed a fact. I didn't deny it and when I read this part of the manuscript to Mary Ann (as I have read every single page to her) she giggled and said, "How could you?"

23
Airport

These days, you are not allowed to board an airplane unless you are the passenger or crew because of strict security, but in the 1970s, I could. When I went onto the plane to get Ray, the flight attendant would announce, "All passengers please remain seated until Mr. Ray Charles has exited the plane."

I was always there eagerly awaiting his arrival (usually on American Airlines), having to hold myself back to keep from running to the plane before I was given the okay. When I boarded the plane I didn't see the other passengers–only Ray. My greeting for him was always the same, "Hi, sweetheart." Of all the words I ever said to Ray, those two were his favorite. I would see his body react, straightening and focusing in my direction. When I reached him, I would touch his face and kiss his cheek, which prompted the passengers to clap as Ray and I made our way to the exit. Sometimes we left the plane via the back exit. I don't know the reasoning for that, considering Ray was always in first class in the front of the plane.

A sky captain was always with me to retrieve his heavy garment bag and carry it to the car. Ray never checked anything–he didn't like to wait at the baggage claim. He just wanted to get through the airport, to the car, and home.

People were always nice to Ray. They would walk on past saying "Ray Charles!" or "Brother Ray!" or "How ya' doing, Ray?" Sometimes people would put their hands out, either forgetting or oblivious to the fact that Ray couldn't see. At those times, I would say "He can't see you" and they would say something nice and move on.

On one occasion, a young couple stopped us. When Ray

asked where they were going, the young man tearfully replied "My younger brother is in the last stages of cancer and we're going to see him one last time." The conversation touched Ray deeply, and he would often bring it up with a sad tone in his voice.

On Ray's return flights, we were always allowed to board first. I sat next to him in an unoccupied seat until the plane began to fill and someone claimed the seat I was using. Even then, the cabin crew was nice enough to let me stand next to him until they were ready to close the doors in preparation for take-off. I would kiss him goodbye and hurry inside the airport to find a window where I could watch the plane until it disappeared into the clouds. "My heart is leaving me," I would think as tears streamed down my face. It was the same feeling I had when I put my little girls on a plane to New Orleans to see their dad.

The next time Ray came, he immediately asked, "How's your mom?" It was typical Ray. He was always very concerned and considerate regarding my family. I had told him in an earlier conversation that Mom had been sick, but she was better. In fact, she now felt well enough to watch him on television the night before.

"I made a terrible mistake," he said. "I did something I never do."

"Watched yourself?" I asked.

"Yes, and I shouldn't have," he said. "The engineering part was very poor. For instance, when the Raelettes were singing with me, they were much too..."

"Loud," I said, cutting him off. "They covered you and so did the band."

"Exactly," Ray complained. "You noticed that too?"

I mentioned that I didn't care for the songs he had selected. Then I told him that I didn't mean to criticize because I was sure he didn't like criticism–no one did.

"Well babe," he responded, "criticism can go either way, constructive or destructive. If you think I don't like criticism, then you don't know me, because that's how I learn."

I could tell that he was a little on the defensive and knew that he was going to explain it all to me. I tried to steer the conversation in a different direction, but he was on a roll. He was on a mission to make me understand why he chose certain songs to sing. I knew I was in for a long discussion–Ray could rattle on endlessly when he was trying to make a point.

"Ray, I don't know anything about your music except that I love it," I said, in an effort to slow him down, but to no avail.

"Babe you gotta remember that 95, if not 98 percent of the television viewers are just like you–everyday people." He went on, "They don't know the technical things, so when someone says 'Hey man! I saw your show and it didn't appeal to me,' I listen. Why do you think the big networks like ABC, CBS, or NBC listen to the public? It's because of the people like you, hon, who are not engineers or technicians." He really was on a roll. "All they know is that they want to be entertained. You forget one thing, Marci. There are many, many people in the world who like songs like 'Take These Chains From My Heart' or 'You Don't Know Me.'"

"Okay, you made your point." I said, but he went right on. Nothing could stop him! I wished I could take back my comment, but it was too late.

"And babe," he continued, "I can wait five minutes and someone will say, 'Hey Ray, you sang all those other songs, but I didn't hear 'I Got A Woman' or 'Hit the Road Jack.' See honey, I do many different kinds of things."

"Ray, I know that," I started to say, but he kept on talking. Finally, I got mad and yelled. "You won't let me talk!"

"All I'm trying to tell you, sweetheart," he rolled right over me again, "is I'm never gonna tell you anything wrong. We've sold over a million records in both types of songs. See what I mean, honey?" Then he started singing, "I feel so bad, like a ball game on a rainy day... We sold over a million of that one too. There's somebody out there buying them, Marci."

Oh...My...God! Finally, he gave me a chance to talk.

"That song is a lot better than 'Look What They've Done to My Song, Ma.'"

"Well, babe, that song did very well, too." Then he said, "We could go on and on about this."

"Well, we're not." I said.

By this time, we were pulling in the driveway. This conversation had gone on through the airport and all the way home. I was ready to end it, but he obviously wasn't.

"A person like me is in various fields of music," he said. "I don't confine myself to any one particular kind. I've had people raise all kinds of hell with me. They write me some very nasty letters. I'm not kidding you, Marci. They say, 'Look man, I don't know who the hell you think you are, singing songs like 'I Can't Stop Loving You.' You ain't no Hank Williams. You ain't no Hank Snow.' I'm just telling you, honey, what I go through."

"Okay, Ray" I said. "Let's stop talking about it. I don't know anything about it anyway. I'm sorry I mentioned it."

Ray had to get in one more little comment before he'd drop the subject. He told me that when *I* was trying to get *him* to understand something that *he* didn't want to discuss, I would say, "'Oh, you don't want to talk about that huh?' But now it's *you* who doesn't want to talk about it. See, Marci, you're the same way." Then he thought for a minute and said, "I don't care if my show was good or bad. When I'm here, I just wanna be with you. Okay, baby?"

Oh my God, yes! It was definitely okay. I was grateful not to have to hear about it anymore. When I mentioned earlier that I would get volumes of information in answer to a question or situation, I wasn't kidding. Ray was compelled to clarify everything in order to give the most complete and in-depth answer possible.

A few days after he left that time, I got a call from him telling me how much he missed me. He said "I love you today." I told him that I didn't like it when he said it like that.

"Marci, I hafta' tell you about today," he said. "God may

see fit that I'm not around tomorrow. So I want you to know how I feel right now."

"Well," I asked, "if you're around tomorrow, will you love me?"

"Sweetheart, like I told you, I love you right now and tomorrow, if I live to see it," he said, trying to comfort me. "Let's just give us this day, that's what the Bible says. Give us this day, our daily bread."

"Well, I think it's ridiculous to stick to one thing in the Bible when you don't stick to another damn thing," I told him.

"Honey, what I feel right now is that I love you very, very much, and you see, if you could halfway understand anything, you would at least realize that it's alright." Then he said "I'm gonna hang up, babe."

"No!" I cried, "No, don't hang up!"

"I just wanted to hear your voice," he said. "I told you, I tried to call you and didn't get an answer. I didn't want you to jump up and say, 'Well I don't know why in the hell you're calling. You told me you just had to have the damn number and damn it you haven't called me in…' (he was imitating me when I was angry) and then I gotta hear a long lecture."

"Oh, my! Do I really sound like that?" I asked.

"Oh, that's the way you sound, honey. I'm telling you how you sound."

Ray changed the subject at that point and asked what I had been doing. I told him I had painted my bedroom and built a bookcase for downstairs. I needed to hide some pipes that went all over, so I sawed and hammered the wood, and the kids stained them ebony. We were all in our panties and no tops–we were ebony colored all over.

"You're my talented girl, aren't you, honey?" he said, clearly impressed.

"No, the things I do are simple," I replied.

"They're simple only because you know how to do them," he said, building my confidence. "You're very modest, Marci."

I told him that my dad had come to look at the bookcases and thought they were pretty good. As soon as I mentioned my dad, I could sense a difference in Rays tone.

"You know...I...I..." Ray had become anxious and was stuttering. He couldn't even say how fearful he was. He tried again. "I...I wonder what...last time I talked to you, you didn't tell me that your Dad...I wonder how he would feel if he caught me there. See you don't think about things like that–you don't have to. What would you do if he knocked on the door? Tell him he can't come in?"

"Sweetheart," I said, as reassuringly as possible, "I wouldn't answer the door. Besides, he doesn't just show up unannounced. Don't worry, you'll be safe. I'll take care of you."

I wish I had reassured him more. I thought that I had made him feel safe and secure when I was trying so hard to convince him to stay with us, but the mere mention of my dad being at my house struck fear into Ray. He somehow had the misconception that dad didn't come to my home, but of course he did. He was my father. I just didn't allow him to control my life.

I would have stood before a firing squad to protect Ray. I would never have let anything happen to him. Ray had already experienced one scary episode in Los Angeles when Henry went to the Coconut Grove. I knew he wanted to avoid another confrontation.

"You think if it's alright with you, it oughta be alright with the world, but that ain't the way life goes, babe," Ray said worriedly. "Sometimes, honey, if a person has a criticism you don't know how far they will take it." His concerns didn't keep him away, however, considering this conversation was in the 1970s, and he was still coming to my house in 1997!

Ray was always calling me asking about certain dates. This time he wanted to know when Easter was. I told him I would check the calendar, and noted how busy he seemed and how grouchy he sounded. He admitted it and told me he was having a terrible time.

Then he asked again about Easter. I asked him what was happening on Easter.

"Nothin', I just wanna know what day it is," he said. So, I told him and asked why again. The reply came as another question, "I just wanted to know. What's today's date?"

"Are you coming to see me? Is that why you want to know?" I asked excitedly after telling him the date.

"I want to," he said, "When is the best time, other than right now?"

"You'll have to decide that," I told him. "You're the one who always gets messed up. It's never me. I can arrange for you to come any time...well, almost anytime. The only problem I would ever have is if the kids' dad would come, but I'm not expecting him."

"Well, honey," he asked, "has he ever been known to just show up?"

"No," I said quickly. "I just meant that he would be the only reason I would have a problem. I shouldn't have mentioned it. He doesn't stay here anyway."

"Ooookay," he growled, and I asked if he would be here soon.

"Yeeaaah...I...I think...I can come pretty soon. I really do, babe."

"But remember, Ray, you thought that before and it didn't work out," I reminded him. "Thanks to my group therapy, I think I've adjusted well to those disappointments, don't you?"

"Yes, baby," he agreed, but still sounded grouchy and sleepy. "Now I'm all the things you've been trying to train me to be." He didn't want me to complain again about not being together enough. I continued on about my newly found strength. "I just hope it doesn't turn out with me just not giving a damn," I told him.

"Aw, no, no, no!" That awakened him. Now he sounded alert. "You're never not gonna give a damn! You see, you can really never go against your true self, honey. And, as I told you, you're not that kind of person. You're never not gonna give a damn."

Obviously, he hadn't understood what I said. I explained to him that I didn't mean about anything, I meant about him.

"Oh! Oh! Uuuh! I get your point, Marci. I hear what you're saying, babe."

After a few minutes, I asked him if he would get the song "The First Time Ever I Saw Your Face" by Roberta Flak. When he wanted to know why, I told him because that was how I felt about him. He told me he would get it, that he knew someone who could find anything. I knew that person was Bob Taylor, his valet. Then he told me that the next time he saw me, he was going to tell me what he had been thinking and feeling. I pleaded with him to tell me then, but he wouldn't. I told him by the time we saw each other, the mood would be over.

"No it won't, baby," he comforted me. "It's never gonna be over between you and me. I won't ever get over you. I'll ring off now and I'll see you soon."

As promised, he did see me soon, and on the trip home from the airport in my brother's Bonneville (I had wrecked my car) we talked about Lisa. She had been diagnosed with anemia, and was taking some huge pills for it.

"So they're very large, huh?" Ray asked.

"Yes," I replied, "and they don't seem to be helping her energy level."

"Well honey, take her back to the physician, I hate to see her feel bad. Lisa's a very sweet girl" he said with concern. "Now that that's said, how's her mother? Last time I was here, you had something wrong with your hip. Does it hurt constantly?"

"No," I giggled, "only in certain positions, and you know those positions."

"Well, I guess we'll have to avoid those positions," he laughed.

"We can work around them," I teased. Then he asked if my car accident had caused my hip to hurt. I told him no, but the accident left me feeling insecure about my driving.

"Are you scared to drive now?" Ray asked, worried. "You know, you're supposed to stay one car length behind."

"I know the road rules," I said. "This accident was my fault, but the first one wasn't. I glanced away–that's what happened. The kids and the dog were in the car and the dog was jumping from the front seat to the back seat."

"Oh, honey!" Ray exclaimed, "You're never supposed to do that."

"I know," I told him. Then I asked him if he had released his latest album.

"We just got the D.J. copies and it will be released this weekend," he told me. The album was "Through the Eyes of Love" and he had brought a copy with him, telling me, "Just in case you might want it."

I did want it. And I wanted something else. I wanted to know what he was going to tell me about what he had been thinking and feeling. He may have forgotten that he said that, but I didn't.

"So what is it, Ray?" I asked him. We were sitting on the side of the bed, and he pulled me close to him.

"I have a strooong... addiction to you, Marci. I just want you to know how I feel. I'm drawn to you like a magnet." I loved hearing those words from him and thinking about it still warms my heart.

24
A Strong Addiction

A few days after he left, Ray called and asked what I had been doing. I teased, "Oh, you want me to tell on myself? Do you really want to hear it? You know how weak I am."

His quick response was, "No, don't tell me." I told him I hadn't been bad, and he informed me that he knew that. He said, "You might be weak, honey, but it's you as a person, it's your whole insides, your innate make-up, that won't allow you to be bad."

I thought…*Ray, it might surprise you to know what my innate makeup will allow me to do (giggle).*

I asked him if he knew he would be working in St. Louis in two weeks on a Sunday night. He said he didn't, that he hadn't seen the itinerary yet. He wondered why he always managed to play St. Louis on a Sunday. "I guess it's a Sunday night town," he said.

I laughingly said, "Maybe they think you're a Sunday night man, you know…Brother Ray."

He laughed and said, "Yeah, right!"

I told him I was going to do some modeling. "I'm gonna be a wood nymph," I said.

"A what?" Ray said.

"Wood nymph. You know, naked in the woods." I repeated.

"You're kidding me."

"I'm not, but you don't need to be jealous, 'cause the photographer doesn't…"

"He doesn't what?" Ray interrupted.

"Doesn't want anything from me. He's my friend. He's someone you'll meet sooner or later," I said.

Ray didn't like the wood nymph idea. He told me not to tell him if I was going to do that sort of thing.

"Okay," I giggled.

I still have the pictures. They were done in good taste. Don Eaker was, and is, a good photographer. When Ray finally met him, he liked him and they became good friends. Some of the pictures that Don shot of Ray and me are included in this book, including the one on the cover.

So Sunday came and went, and no Ray. When he finallly called, he said he was trying desperately all last week to reach me.

I said, "Well, keep trying. Maybe I'll get back to my normal, sweet self."

"Oh, you're always sweet," he said softly. "You know, honey...you know how it is with you. There's just some people–you know, whatever they do, or whatever happens, or how mad they can make you, or how disgusted you can get with them...there's certain people in this world, no matter what...it...it's...I guess it's like a strooong addiction. You know, it's bad for you but you can't leave it alone."

I giggled and teased, "Oh, is that right? I get your point. You think I'm bad for you."

He hurriedly said, "No! No! I don't, baby. I...I...I...can't help myself. I'm just crazy 'bout you Marci." Then he said, "Aww shit! I'm not s'posed to tell ya' that, but it's true. What can I do?"

I told him I was sorry he hadn't been able to reach me.

He said, "Well, that's alright, babe. I...I...don't know, I guess the moon must have been...whatever, because I wanted to get you very, very badly and I don't...I don't know what came over me, you know, I don't know what happened to me." Ray sounded sad and disappointed.

I told him I had been thinking about him, really thinking about him especially hard because I thought he was going to be here and I wondered why he hadn't called me.

Ray said, "I thought we were gonna be there, too. But I told you I wasn't sure about the date. I hadn't seen the itinerary. That date was so close to the beginning of our tour. I would remember the first couple of dates and I didn't remember St. Louis being on there. As it turned out, it was on there, but there was a question about it. So I thought I'd wait 'til I knew we we're actually gonna be there, then I could call you and give you the details. If we weren't gonna play St. Louis Sunday, that meant we were off, right? So if we were off, and I would have Sunday, Monday and Tuesday, I was just gonna…

I interrupted, "Oh, brother!" I was gone and I had missed him!

He continued, "If you let me, I was gonna come see you those three days."

"Oh my God! That really upsets me," I cried. "I think you did that on purpose!"

"Awww, honey, come on," he said.

"I think you just got even with me for not staying home," I teased.

Ray wanted me to know how badly he wanted to see me. He said, "Well, you know, I really wanted to see you, so I thought…if I wasn't gonna work Sunday…and ya' see what happens, since I couldn't get you…I didn't know whether…" (Sometimes he wouldn't finish a sentence and I had to piece together what he meant).

He went on, "And what really got me is–when I called in the evening and still couldn't get you, I thought maybe you took the kids and went to Kansas City. But then I thought the kids were in school so that didn't make sense. Well, you know I was tryin'…see Marci, when a person's trying to be reasonable you think of all kinds of things, but most of them you can rationalize. So in my mind, I figure something's gone wrong…no that can't be…but then you get worried. You start thinking, 'My God, I wonder if something's really gone wrong.' You know, in the winter people have a lot of fires."

I told him I didn't know he thought about those things.

"Sure," he stressed.

The phone was clicking and making a buzzing sound, which upset Ray.

"This stupid phone," he said.

Finally, the operator cut in and told Ray she was testing something. It finally cleared up.

Ray continued on. "I was telling you about the fears I had about you."

"I'm very happy to hear that because I never thought you worried about me."

"Why?" Ray asked, in a perplexed voice.

"I just never thought you worried about me," I answered.

"Marci," he said, after analyzing that remark, "You know what it is?" he asked. Then he answered his own question. "You don't think I give a damn about you. So, I understand why you feel like that, because you really don't think I give a damn about you."

Laughing, I said, "Yeah, I don't know if you do."

Ray said, "You don't think I care, but you're totally wrong. I guess I'll live my life trying to convince you that you're wrong, and it's probably one of the few battles I won't win."

I said, "You're probably right!"

"Yep," he assured me. "You know I won't give up on it. I'll keep tryin'. One day I might accidently get through to you."

"How do you think that's ever gonna happen?" I questioned.

"Well...I don't know...But you'd be surprised sometimes what circumstances can do." He often said things like that to me–time, patience and circumstances can take care of many things.

I told Ray that he reminded me of a friend of mine, John, who could change his thoughts to peaceful thoughts. Ray said he thought it was pretty hip that my friend didn't allow unhappy thoughts to clutter his mind. I told him that John had meaningless affairs, according to him, but that one kind of got to him. He had a child by her. They broke up and it hurt him, but he just wouldn't think about it.

"You do that, don't you Ray? How do you do it?" I asked.

"Yeah," he said, "Uhhh, what it is...psychiatrists have known this for years, honey, that people can block things out of their minds–like little children, you know, things like bad memories. It's just somewhere in their subconscious. Sometimes you get a kid and he goes through certain things and you can't figure out what it is, maybe something always seems to frighten him, but if you trace it back, you'll find that it was some bad experience, and unless you really probe his mind, you can never get it out of him. The thought won't surface. And uuh...I think what someone does with that kind of thing is to try to put it somewhere in their mind, a portion of the mind, and then cover it up with other things, you see, so they don't get so hurt. Otherwise, if they don't, well, every waking hour that they have, you know, they're sensitive to that bad thing."

I regret how little attention I paid to what Ray said. Now as I remember, what he was really saying was that this was the way he handled his sad childhood and early adult years.

"Ray, I wish I could do that. For the last three and a half years, you've been all I could think about. Like, why you did the things you did. I just never thought you cared. But I've been able to overcome it, somewhat, thanks to group therapy."

He said, in a soft sweet, loving voice, "I don't care what you think. Well, I do care what you think. I take that back. You don't believe me, but you're just my sweet baby. God, I'd love to see you. Where are you right now?"

"I'm in the rocking chair," I answered.

"In the rocking chair," Ray said in a high pitched voice. "Isn't that sweet; sitting in the rocking chair. I'll bet you look pretty."

"I don't know how pretty I look," I said, "but I smell good. I took a bath and put lots of good smelling lotion on."

"You always look pretty, baby, and you always smell good," he said sweetly.

Our phone conversations always drifted from one topic to another. I told him that I had the creeps the night before because I read a ghost story in the "Enquirer" which scared me.

"Why do you buy it, babe?" he asked.

"Because I'm curious and it has a bunch of garbage in it. The story I read was gory and scary. I'm more afraid of things I can't see than the real things I should fear. I'm terrified of ghosts and I don't want them in this house."

Ray howled with laughter. "But, Marci, you say that like you can do something about ghosts. He mimicked me, 'I just don't want 'em in this house.'"

"Well, I don't," I said.

"How do you know? They might be nice," he teased.

"Noooo," I said.

"You may encounter a real sweet ghost," he said.

"Poltergeists are the funny ones, and I don't want them either. I don't want the gory ones or the cheery ones!"

Ray said, "Oh wow!"

"I wished you were here last night. You could have held me. I left all the lights on," I told him.

"Now the lights keep the spirits from coming in, right?" He was splitting his sides laughing. But he began to get serious. He said, "Things like that usually go back to when you were a child. I know when they wanted to get you to behave, they'd tell you hate's gonna get you. And kids are fearful of that. When I was a kid I...I was always scared of the ambulance, or anything with a siren. I never cared for fire engines because they had that sound on them. I think the reason I didn't like it was because my grandmother was in...you know...was in one of those hearses and...and...I didn't like it."

Writing these memories and word-for-word conversations, I'm reminded of the fears Ray had as a small, sightless boy and all of the adjustments he was forced to make in his little-boy-life. Having to leave his home, Mama, friends and relatives at the age of seven, then board a train all alone and just leave had to have been devastating for a little boy, much less a blind one.

I remember what heartache I felt when I put my little girls on a plane to New Orleans at that age, and that was just for a visit. I couldn't imagine sending them away to live.

My heart is filled with empathy and sympathy for Ray and his young mother. She did the right thing for her little boy, even though it must have broken her heart, which was already broken from the loss of her younger son, George, who had drowned at the young age of 4. It was very possible that poor Retha could have expired from sheer heartbreak at such an early age (her early thirties).

It had been about three weeks since Ray had been to see me and that was too long for me. Rather than complain, however, I took a different approach. I began telling him about a neighbor who had taken an interest in helping me improve my property. He was doing pretty major stuff, like laying flagstone on my small concrete breezeway and building a plant container with railroad ties and filling it with soil and a small evergreen bush. Then he built a small landing and step leading to the outside patio. The flagstone part was covered. One morning, I looked out and saw that he had cut my spindly hedges and layered mulch on them. They looked beautiful. When they grew, they were much thicker, greener and prettier than before. I had never even thought about having these wonderful improvements done, and I loved it.

"You better be careful, babe," Ray warned.

"Why?" I asked.

"Well...you know some people...uh go off their rocker... when they see certain things or things hit 'em wrong," he warned.

"You mean like you being here?" I asked.

He said, "Well, you never can tell about it. There's some crazy nuts, babe, and yeah, like my bein' there is one of them."

"How's he gonna know?" I asked.

"Well, lets put it this way, I mean, after all, I don't figure that it necessarily needs to be a secret as far as he's concerned you know. You can't seal up everybody." He wasn't happy. Then I made the mistake of telling him that my neighbor was divorced.

"Oh, he's divorced?" Ray asked.

"Yes, for two years," I answered.

"And what about the man down the street?" Ray questioned.

"Oh, Melvin, the one who repaired my lawnmower? I never hear anything from him. His daughter's out of the hospital now and I guess his wife's there all the time," I said, trying to ease his mind. It didn't matter. He continued, still troubled. "Well...I guess...you know when a person is determined to attain something, or someone, he may resort to many, many things."

"Well, damn it." I said. "If you were here taking care of what you're supposed to, I wouldn't have these problems. They see me raking and working and I guess they think, 'Why not try.' You gotta give them some credit, you know. I'm not the ugliest thing in the world."

"I never implied that, my dear." Ray was defensive. "I know better than that, Marci." Then he said he would be here in the morning. Just as I thought, the conversation triggered the jealousy in him.

I kept it up, "You better tend to business. Either tend to business or suffer the consequences." Then I said, "I have to shampoo my hair. I was too tired last night. I've only had two hours sleep."

"Why?" he said. "Never mind, don't tell me. Let me get another cigarette." I guess he was afraid I would tell him someone else came to help me!

The neighbor who did the nice things for me was never anything more than a friend, and still is. We went out to dinner and had drinks together. He came for Thanksgiving and we visited on other occasions, and we had lots of fun. He was like part of our family. He moved out of town and I rarely see him now.

I told Ray that I had gone to my friends' horse ranch and stayed too long and had to rush home, bathe the kids, put them to bed and then I couldn't sleep.

"Say that again!!" he said. He wasn't happy with me.

I asked if he had tried to call me again. I was giggling.

"Oh, maybe I misunderstood what you said. I thought you

said you only had two hours worth of sleep," he said.

I told him I did say that.

"And I asked you how did you manage that, and you said you did what?"

I told him again that I went to my friend, Ona's, ranch.

He just couldn't get it straight. "When was that?"

"Last night," I answered.

"Well that don't...that don't make much sense, does it? You mean last night?" He couldn't get what night I meant. I don't know why. I was clear about it. Maybe because he was so irritated and he just couldn't figure it out.

Finally I said, "Mom had the kids all day. I picked them up about seven o'clock and went to the ranch."

"Oh," he said, "She didn't work yesterday?"

"Ray, you know she's off on Wednesday."

"Oh, yeah," he remembered, "Then you came home and got right on the phone."

I was surprised. "How did you know?"

"How'd I know!!!" he sounded exasperated. "I told you I've been tryin' to call ya', didn't I? And the line just stayed busy. You were on the phone just yakkin."

I said, "I wasn't on the phone very long."

"Well, I got news for you. You might not have thought you were on the phone a long time, but I called you three times during the Dick Cavette show when the commercials came on. You don't have to believe me, but you know I'm not gonna say something just to be saying it. After all, I didn't have to say it, you know. I'm telling you, you were on the phone."

By now I was so tickled, I was just laughing at him, but he wasn't thrilled. I asked if he was up for the morning.

"Yeah, I might as well be," was his short response.

"Are you tired?" I asked.

"I could go either way," he said.

"Now you're gonna be tired when you get here and so am I. What time do you leave tomorrow?" I asked. He said he hadn't checked yet, but he would let me know so I could make arrangements for someone to pick up Mitzi if I had to be at the airport when she was getting out of school.

He gave me the flight number and time he would be in after making sure I was awake enough to remember.

"I'll be there, Ray," I assured him. "I'm never late."

"Okay, baby," he said sweetly.

He was here for only one night this time. There were many times like that and there were many times when he was here for three, four or five nights.

Ray fit so well into our lifestyle. He once said to me, "I don't want you to change anything because of me, honey, just do what you normally do." And that's what we did.

Ray was back again in a week. I had told him on the phone that the kids were in New Orleans and that I had been crying.

"Oh, babe, are you alright?" He was concerned about me being sad.

"No," I answered. "I drank too many Margaritas." He wanted to know where I went, and I told him some Mexican place. Then I asked him to please come here or let me come to him.

He promised, "Okay, babe. I'll see what I can do."

"I hope you know how serious I am," I said, kind of crying.

"I do, babe. Let me work on it, baby. Okay?" he asked.

"Don't work on it too long, Ray." He didn't. He was here right away, trying to soothe my loneliness. I missed my kids something awful and he understood.

As we snuggled together and he lightly touched my face, I felt his body tense. "You've cut your hair," he said.

"I only cut the front," I said. I had cut some bangs.

"Now what did you do that for? You're rebelling against me?" he insisted.

"Nooo, I'm not," I said. "If I had been, I'd have cut it all off."

Ray laughed. He seemed to find me very amusing.

"I'm going to color my hair red, Ray," I said.

"That won't become you, honey," he informed me.

"How do you know? I do have that red head temper," I admitted and giggled. Ray laughed and laughed.

I told him he wouldn't think it was so funny if he were ever on the receiving end of my violent temper.

"I don't really wanna know all that, babe. I don't know how you can let yourself get that mad, Marci."

"Well, you need to know it. You can't go through life just taking all the honey." After reading Michael Lydon's book, it was clear that Ray had done just that.

25
Poetry

Ray and I were talking on the phone, discussing how his day was going. He told me he had a rehearsal, then he was going to the Senda place to have his electric piano looked at. He took it on tour and used it from time to time, but played it only on certain songs. As busy as he said he was, I still asked if he wanted to hear some poems I had written about him. Being the sweet, gentle man that he always was with me, he said, "Yes, baby, I do."

I've written many poems about different subjects, but only a few about Ray. This one is about his name.

> To some a ray is a ray of sunlight in a time of darkness.
> To others, a ray is a ray of enlightenment in a time of need.
> Still to more, a ray is a ray of beauty into their dull lives.
> But to me, Ray is everything. He is my life.

He asked if that were true. My response was, "Maybe." But it was true. He knew he was everything to me–still is.

"Read the next one, babe." Ray said. I knew he was eager to get to the Senda place, but I continued on, "Okay, the name of this one is "My Man."

> I've got a man who's crazy for me.
> He thinks I'm fine even though he can't see.
> He loves to feel the smooth of my skin.
> That simple touch does wonders for him.
> He likes to feel his hands on my hair,
> And I'm sure that's something not so rare.

But for him, it's special. Everything is.
And everything I have is his, just his.
My body he wants so close to him.
And he's issued an order. I've got to stay slim.
But he's the boss and he's gentle and kind.
And the need to please him never leaves my mind.
We also do talk. I have to confess
And both agree things are quite a mess.
But when we're together we don't worry, you see,
'Cause then I've got him and he's got me."

I can't believe that I wrote this mushy poetry...and actually had the nerve to read it to Ray Charles! And I didn't stop with two–I read another one. As I'm looking back, I'm thinking, *Oh Lord, Marci. Stop!*

Ray just kept listening, and when I finished reading he said, "Yeah, babe. Those are awfully nice. I think I could take a combination of the two of those–I'd like to uh...uh...yeah. Why don't you send both of them, babe." He was going to "fool around" with the lyrics for a song. I never did send them. I didn't want to punch them out in Braille with a stylus. Ray said I didn't have to, but I didn't want anyone else reading my mushy poetry and transcribing it for him. So here they all are in a book, when perhaps they possibly could have been, with some embellishment from the master, a Ray Charles' song.

༒

My kids were still in New Orleans and Ray was coming for the second time since they left. I told him that Henry was driving them back because he was bringing their cousins for a visit.

"Oh, he's gonna drive 'em up. Okay, if you're sure, I'll tell you what we'll do. We'll ah.. ah...we'll call Thursday night, and if he's still there, fine. I will have already been there all day. We'll call just to be sure." Ray had it all figured out.

"You're really afraid of him, aren't you?" I said, and I wished I hadn't. Ray was sweet and gentle, but he was also very mas-

179

culine. I realize looking back that me saying that made him feel powerless, diminishing his masculinity.

He responded by saying, "Naw, honey. It's not that I'm afraid. I'm really and truly a pacifist. Honest to God. That doesn't say very much for me, but it's true. I don't like nothin' unnecessary and if there's any way I can avoid it by prevention, that's what I do."

I thought he should have had more confidence in me. I told him again that I would never let anything happen to him—that if anything were to happen, it would be to me.

"We...we...well...you...you're talkin' as if it were gonna happen to you, it would be alright with me. No, no. I don't want anything to happen to either of us, honey, and especially, particularly, not to you. I do have confidence in you, Marci. If I didn't, I wouldn't be with you."

"I hafta check on American Airlines," he said. "As a matter of fact, hold on a minute, babe. I'll do it right now."

I had a friend picking me up for lunch and he was at the door. I yelled from my bedroom, "I'm on a long distance call. I'll be ready in a minute."

Ray was back on the phone and heard me. He asked who I was talking to.

"I'm going out for lunch," I told him, "and I'm in the bedroom with no clothes on. So if you don't want him to see me..."

"No, I'll hang up right now, babe," he said, irritated as hell. "You say you're gonna meet the plane? You know you hafta be at the airport at 6:00 a.m.," he continued.

"Oh! You're taking your life in your hands, riding with me at 6:00 in the morning," I giggled.

"We'll let Bob drive," Ray said.

"Okay, then, I'll neck with you in the back seat," I teased.

"Okay, neck with me in the back seat. Now I told you, it's Thursday morning, didn't I?" he confirmed again.

Then it hit me that he said Thursday morning. I was upset. "Thursday morning?" I complained. "You said you were leaving tonight."

"No," he said.

"Yes, you did," I argued.

"I did not. Thursday morning at 6:00 I'll be there," he reiterated firmly. "And Marci, maybe you should put some clothes on."

"Well, you like me with no clothes on. Maybe he will too," I giggled.

"I kinda figured there were certain things that were strictly for me," he said.

"Oh, Ray. You are being selfish wanting to hoard everything just for you," I teased.

"Honey, I can only tell you how I feel," he answered.

"Okay, I'm going to lunch and then swimming," I told him.

"You...you...just got to be...you just must be tempting," he fretted.

"I won't wear any clothes with you either," I continued teasing.

"I don't really appreciate you doin' that with...around other men...uh...uh...do I make myself clear, babe?"

"Yes, Mr. Charles, you do," I answered him. "Quite clear."

At 6:00 on Thursday morning, I met my sweetheart at the gate. I didn't go on the plane because his valet was with him. I dropped Bob off at a nearby motel where I had made earlier reservations.

After hanging his coat and clothes in the closet, Ray sat at the kitchen table drinking coffee while I made pancakes and bacon for breakfast. I cut his pancakes, covered them with maple syrup and poured his milk, then joined him. There was something that I wanted to bring to his attention.

"Ray," I said. "Do you remember my neighbors, the teachers?"

"Yeah, babe, why?" he said, while feeling with his left fingers for his bacon.

"Well they think you're a ladies' man. She told me you have been connected with women for years."

"What!!!.... Well, how does she know?"

"Magazine articles." She also said that's one of your trademarks."

"I said I had never read that about you, but she told me I didn't read the right magazines. I asked her which ones they were and she told me Ebony and Jett. Those are magazines I've never read."

"But!...," Ray said, "You notice, honey, you heard that from people who never talk to me. That's not been said to me. Thank the Lord. I can't understand why a person would want to hurt your feelings by saying something like that. I think we're both old enough not to worry about what people say."

I agreed and let it drop. I really didn't know anything about it. All I was ever concerned about was him being married. I felt guilty about that and it was a constant concern for me.

Having been raised Baptist, I knew I was bound for hell fire, being in love with a married man. My conscience was nudging me to do something to relieve my guilt, but what? I loved him so much. Between the gossip, the guilt and my love for Ray, I was an indecisive and emotional mess. My constant companion was my emotional fragility. I couldn't allow myself to slip back into what I considered insanity.

After washing the breakfast dishes, I joined Ray in the living room where he was sipping coffee and smoking his KOOL cigarette. We had decided to listen to some of his albums. When I turned the stereo on it sounded terrible. I had no idea what was wrong, but Ray did. He asked if I had a new needle. I didn't, so he told me what to get at the store. When I returned, he worked on the stereo for about ten minutes and it worked.

We danced to slow tunes, not taking steps, but standing and swaying back and forth. We did that often. I would put my arms around his neck and he would hold me close. I miss those sweet times.

Ray could do things that some sighted persons were unable to do, and fixing the record player was one. Another was to fix a leak under the bathroom sink. I brought him tools and some gray putty that he said would work. He got under the sink, found the leak, took the pipes apart, smeared on the putty, put it back together and tightened it with the monkey wrench. He asked me to turn the faucet on, and when I did, there was no leak. Ray had fixed it. He was proficient, brilliant, and a true gentleman–so, so, sweet to me. I loved him with all my heart. I still do and will until the day I die.

As midday came, Ray said we should call New Orleans to see when Henry was leaving. We found that the plans had changed, and now my kids were flying home the next day. The cousins were not coming. Ray coordinated his departure time with Lisa and Mitzi's arrival time so I wouldn't have a long wait between the two.

Now Ray could relax since he knew Henry wasn't coming. We enjoyed a nice dinner, watched television, and had a blissfully romantic evening–until I began to complain about him being married. I told him it made me unhappy to the point that I was thinking of breaking it off between us.

We spent the night loving and holding each other. But Ray was sad, asking me to please not shut him out of my life. I think that had I not been so insecure with Ray, we would have had an even better relationship. I was always ambivalent, never knowing whether I would stay with him or leave him. I was always keeping him on edge–not meaning to, just being afraid because I loved him so. I wanted a quiet conventional life, but I chose an unconventional, complex and, I suppose, mysterious man to love.

I truly had no idea what he did when he was not with me. I thought he was with his wife. I once said to him, "You get everything you want. You have me wrapped around your finger." He responded, "I couldn't do that if you didn't let me." After that I sort of kept him guessing. Although I knew I was the other woman, I also knew that he was jealous and didn't want to share what he considered his.

The next morning we went to the airport, but this time Ray and Bob went to their gate and I went to a different gate to get my kids. I had always walked to the gate with Ray, and it felt strange not doing so, but I was eager to see my little girls.

They were supposed to wait with the flight attendants (in

the seventies they were called stewardesses), but when they spotted me, they came running. The attendants knew by our happy reunion that I was their mother. I overheard one say, "There's no doubt who she is."

On our drive home, Lisa and Mitzi filled me in on their wonderful visit with their Dad. They stayed with either Henry and Darlene, (yes, he was still with her), Grandma Cuka and Poppie, or Delia (Aunt Doo) and Uncle Jake. Theirs was the fun house. Ten cousins lived there.

It was routine that on the day they arrived in New Orleans, their grandma would cook a big Mexican dinner for them. They loved her cooking–everyone did. Who wouldn't love authentic Mexican food, including homemade tortillas that she slapped from one hand to the other and threw on a hot grid? They were delicious!

Henry would always take the kids to Audubon Park to feed the ducks, go to the zoo and play on Monkey Hill, and go to Lake Pontchartrain for the rides. Sometime before they left, he would take them to Lake Shore for crabs. They would buy a bucket full, which they poured onto a table covered with newspaper, that they would eat until they were stuffed.

But the main event was the messy, exciting and always-fun watermelon fight. This master of events took place in Jake and Delia's backyard. Henry provided the watermelons, all of the cousins sat in the grass eating them and then everyone started throwing the rinds, smearing them into their faces, hair and all over their bodies. Then some crazy person, either Aunt Doo or Henry, would turn on the hose and let them run under the water, making it even more slippery and fun.

On their trips to New Orleans, Henry took the girls to different places – Jackson Square, the French Quarter and Marti Gras. My kids were truly entertained by their doting and adoring dad.

I was so happy to have my little girls back. I was sad and lonely when they were gone for a month. My friends have asked me why I let them go. They had so much fun with Henry, and they had so many cousins, aunts and uncles to maintain close relationships with. I've never regretted it.

Lisa and Mitzi are in their forties now and when we get together with their cousins, they have such wonderful memories to recapture with one another. One will say, "You'd better listen or she would get the hair brush after you." Another cousin said, "How about when she would pull your ear." Oooh! They all complained in unison. They were talking about their Grandma Cuka.

Now my girls were home, back to their regular routine, and getting ready for school. I had my babies back. Things were the way they were supposed to be. Nothing was missing–except Ray.

When my kids opened the closet door to hang their jackets up they said, "Mom, the closet smells like Ray." Ray's aroma lingered for days after he left, and we loved it. The fragrance of Cannon Cologne was soothing to us.

They felt the same about their Dad. Henry always smelled good. He wore expensive cologne with a not-too pungent fragrance. Years later, Lisa brought Henry cologne from Paris and he loved it.

I particularly loved the smell of Cannon cologne. It seemed so much a part of Ray. I was seduced by its aroma, and when we touched, I always knew he was the Alpha and Omega for me. Anyone else paled in comparison.

By all accounts Ray Charles should have been unattainable to me. But he was here at any given time, lying next to me...whispering, touching and loving me. My sweet, gentle, soothing man–I was drowning deeper and deeper into an emotional bliss that I couldn't remove myself from any more than I could have pulled myself from quicksand.

Ray's shaving kit was still in the bathroom. He had forgotten it. I left a message for him and as soon as he heard it, he called. I told him I was leaving immediately to Fed-Ex it to him. That was the only time in thirty years that he ever forgot anything.

Two days after I sent the kit, Ray called. It didn't get there. He wanted to know if I put the zip code on the package. I told him I did.

He said he would keep calling the Fed-Ex office.

I asked him when he would be back. He said in a week or so. Then I asked, "Are you sending me some money?"

"I guess so," he said disgustedly. "I knew that was the next question. I told you I would, alright?"

"And you knew that was the next question," I said. "Well isn't that alright?"

"Well, look I…uh…uh…don't matter whether it's alright or not … anyway hon, I'll call you when I get the kit… uh don't you ask whatever you want anyway?"

I said I did but that I'd prefer he didn't get so frustrated about it. I should have helped him pack, then he would have had his kit. Of course, I had checked his kit before I sent it off, and found a turquoise tie clasp that I asked him if I could have.

"How did you know it was in there?" he asked.

"How do you think?" I answered giggling.

Ray had told me what he expected about privacy in his marriage, which was that he had his drawers and she had hers. And I guess no one checked the others drawers. He knew that would never happen here.

Ray just laughed and said, "Yeah babe, you can have the tie clasp."

Don Eaker, my dear, talented friend, made it into an unusual pendant for me. It was so special, made from copper, silver and turquoise, in the shape of an upside down wishbone with Ray's tie clasp dangling from the center. I absolutely loved it. What made it so special was the fact that it was uniquely designed and artfully crafted by my friend from a piece of the-love-of-my-life's jewelry-the perfect combination.

Sad to say, I don't have it anymore. It was stolen in a burglary. I do have pictures of myself wearing it though. I'm grateful for that. Ray, too, was impressed at what Don did with his little piece of turquoise.

Ray was back to see me in about a week, just as he promised. He was sitting on the couch and I was busy in the kitchen. When I went in the living room, I was surprised to see him holding my fairly large, ceramic elephant, with very delicate four inch long tusks. We had already broken one tusk and glued it back on. The other end table held the large mother and baby elephant. They were a one piece unit.

The elephants were a gift from my neighbor, Linda Albright, and were a recent, new addition. Ray, being Ray, noticed them and was checking them out. He had such a gentle touch that nothing he looked at was ever damaged. He made it a point to know what objects were on the tables, dressers, etc. Ray was inquisitive and curious. It made me happy to see him enjoy sculptures, and I loved giving him detailed descriptions.

We also loved singing and playing the piano together. We would often all go downstairs into the family room and sing, while Ray played our old studio upright piano. I bought the piano for Lisa and Mitzi to take lessons–and they did for a few years. It was a fun added bonus when Ray played. The kids and I sang songs like "Yankee Doddle" and "Frankie and Johnny." I changed the lyrics on that one from, "But he done me wrong" to "But Ray done me wrong." Ray protested vehemently "No, no, no!!" He played "Three Blind Mice" as if it were a scary movie. It sounded very dark and gruesome, especially the part where "She cut off their heads with a carving knife." The kids and I were making ghastly noises. Ray too. He was going, "uuhmmm, uuhmmm" in a deep voice and getting such a kick out of scaring us.

All too soon he was gone again, and we were left with sweet memories and the lingering aroma of Cannon Cologne.

26
Ray - On Marriage
∽⚬∽

Lisa, Mitzi and I were still riding our horses on weekends. We were riding in parades around town and just pleasure riding with my brother and dad. They trailored our horses from the barn to wherever we needed them to be.

Lisa was always the real horsewoman. She went with my dad and brother on week long trail rides. Mitzi wasn't into horses as much as Lisa, so she and I stayed home.

We were a pretty active family and were constantly on the move. My kids took dance and piano lessons and Lisa took modeling lessons. They were in many recitals. My dad called us 'Movers and Shakers.'

We were gone so much that Ray had a hard time connecting with me. I didn't have an answering machine (it would be twenty years before I got one, not until 1991 when Lisa moved to Los Angeles).

When Ray finally did reach me, he asked if we had gone to Kansas City. I told him I hadn't but that I was going to go to New Orleans soon.

"Oh, when ya gonna do that?" he asked.

"Right away...probably within a few days," I told him.

"Oh yeah, okay," a long okay. He wasn't happy.

"My...hus...ex husband's brother passed away and he wants me to bring the kids and be with him for condolences, I guess."

"Heh, heh, Oh! Really?" Ray was being cynical.

Henry had a brother living in Mexico. When our kids were very young, we went to visit him. He provided us with our own apartment and had tons of new toys for our kids. He spoke Castilian Spanish beautifully, and was suave, elegant and dangerous, (but not to us). I told Ray that the family was having his body shipped to the States.

"Why would they do that?" Ray asked.

"Well, it's cheaper to bring him to the States than for everyone to go to Mexico. Fernando, that was his name, was deported. I liked him and kept in touch via letters."

"Oh, you can't live here, but you can be buried here?" Ray said.

"I guess so. They're shipping his body here," I answered.

"Hmmm," Ray said after a long hesitation.

"What is it?" I asked.

Ray was quiet for a while. Finally he said, "I'm trying to digest that."

"What is there to digest, Ray?"

"I guess...probably nuthin," he said. I knew he wanted to ask a lot of questions, but he wouldn't allow himself to. He really didn't like me going to New Orleans. I knew he wanted me to elaborate more about seeing Henry, but I wouldn't volunteer anything.

I changed the subject instead. I asked if he had been traveling. He told me yes, that he was going to Israel and would be gone about a week and a half. He was filming a documentary or something.

"I'm not up on it," he said, "but I think they want to inter-weave it into something that relates to my music. I hafta first get over there and see what it is they're after. It might be pretty good. I don't know. It'll probably be a lot of hard work."

I asked if he had been to Israel before. He said that he hadn't, but that not too long ago, he had been to Beirut, Lebanon which was only sixty miles or so from Israel.

I asked if he had been to his office yet because I had sent him a surprise. He said he hadn't, but that he had called and was told he had a package there.

"I sent you a candle, some incense and an incense burner like mine. You know—the one with the little bell that you liked? It's not exactly like mine. I couldn't find another one, but it's similar. If you don't like it, you can have mine. I just didn't want to send something used."

"Thank you, baby. That's sweet." He always appreciated every little thing I did and enjoyed getting things that he could see by feeling. I truly did love to give Ray special little things that I knew he would like.

I was growing more and more weary about Ray being married. I couldn't get it off my mind, and we were not making any progress towards a solid relationship. I was in my early thirties and I wanted more than he was giving me. More time, more security...and commitment. I thought about the possibility of marriage–if not to him, then perhaps to someone else. But the idea of "someone else" was unfathomable to me. I didn't know if I could give Ray up.

I finally told him I thought we should stop seeing one another–that our relationship was driving me crazy.

"I'm driving you crazy?" Ray asked.

I told him no, not him, just everything. "We don't see each other enough for me and there's nothing to hope for." I said, "I've talked and talked about the way I feel, so you know. And you've made it perfectly clear that you don't want to get married again, and it's important to me."

Ray stammered and never really said anything. "Well... honey. I mean uh–you know as much about this as I do, probably more. Uh...uh...you know...uh you're right though. It's probably important."

I kept right on, "Yes, it is to me. You and I don't think alike. You're already married and it bugs the shit out of me, and I think you're gonna always be." I couldn't shut up. He tried to interject but I wouldn't let him. "And you don't think marriage is anything. You don't respect it."

He tried to tell me how he really felt about marriage.

"I didn't say I don't respect it, honey," he said, "I think you misunderstood. I said I think it's alright as long as people don't try to use it as a tool, and far too many people do. That's probably why the divorce rate is so high. They tend to feel 'now we're married and I own you.' Ain't no such thing as that. I mean, you can't own people like you own furniture."

"Yes, but Ray, don't you think if you feel that way, you should untie yourself?"

"Honey," he explained, "I think the main thing that we ought to do is love one another. It's the greatest thing…I mean…to me that supersedes…is that the word? I mean that takes precedence over marriage. It's how much two people can genuinely love one another and respect one another. That's what counts."

I told him I agreed with him.

Ray went on with his marriage philosophy. "Now when you take a…a…piece of paper and start waving it over somebody's head, to the point where you have some kind of threat going…like you will do that because you're married; then the whole thing is defeated–you're not 'sposed to do it because you're married–you're 'sposed to do it 'cause you wanna."

"I feel that way too, Ray. But even so, there are certain things you shouldn't do when you're married."

"Well, you see, honey, the whole point is–if you really dig the person you're with, being married isn't gonna cause you not to do things. What's gonna keep you from doing it is how you feel about the person you're with."

"I understand, Ray, but it's not fair to either woman. If your marriage is at that point, you should do something about it. If your marriage is that bad, then possibly neither of you are happy."

Ray was hell bent on making his point. "Which is what I just said, babe. When two people are into each other a hundred percent, then the things you're thinking they shouldn't do, they wouldn't do anyway. Not because they're married, but because of the way they feel about each other, just as we do."

"Ray! You're completely missing my point! I know we have that or I have it. I don't know about you because I don't know what you do. I only know about me, but I do know that you're married to somebody else and it's disturbing to me. If you weren't married, maybe things would be different. I wouldn't feel this sadness. I don't like you being married to someone else. To me, marriage is something, whether you want to recognize it or not. You do have a wife. She's there!"

"Okay, Marci. It's an institution. It's just an institution. That's what they say, isn't it?"

"Ray, I think two people can live together forever and not be married, but I don't think one of them should be married. You didn't like me being married. You were eager for me to be divorced, because you didn't want me to have a husband and have you too. Remember?" He had been very insistent about me getting a divorce. Ray wasn't eager to pay for anything, but he was glad to pay for that. (Thank God it didn't cost much, or he probably wouldn't have).

"Well, hon. I told you once before, if it were possible for you not to be married, then it shouldn't be that way."

"Anyway Ray, I wouldn't want anyone to leave their wife because of me. But I don't want you married. I don't want to share you anymore than you want to share me."

"Like I told you, babe, I told you very frank. I don't know what my status is, but I know this–if my wife and I separate, I wouldn't marry anybody. Like you said, we have two different philosophies about it. I...I...I just feel that many people, un-fortunately, use it as a weapon–you know–a tool of blackmail or something."

"What? Blackmail! Oh Christ!" I said in utter disbelief.

"Yeah, really, babe. You see so much of it where people... uh...instead of thinkin'...well the main thing is how much we love each other...you know they..."

I interrupted him. "I don't think we love each other. I think I love you!"

"Okay..." this was that defeated "okay" that sounded so down. "I guess I can't do very much about what you think. You know, I've told you enough how I feel about you, and if you don't see that, well then you just don't see it. I can't do nuthin' about it."

I told him I knew we couldn't do anything except see each other more–that that would help prove his feelings for me. I didn't see how it could happen unless we lived in the same city, and that wasn't happening. I would never do that again!

"Well, that would be helpful, obviously. But I don't think that would be the answer because you know...like you were saying to me about this marriage thing, that's an obsession with you. You know, and...uh...it's just uh...I mean, even if we were together more, that would still be a hang up. I would refuse to get married and you wouldn't like that–and there we'd be."

"It's never been a hang up for me, Ray. I just don't want *you* married! I don't like being with a married man. I do respect marriage. I don't care whether you do or not. I think it's important to people.

"I didn't say I disrespect it. I just said...I..."

I wouldn't let him finish. "Well, you don't respect it, and you don't want any part of it, but you *are* married, and you *would* have married Louise. She didn't marry you." Louise was his first love.

"Well, sweetheart, you know the way I feel about that–the same way I feel about a lot of things I've done. As you well know, I've done many, many things in my life, that I've found better, or at least for me, better not to do–so just because I did something twenty years ago, doesn't mean I would do it now. That's the whole point." Ray said that to me more than once throughout our nearly three decades together.

"Ray, I feel upset all the time. I think it would be better for me if we stopped seeing each other. I'm back in group therapy. I think I should get out of my house, start going out, activate my social life." There was a long silence. "Come on, speak up." I said.

"Yeah, I'm here." This was how he handled disappoint-ment. He sounded so sad, but he never did hang up on me. He just tolerated my drama. "Okay, Marci. I heard you and I understand you very well. You made yourself extremely clear–perfectly clear–absolutely clear."

"Ray, the ultimate to me would be if you put yourself in a position to be with me."

"I heard you," he said.

"Now you're tired of talking about it, huh?" I continued to nag.

"No, I just...I really should get up now. I gotta leave outta here by ten. And uh...you tell the kids hi for me...least you can do that. Take care of yourself, Marci. I love you, baby."

I was so upset and frustrated with Ray, but I couldn't just let him hang up. So, all of a sudden, I switched gears and changed the subject, which I often did when things got uncomfortable with him.

"Oh, Ray, I got a chess set." I said out of the blue. I know he was grateful for that, even if he did think I was a little crazy. God knows, he didn't want me fussing about marriage anymore!

"You did?" He was happy to hear that I had gotten a chess set, being an avid chess player himself.

"Yes. Lisa and I are learning. She's much better than I am." I've never been a game player. I like to move around, not sit at a game. I do enjoy a good book, but only before going to sleep.

"Lisa will be a good person to practice with, sharp little girl," he said. "You know, I'm crazy about them."

I knew he cared about my girls, but I also knew why he said that. He thought I was on the verge of telling him not to call me anymore. That comment was supposed to make me feel bad. Mean ole' Marci!

Mitzi learned to play chess too. So for a few years, we always had a chess game going and sometimes when Ray arrived he would finish one of our ongoing games with me. I always won (but only because he let me).

Ray told me the main objective is to get your partner's king before he gets yours and to learn how the pieces move. We discussed how the Bishop, Knight, Rook, etc. moved. When we got to the Queen, he said, "Naturally you should know the Queen, 'cause she can..."

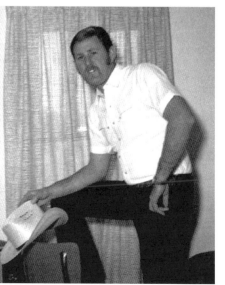 

Left to right, top to bottom: Series of three photos of me at age 20 taken by photographer Bernie Thrasher; Photo of me, taken by Peter Patrick, that appeared on the cover of The Guzzlers Gazette magazine, early 60s; Me, my date Johnny Friedman, Pat Aluisa and Mary Ann, early 60s; Photo of my brother Don taken by Don Eaker, mid 70s; My mom and dad, mid 50s.

Left to right, top to bottom: Henry and Lisa in white mustang (which I sold when I moved to Los Angeles), mid 60s; Henry, Lisa and Mitzi, 1967; Henry and I, 1968 (I'm wearing the suit I wore when I met Ray for the first time.); Henry and I in Mexico, 1966; Henry and I dressed up for the Mardi Gras ball, 1966; Lisa and I in front of house on Gretna in New Orleans, 1967

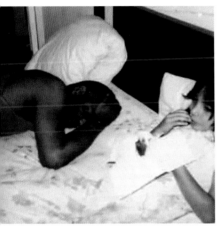

Left to right, top to bottom: Ray, 1969; Ray and I, August 11, 1971; Ray, Mitzi and I in 1972 (notice my portrait of Ray in the background.); Ray napping while Lisa has a snack and watches TV, 1972; Mitzi, Ray, Lisa and her friend Liz going to dinner; Lisa (8), Ray and Mitzi (6), May, 1972; Mitzi, Ray and Lisa going to Red Lobster for dinner, 1973; Naptime on my couch.

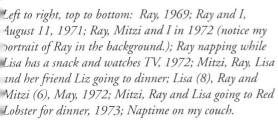

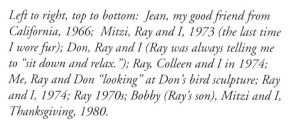

Left to right, top to bottom: Jean, my good friend from California, 1966; Mitzi, Ray and I, 1973 (the last time I wore fur); Don, Ray and I (Ray was always telling me to "sit down and relax."); Ray, Colleen and I in 1974; Me, Ray and Don "looking" at Don's bird sculpture; Ray and I, 1974; Ray 1970s; Bobby (Ray's son), Mitzi and I, Thanksgiving, 1980.

...eft to right, top to bottom: Diablo and I; Ray, 1980; ...ay and I, May, 1980; Don, Ray, Bobby and Colleen in ...allas, 1981; Ray and I, 1981; Bobby and I, 1981; ...isa giving Ray a kiss on the cheek good-bye, 1980.

All of the photos on this page were taken in 1981. Left to right, top to bottom: Ray and I; Don, Ray and Colleen; Don and Ray; Lisa, Ray and Lisa's friend; Ray and Mitzi; Ray and I.

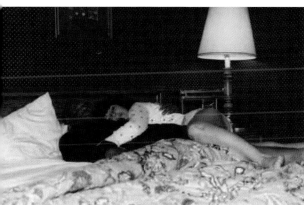

Left to right, top to bottom: Ray packing to leave,1981; Ray "looking at" my elephant sculpture,1981; Ray and me snuggling, 1984 (It was during this visit that Ray paid off by house, unknowingly!); Lisa and friends in Los Angeles, 1992; Ray having a relaxed cup of coffee; Ray's manager Joe Adams and I, 1992; Ray in my bedroom in Kirkwood, 1992.

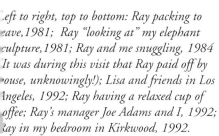

Left to right, top to bottom: Ray and I, May 1992; Mitzi and I, Variety Club Charity Gala, 1997; Lisa, Mitzi and I at the Charity Gala. (This was the only dress I could find–Ray bought it for me, but I hated it.); Our little family at the Charity Gala; Ray, Lisa and her husband, Tom at the Charity Gala. (The Variety Club Gala would be the last time I would ever see Ray.); My beautiful family now, taken during our 2010 trip to Hilton Head, South Carolina. Left to right: Chase, Mia, Mitzi, Peyton, Lisa, Tristin, and Me. (Not pictured: Josh Foster, Mitzi's husband).

"Go anywhere," I finished for him.

"Tha...that's right!!!! They can do anything they wanna do," he said.

I said I wondered why they made it like that.

"Well, because it's true." Ray said without hesitation.

Lisa had a little girlfriend named Liz who Ray had met since she was often at our house. I told him that Liz was a pretty good chess player. He said he was glad because then she could help Lisa. I told him Lisa had already gotten Liz' king.

"Oh wow!" Ray said. He added, "Lisa told me Liz was her best friend."

Liz helped me learn the game. I had the "Beginners Chess Book" but I was truly lost without Liz' help. Ray said chess was a good tranquilizer and would teach me patience, which I'm sure he thought I needed.

He asked me who taught Liz to play chess and I told him her Dad had taught her. According to Liz, he had carved a chess board and all the pieces.

Ray was impressed. He said that his stage manager carved him a set out of wood, and that his road manager, who was now deceased, had made him one out of nuts and bolts.

"You've never seen anything like it in your life. He did it all by himself," Ray said. Ray absolutely loved that set.

Ironically, I had just bought two little statues made from nuts and bolts. Their bodies were long spindle screws with screws for arms and legs, and bolts for hands, feet and head.

"Oh, Wow! Well I...I almost...I started to say I...if I ever get to see it...I guess I won't now...the way you're talkin...But I would love to see them. You know, honey, things like that fascinate me...they really do, Marci."

"You can have them," I said.

"Okay, baby, but don't you want them?" he asked.

"I like them, but I'd rather you have them because you don't get a chance to get out and see things like I do." I was happy for him to have them.

"Well I...I...they're the kind of things you know...I love any form of artistry like that. I guess that's why I like pop art."

"It's amazing how someone can take all kinds of tin and metal and cans and pop bottles and when they get through, they come up with some fantastic things. See, for me, it's very good. It's a lot different than say...a picture. A picture I can't...can't see, ya' know, but a sculpture, I can touch and tell how it looks."

I told him about my friend where I grew up, Tom Runnels, who was a great sculptor. I described some of the wonderful sculptures he had done, including a life-sized horse.

I told Ray I should have shown him the beautiful wood carving my friend Don Eaker did. My brother bought it from him and gave it to me for Christmas. It's a raised Magnolia, carved from wood and it still hangs in my living room. It's elegant looking and very beautiful. Don used to make Lisa, Mitzi and I gold nugget necklaces and rings. We loved them.

His wife, Colleen, is creative too. "She's a hooker," I said, shocking Ray.

"A what?" Ray exclaimed.

"She hooks rugs," I said, easing his mind, "and she hooked one for me." I had that rug for years.

Colleen is artistic. She also made me a beautiful stained glass sun catcher that I still display it in my bathroom window.

Don was so talented. He was such a gifted photographer. I have many photos he shot of me, a lot of Ray and me together, and even one of Willie Nelson and Ray that Don took while visiting Ray in Dallas, Texas in the early eighties.

As we continued our phone conversation, which often went from subject to subject, I asked Ray if he was playing in a club. He said that the place where he was currently playing was more like a theatre since the stage revolved. He said most of the places he played were theatres in the round, but if he had his "druthers," he preferred the concert hall. He didn't care for theatres in the round because there were people all around him, and from time to time, there were people at his back. He didn't like that.

He didn't like to play clubs because "folks talk too much."

"You're never gonna get people to be quiet," he said, "unless it's a supper club, like the Latin Casino right outside of Philadelphia in Cherry Hill, New Jersey. They have excellent and expensive food, so folks come there to have their dinner and see the show. In that case, they're quiet."

He also liked the Coconut Grove. He said, "The people are eating while you're on, and the prices they charge–you can almost rest assured the people you get in there are pretty cool."

I told him I saw him on the Carol Burnett Show and Bill Cosby's show. Ray said he really wanted to see the Cosby show. He said, "Cos is a pretty hip fella, and very, very smart."

"You have a really good rapport with Carol," I told him.

He said it was that good mutual thing and that she was a fabulous entertainer.

"She can't keep her hands off you," I said.

"I figured you'd see that," he laughed.

"It doesn't make me jealous, Ray. You can tell she likes you so much and I like that."

"Yeah, I guess she does like me," he said, being very shy.

"She just caresses you and kisses you when she sits with you at the piano."

"Yeah, Carol's a very sweet person, babe, ain't too many like her."

Even though I know he had hoped to avoid it, we ended our conversation with me confirming that I thought it best not to see one another anymore, or at least, not for a while. I was just so frustrated.

I felt like he was coming to see me when he damn well pleased. I didn't feel it was regular enough. In fact, I thought the distance between visits was getting longer, and it was making me unhappy. It was in the latter part of 1972 when I began seriously trying to break up with Ray. I knew I needed to move on, to build a life for myself, but it was the hardest thing for me. I didn't know what I was to him, but I knew what he was to me. He was my true love.

27
Weighing Heavy on Ray's Mind
❧

The last part of 1972, I stopped seeing Ray. Then he called late
one night asking me if I wasn't ever going to let him see me
again. He was so down. He sounded pitiful. I had never heard
him like that before. He told me he wanted desperately to see
me, that I was weighing heavily on his mind. We talked for
over an hour that night. He sounded sad and mournful, but I
refused to see him. He was convinced that he would never see
me again, although I had not exactly said that.

He said I had been in his mind, his head and in his body
and he didn't know what was wrong with him. He called again
the next day, still feeling the same way, but I still wouldn't agree
to see him.

Years later, I read in a book that during that time, his marriage was beginning a downward spiral. That must have
bothered him, even though it probably was his fault. He was
about to lose me, his records were not selling well and he was
losing his beloved Tangerine Record Label.

It shocked me to learn that Ray's records were not selling–he
was in a slump. He was so dedicated. He had a relentlessness
about his music, and he maintained his own style and integrity
always. He blazed his own trail from beginning to end. I always
felt that Ray's delivery of a song was profound. I could hear
the story he was telling, and I could hear his heartbreak and his
happiness. His music echoed him, and I absolutely loved it.

I'm glad I didn't know about the disappointing record sales
at the time. It makes me angry even now as I think about it. I
understand why he seemed so depressed, but he never once
complained to me that his records weren't doing well. He felt

that his music was good. He would not have produced something he didn't believe in because his integrity would be on the line. To me, there was never a question about his belief in his music. I can't imagine even one Ray Charles' song not selling. To me, he was "the best of the best."

He took me seriously about not seeing each other. He called several times, then stopped. I knew he was going to Israel. He said it was only for a week and a half, but I hadn't heard from him for a few weeks. I didn't call him either. I thought, "Okay, let's just do this. No matter how much it hurts."

Once in a while, Ray would send me money. Usually if he didn't come to see me for a longer interval of time, he would send a couple hundred dollars. Sometimes I reminded him, but I hadn't spoken to him. This time, he didn't send anything.

Now, as I reflect back, I realize that to him, sending me money during these occasional absences was to keep me pacified and on the hook, while he was off doing whatever.

I know that he dreaded calling me after he had neglected me for a time. Fearing that I would have changed my number, or that I would hang up on him, or as he called it, "go off on him."

Finally, I did get a sad call from him, and he sounded so low he could barely talk. There is no way that words could describe the depth of loneliness and despair that I heard in Ray's voice when he was down. I don't think there is anyone in the world who could sound as sad as Ray Charles when he was in the doldrums.

It was one o'clock in the morning when I answered the phone and heard, "Marci, baby, I miss you something awful. You don't believe me, but it's true."

Groggy from being awakened in the middle of the night, I yawned and said I did believe him, that I thought he meant what he said at the moment, but that he was inconsistent.

He said he wanted to explain something to me. That he just wanted to tell me how heavy I was leaning on him, but that it didn't seem to go over too well with me. He said he thought it was fair for him to tell me. He compared it to talking to his mother as a child–if he told his Mama, "Look Mama, my leg hurts or my stomach hurts or whatever it is that hurts me...once I say, 'Mama, it hurts me,' that's all I can say. Now I've told you." This was his way of telling me how badly he was hurting.

I said I believed him and that I probably was on his mind right now, but a few weeks had gone by that obviously I hadn't been on his mind. But I said I believed him at this moment and was glad he called.

"Okay, baby," he said. "You go back to sleep. When you're awake I'll call you back and talk to you. You sound like you're tired and sleepy. I am too. But God! I...I...I've missed you. I don't know what the shits wrong with me. You've really prayed heavily on my mind, in spite of the fact that you don't hear me...you don't hear me at all."

"I hear you, Ray, but it doesn't do me any good. It just does not sustain me. I've made myself accept things for what they are and I'm trying to live with them."

"Okay, Marci. I didn't mean to shatter your...whatever." He was on the defensive.

"Ray, you haven't shattered me. You couldn't. That happened to me a long time ago." He knew what I meant–the rejection in California. That *did* shatter me.

"Well...okay, babe," he said. "Will you forgive me?"

"Whatever happened to me, I brought on myself, Ray. I don't have anything to forgive you for."

"Baby...I'm sorry, babe. You don't believe me, I know, but...I'm...I'm..."

"Ray, I do believe you. I don't want to hear that you're lonely and depressed. I'm not the kind of person to want you to be unhappy."

"Okay, Marci. I...I...don't know what to say to you. I...I just don't know. I kinda got the feeling tonight that..." He thought that I had ended our love affair, and he was struggling to find the right words to say to me. He continued trying to convey his serious message to me.

"You know, Marci, if I...believe me or not, if I tell you something it's at least worth listening to, if for nuthin else. So if I tell you you've been praying on my mind, weighing very, very heavy on my mind...I mean that, even if you don't believe me."

He was frustrated because I never did believe he cared for me the way he said he did. He continued trying to explain his feelings.

"I'm just telling you what's really been happening to me. You know, there are certain things, Marci, in one's life that we can try to act like it don't exist or it never happened, that's good in theory, but it's...it's not true in reality. And the way I feel about you, regardless of what you might think, there's no way in the world I can just literally act like it never existed or act like the whole thing was a mistake."

I said that I *did* think it was a mistake.

He said that he didn't and that's where we differed. "Right there, that is where we draw the line," he said. "I just wanted you to hear me, babe. I...I...I...miss you something awful and...and you've just been in my mind, you've been in my head, my dreams, you've been in my body and I don't know what the shit's wrong with me. Maybe I'm deteriorating or something."

I told him that that was exactly how *I* had felt at different times, but he was going on and on about himself and *his* feelings.

"Marci, before I die, and I don't mean to be morbid about this, but I'm just tryin' to tell you something. Before I die, if you can... even if I'm sixty years old, before I leave this world, if you could somehow find it in your heart ah...ahhh...I would just like to...at least...get a chance to...to look at you. Now uh...uh...that's a wish, honey. It's not a demand or it's not anything that I'm insisting upon. It's just something I wish could happen."

"Ray, you've never said things like this before."

"Well, I'm saying it now." He sounded like he was crying.

"You're scaring me, Ray. Are you ill, feeling bad or something? I'm worried."

"Whether I'm sick or not, that's not the point. I just wanted to tell you...that uh...I wish I could see you. That's all."

I could feel myself weakening. "You always seem to know just what to say to me, Ray."

He asked what time I would be home tomorrow. I said about 3:45 p.m. By now, we were both sniffling. He said, "Well, that seems strange. I couldn't get you today. I called at that time and you weren't there."

"I'm glad you got me tonight. I had lots of things to do this evening. After work, I took Lisa and Mitzi to the pizza place for a birthday party. I sewed their dance recital costumes and then I ironed. So I was busy. I hadn't been in bed long when you called."

"I'm sorry, baby. I...I just felt I had to talk to you. What time did you say you pick up the kids from school?"

"At 3:45 every day except Thursday. The kids have music lessons on Thursday."

"Okay...alright, baby. I...I will talk to you tomorrow."

"Ray, don't tell me that if you don't intend to do it. You know how I am about you keeping your word."

"No...I won't tell you nuthin else, I've already told you what I wanted to tell you. I told you, you're weighing on my mind...you've been on my mind...I really would like to...I wish like hell I could see you, but...uh only you can say the answer to that."

"I'm afraid," I said. "I don't like the way things are."

"Okay, honey. Alright. That's a nice way of putting it to me. I ...I understand."

"Ray," I said irritated. "Don't twist it around to suit your purpose. I've been through this be..." He interrupted, "Marci...Marci, you know, I know how it's been."

We were both teary. I told him that when he went to Europe and I didn't hear from him for weeks, it bothered me. After that, he started calling me from everywhere–Japan, Italy, everywhere. I also told him that I'd been trying to overcome this feeling I have for him.

Ray said he could only tell me how he felt, but that he guessed I was trying to let him down easy by telling him in a nice way that I didn't want to see him anymore.

"Oh come on, Ray. Don't play games with me. Don't use that psychology on me. It doesn't work anymore. You know who you're talkin to."

"I...I...I hope you don't think I'm playing games. I'm deadly serious in what I'm tellin you, Marci. And honey, it's not psychology. Marci, please listen to me."

"Ray, you know I'm not telling you in a nice and easy way that I'm through, that I don't care about you anymore. You know me. If I felt that way, I'd say it plainly, because you deserve to get your feelings hurt. Mine have been."

He began talking to me so softly and pitifully, "So what does that mean, Marci? Are you saying to me I...I...I can't see you any more? Tell me, Marci, if that's what it is. That's not what I want and I'm sure you know it. Marci...Marci...I'm really sayin' something to you. Believe me, I am."

Ray had an innate ability to phrase his songs so that his listeners could understand the message he was conveying. It's hard to imagine, but he was even more compelling in a verbal battle, especially if he thought he was losing. He could make his voice so mournful and sorrowful that I just wanted to glide through the phone and place myself next to him so that I could cradle him and whisper soothing words to him.

I really wanted to tell him to come see me, but I wouldn't allow myself to give in. I had been through this before. Ray had said to me a thousand times, "You don't have to say things, because actions speak, Marci." I reminded him of that and added that actions speak to me too. I said, "Words are nice and I love to hear them. In fact, I've heard more tonight than I ever have. But your actions are not proving much to me." He acknowledged what I said with a defeated sounding ooo...kay.

I told him that I didn't want to be unhappy and I didn't want him to be unhappy either. He responded with, "Yeah, alright baby. I don't know what's wrong with me I just...just."

I told him that he he sounded so sleepy, he probably would forget he even talked to me. That caused him to get very frustrated, he said,

"No, you know...well I... Marci...I really think that if I felt I couldn't even remember talkin' to you, it would be an insult to me and to you, too."

I said I thought that the reason I hadn't heard from him for so long was because he got upset about me asking if he were sending some money. He said no, that he didn't even remember it. I told him, "Well, just so you know, I don't want your money, and I'll never take a dime from you ever again. Never, not ever. You should be grateful to hear that."

"Oooh, Marci, don't you know, I know when you say things like that to me, you're saying it in a hostile way, or whatever that...that word is? Honey, you got any other bad things you wanna tell me?"

"I'm not being hostile, I'm being honest. You have it in your head that because you're a movie star, a celebrity or whatever the hell you are, that everybody wants your money. I don't want your money. I don't give a shit about it."

Ray was trying to talk, "Marci how can you sa...Marci..."

I was so frustrated with him at that point, I just wanted to lash out. "I'm saying it because you're so conscientious about it. You're so scared you'll have to help me a little bit. But you don't have to. I don't need it now. I want you to know that. I don't need it. If I just wanted money, I sure as hell wouldn't have stayed with you. You're not the only millionaire I know."

"Marci...you wanna tell me what you're really tryin' to tell me? Or do you think I...I don't deserve to know?"

I said that I had said everything I wanted to say.

Ray said, "No th...tha...that may be all you wanna tell me, but that ain't all I'm asking. And you know it."

I asked him if he wanted to know if I still loved him. I said the answer was yes. And then I asked if he was trying to ask me if I was pregnant. The answer to that was no, no–hell no–and that I never would be.

"No, no, that ain't what I'm asking you, Marci. Now you know better! Come on! You know what I'm tryin' to find out from you, babe."

"No, Ray, I don't," I said, but I really did know. He wanted to know if I was really through with him. I thought he should just stop beating around the bush and have the guts to say, "Are you through with me?"

He went on, "I hafta know Marci. I have to know it. See, you didn't just say that for nuthin." (Meaning all the things I said about trying to stay away from him and what I said about the money). "I mean...I...I'm guilty of doing a lotta things to you, but I've never insulted your intelligence–that's the one thing I didn't do. At least I deserve that."

I abruptly said, "Oh yes, you certainly have, but I've let you. I've let you play me for a dummy."

Then he said, "Ooooh, Marci...come on...I think that's unfair."

I kept right on, "I don't care what you think. The truth of the matter is that I have allowed you to do whatever you wanted to do with me."

"Your wrong, babe," Ray tried to get a word in, "I've never I...I..."

"But you didn't manipulate me, Ray. I've allowed you to do it. I want you to know that, too."

"Okay, okay, I know better than that, babe. I've not tried to manipulate you," Ray said, but I didn't pay any attention to what he said. I was on a roll.

"You haven't been such a Don Juan. It was only because I loved you so much, and believe me, no other man has ever done that shit to me."

"I have never done that to you, Marci."

"Shit!! Huh!!," I said sarcastically.

"Okay, huh. I heard your "huh" Ray said, "but I never...I never...it may be because you don't think too much of me. That's why you're saying that, but I never did that to you, ba...I never insulted your intelligence."

"Oh, brother!" I said. "You've treated me like a school girl, not like a woman. You knew I'd always be around and I always have been. That's the sad part!"

"Which is to say what?" Now...now Marci, we're gonna get at what I've been tryin' to ask."

I said I didn't think anything was ever settled between us, that it seemed like a rope was hanging between us, always on the verge of breaking, but never did. I told him that I was bitter as hell and, furthermore, I didn't know how I would treat him if I *did* see him.

"Alright, Marci," Ray said sadly, "Alright."

I told him that I didn't know what the hell he wanted, that if I knew, if he leveled with me for once in his life, maybe I could do it. I said, "Maybe I could be whatever you wanted...you know if you want just an affair..."

He stopped me, "I only want...I just want you to be yourself, Marci. That's all. Just be you."

"I'm always myself, Ray, but it's disappointing when I don't hear from you on time. Don't say it if you don't intend to do it. I'd rather hear the truth. You know the way it really is. I can take that. Just like if you had cancer and you knew you were dying, but no one would tell you and you were just hanging. You'd be better off knowing. That's how I feel. I just want to know."

It's ironic that I said that to Ray all those years ago. Thirty-four years after I said it, cancer took his life.

Ray said he agreed with me, and asked if he could ask me something, then he changed his mind. I said it was okay if he didn't want to ask me, then he said, so sadly, "What can I do, Marci? I...I...I..."

"Nothing, Ray. There's nothing you can do."

"Marci, if you're saying to me, look...and I...I'm sure you're saying to me what really is the truth. If you're saying to me, 'I'm so bitter, I don't know how I would respond if I looked at you right now'."

"Yes, I am Ray."

Ray's response could have been a short and simple, "Will I

ever see you again?" but instead it was the following, which is typical Ray and word for word–verbatim.

"Can I...alright...let me say this in...in desperation...or...or whatever, I don't know the right word. I...I...I do need to know. Like you say, you need to know things, or at least you would like to feel that you have a good idea about things. Are you saying to me I'm...I'm...I should never attempt...or it's impossible or whatever...I don't know the right terminology or the right thing...but if you really broke it down into the smallest term, would you say that I will never see you no more?"

Ray could hardly bring himself to ask me that question. He knew that I wasn't happy and wanted to separate myself from him. It was a matter of whether I could or not. I told him that I didn't know how I was gonna feel, that I was hanging by a thread and it could break at any moment. I also said that I had had bad luck ever since I had been involved with him. It had been four years and things were no better.

"You're right, Marci. When you break it down, you really are right. There are certain things that follow people. People who are prone to certain things. And I kinda...you know, maybe you're right. Maybe that's something that follows me."

"Ha! Not you! You haven't had the bad luck, Ray. Everything you touch turns to gold." (I didn't know yet all the problems he was having and he didn't tell me.)

"Well, let me put it this way. Maybe it's something that follows us. Is that better, Marci? I'm talking about us, Marci."

"Bullshit! It's been me. You've walked right off from it. You walk away. I'm the one whose stuck, every damn time. Stuck! Stuck! I couldn't even get ahold of you." I was thinking about the time that I had had car trouble and couldn't even call him. I couldn't call him with just everyday problems, and it was so frustrating for me.

"Tell me something, babe...please tell me." Ray pleaded to no avail.

"No, I'm sick of this ache. You can go to work and get away from the ache. I can't."

the past two weeks, I've been trying to call you, but I guess my timing's been off. I try not to call you in the middle of the night and I'm scared to death when I do, but I had to hear you. Now I've heard you. I...I...guess I'm satisfied."

"Are you?" I asked.

"I guess I'll have to live with what is," he said.

"I know you can, Ray. I have no doubt about that. I've been the one who's had the problem with that. You haven't."

"I don't know what you mean by that, babe. When you say you've had the problem, I guess maybe I don't know what the hell I've had then. But alright, babe...whatever. I...I just wanted to tell you you've been weighing me down for at least a half a month or more–weighing me down very bad."

I told him that I had a difficult time believing him, and maybe I didn't even want to believe him.

"You know, Marci, I think, you think, I'm some kind of sub-human or something."

I said I didn't think he cared deeply enough for me.

"That's too bad, Marci. I'm sorry about that...alright... Okay...alright...well, I'm very sad...it's a pity that you don't really know that. Alright, babe. One of these days maybe, and it will be a very, very slim chance of maybe, I'll be able to convince you how deep my feelings are for you."

He told me over and over that I was endlessly runnin' round in his head.

As we said good-bye, I still didn't agree to see him. *You've lived without me for a few weeks and it didn't seem to bother you...never even a phone call during all that time, so now you can live with me "weighing on you" for a while longer. I'm not feeling much sympathy for you right now.*

209

28
Loneliness & Politics
ঔৣৎ

Ray called me every day, telling me how much I was weighing him down. One time when he called, he was trying to pinpoint the best time to call me.

"I just tried to call you back," he said. "What time would you uh...normally get back from picking the kids up–around four or four fifteen?"

I told him yes, but on this particular day, I told him that I had taken Lisa and Mitzi to a department store to look at toys, but mainly for them to buy a Christmas present for me. Since I didn't have money to waste, and didn't like stuff I didn't need or want, I gave them a choice of three things that I really wanted and they could still surprise me.

"You know, practical Marci," I said.

"That's awfully nice, babe. That's a very good point. That's sensible. The practicality of it is irrelevant. The main thing, I think, is that it's quite sensible. As a matter of fact, you've given me an idea."

"Really?" I asked, thrilled that he thought I was so sensible. In spite of our relationship at the time and the fact that I did not want to see him, I still needed to hear his voice and I loved getting his approval.

"Oh yeah, because I...I...I never woulda thought of that. That's very hip. Say, here's three or four things that I really would like. Any of them would be very nice for me. You decide between you, which one you think I should have. I think that's very...that's awfully nice. Which means it will be a surprise because you don't know which one they're gonna decide on. I think that's good, really good."

I told him I was glad he thought so; that the kids liked the idea. After they found the "perfect gift," they took everything to the basement and hid their presents from me. I giggled and added, "As if I can't go down there and find them."

"But you wouldn't do that, would you? I don't want you to disappoint me that way." Ray laughed. He thought they were so cute.

"Oh, you know I wouldn't do that to them, Ray. They can tell if I'm really surprised."

I said he sounded better than the last time I had talked to him and I was glad. I didn't like hearing him say he was depressed.

"You know strangely enough Marci, aaaah...I'm not sure...what it is. Uuuh...I...I...to be very factual with you...I'm not sure its depression. Maybe it's...loneliness or something. I don't know what the hell it is...I guess maybe depressed may be the wrong word, because I don't know if I'm really depressed."

"Well, sweetheart, loneliness is very depressing. It's the same feeling, but you don't have to be lonely, do you?" I asked. He gave me the following l-o-n-g answer (so typical of Ray!).

"It's not a question of *having* to be, honey. It's a question of what is. You know you can't uh...uh...you know sometimes...uh Mother Nature or fate or life itself...uh...uh sort of dictates...uh even...you know...even the most...uh you know, uh people who are always very alert or always very careful and...and you know, very protective uh…but even so, I don't care how careful one may be if you're human, there comes a time...somewhere in your life where you...uh...that's why I said lonely. Because you know you begin to all of a sudden feel for something or someone, and that's different, you know, because there's just no way to describe that. I'm not sure what your s'posed to call that. I don't know. I said loneliness because I think when something hits you, or something strikes you and uh...uh someone leans on your mind...or weighs on your mind," he kept saying how heavy I was on his mind. This was the third day that he pounded that into my head.

I thought he was feeling a longing–a yearning and sadness, and I knew that feeling very well. I told him that I had experience with that feeling, thanks to him.

"Oh, okay...I'm sorry I...I," but I didn't think he was really sorry–not for me anyway–maybe for himself. He had tunnel vision and once again reverted right back to his own feelings.

"So I...I don't know...what word is correct for that...wh...when you're weighted down, or is there a word?" He seemed surprised by the heartache and was desperately trying to understand it.

"I don't know what the word is. But I'm a pro on that aching feeling," I told him. There was a long period of silence, then I continued, "But you *can* live with it and eventually it subsides–somewhat."

"Well, honey," Ray said, "I guess uh...most feelings...in general, even if your mother dies, which I know happened to me...uh...eventually life itself will cause the sting of it to go away."

I agreed with him. Then he said, "Marci, you're the sweetest woman in the world, and the most stubborn! I wonder if it's because of your birth sign?"

My *sign* is Taurus the Bull. My *problem* was Ray the Bull-shitter! He was right about me being stubborn, though. Once I make a decision about anything I can't be convinced to change my mind. Even Ray, who had more influence on me than anyone except my kids, couldn't do it.

I had mentioned to him before that I had seen him on the Cosby show, and I had just seen him on another Cosby show.

"Yeah, I was just tryin' to remember, since you said that, what show it was. You know, when you do television, as I told you before, when you film it, it's so far in advance, that by the time it airs, you've forgotten what it is." Then he asked, "Which one did you see? What was I doing? Just give me an idea and I..."

"It was at the Carnival," I reminded him.

He was excited, "Oh! Okay, okay, okay, I gotcha. I gotcha, the thing with the gun." Then he laughed. It was a very funny segment.

I said people would think he could see after that show. He laughed and said, "Yeah, they probably will."

He asked when it aired and I told him it had been a few nights before. "The kids rushed in the kitchen and said, 'Mom, Ray's on.' I didn't know you were on. Five people called to tell me and I missed your first song." That happened every time he was on television.

He said that he had filmed that show three months ago (still in 1972), and had already done another Cosby show. He said folks would approach him and mention things about the show and he wouldn't know how to respond because he had finished it so long ago.

Cosby was great, but I really enjoyed seeing him on Carol Burnett's show. This is what he said about Carol, who was so special to him.

"Well, she's so good herself, honey. I hafta tell you...I've said this to you before, she's so great. There's just no way in the world I can over dramatize...aaaah..how I really feel about her. She's a very fantastic woman. You know, I was doing a thing for aaaah..sickle cell. We were trying to raise some money, and I called her up and said, "Well look, it's my turn to try to raise money for sickle cell...I would like to know if you can just come, you don't hafta perform, honey. All you hafta do is walk on stage and say, 'Hi, I'm Carol Burnett.' That's it. Finished. And you know, to show you how great this woman is, she said, 'Ray what I really want to know is, what should I wear?' Can you imagine? Isn't that great? I thought that was so sweet. So you see, babe, there are still some wonderful people left in the world."

I also really liked Carol and I loved her show. I said, "It was very sweet," and I agreed that she must be a nice person. (Later, in 1993, my daughter, Lisa, confirmed just how nice Carol was when she made an appearance on her special as a Cher look-a-like. Lisa worked for the Ron Smith Look-A-Like Agency in Beverly Hills, California. Lisa said that Carol was down to earth, super sweet and that she made her feel very comfortable).

Ray continued, "Both of them, Carol and her ole' man, Joe, are really nice people. And she brought her whole family down last time I was on her show. She had...at least the two little girls and they're just darlin' little kids. They really remind me very much of your girls. Really nice, very sweet little kids. And you know, when you see children who are children, I really like that. I...I detest little kids who try to be grown. I have no use for that. Just like you're raisin' your kids–they're just little children. You know, that makes you love them. I love that. I really do. I guess I'm just not as modern as I oughta be. I haven't gotten to the place where I think children ought to be adults. Uh...once they become adults that's fine. But when they're children, they really oughta be children."

"I make my little girls be children," I said when I finally got a word in edgewise.

"And...I...I love that. I really do," Ray said. "Most of the time, as you well know, you see kids who are so grown you almost hate them if you're not careful."

As I think about that remark, I wonder whose kids he almost hated. That sounded strange coming from Ray, who was always so sweet and gentle with Lisa and Mitzi.

He asked what I had been doing. I told him that I'd had teacher conferences, and he wanted to know what was wrong. I explained that it was just routine–we had conferences twice a year and every parent goes just to see how their child is doing.

He wanted to know what they were really for. He said you can always find out about your child.

I told him it gives parents a chance to connect with the teacher, ask her questions, etc. She can point out the low points, or bad behavior or maybe compliment you on your kids. I told him I thought it was a good thing, and I liked it because I like to know what's going on.

Ray was innately a curious man, but I really appreciated the interest he showed in my kids. I can't say it enough. He really had me with that. Well...he had me anyway.

Then I asked him if he voted. He said that he had voted in the primaries, but when Hubert Humphrey didn't win, he didn't vote anymore.

I told him that I had heard he went to see President Nixon, and asked him if that was true. He said, "Yes, but I didn't go to see him about anything political."

"Everyone, including me, thought you voted for him," I said. "It was in the newspapers." That irritated him, and he responded with...

"Well, I guess if I went to see the President of Russia, they'd think I went to vote for communism, and why would you think that anyway? You know I..." He meant that I knew he was a Democrat, but knowing Ray so well, I thought maybe he chose to vote for the man and not the party.

I told him I didn't know why I had assumed that...I hadn't even seen the article. Mary Ann had called and read it to me.

Ray was still upset. "Well, I'll tell you a little something that may shock you, well...maybe not shock you, but at least help you to rationalize what happened. What the paper probably didn't tell you was I didn't *go* to see Nixon. I was invited. Okay?"

"Oh, I know," I said.

Ray was still defensive. "Now, I don't know how many people, if they were invited by the President of the United States to go to the White House, would refuse to go see what he wants."

I said I hadn't heard anyone criticize him.

Ray didn't even hear me. He said, "But...I...I hafta tell you, you're not the first person who's said that to me. I got all kinds of calls from people who said, 'Hey Man, I never woulda thought it.' And I said, 'What the hell are you talkin about? I've been a Democrat all...and even if I was ah...you know, if I was gonna...Nixon, I guess is..."

"He's alright," I finished his sentence again.

Ray's conversation was all over the place. He jumped to the next sentence before he completed the first one. I was still laughing at him saying, "Man I never would of thought you'd vote for Nixon."

Ray went right on talking, "He's a politician, but certainly my man was Humphrey 'cept he didn't win and I'm not a Nixon fan, but the man invited me to the White House. He invited me. I didn't call him up and say, "Hey Nick, is it alright if I come by to see you? I'm sure he woulda said, "Are you crazy?""

Laughing hysterically, I said, "I don't know. He might not. I called you and asked you to come see me, and you didn't say "Are you crazy?"

"Well I...I think it's probably...a...a little bit different," Ray laughed.

"No, I don't think so. From my position, it's about as impossible to get through to you as it would be for you to get through to him."

Ray said he would go to the Kremlin if he was invited, and if he was in Rome and the Pope invited him to come to the Vatican, he would go. He said, "In other words, what I'm saying to you, honey, is I don't feel that that has anything to do with my religion just because I go talk to a person."

"Ray, I don't care who you voted for. I think people have a right to vote for whomever they please."

"Well, I didn't vote at all, because I told you my man didn't win," Ray said.

"I did," I said. "I voted for McGovern and he didn't stand a chance."

"Well, I knew that, honey."

"I did, too," I said, "but I just wanted to make sure I voted."

"I didn't vote for McGovern," Ray said, "because I voted for Humphrey in the primary and he didn't win so...after that...well, see first of all, honey...after Humphrey didn't win...I really didn't care for McGovern. You know, what really turned me off, there were a couple of things, I'll tell you something, uh...sweetheart. When a man says to me, or at least makes himself public and says, "I don't care what anybody tells me," Ray was quoting, "I am for this man (meaning Thomas Eagleton in the 1972 presidential election) a thousand percent, not a hundred percent, but a thousand percent, then when the pressure gets hot, through his aids, he forced the man to retire. I'm...I'm sorry, honey. That really turned me off with McGovern."

I said, "That turned me off too, but I can't stand Nixon."

Ray said he couldn't either and that's why he didn't vote for either of them. He said he felt there was no point in being a hypocrite to himself.

In the 1972 election, Eagleton, McGovern's running mate, had undergone treatment (including electroshock therapy), for manic depression. Hearing this, McGovern dropped him as his running mate. Ray thought McGovern was so wrong for turning his back on Eagleton because he had a breakdown.

Ray said McGovern was very hypocritical because he didn't want the man to get help. Ironically, Ray didn't think *I* should go to group therapy for my mental issues. He could accept Eagleton's problems, but had a difficult time accepting mine!

Ray couldn't get over McGovern's hypocrisy. He said, "I mean after all, the man said, 'I feel overtired and I went somewhere and tried to get some help,' and McGovern said, 'Well once you've done that...okay...well...' and he turned his back on him. 'That really hurt me. I thought, 'Well, hell, if he's gonna do that, ...I...I don't think he's too good for me.' Plus, there were a couple of other things I didn't care for, but *that* was the main thing."

"Well," I said, "all he did was establish Eagleton. If he ever runs for office again, he'll win hands down."

"I'm sure he'll win anything he...because...and at least the man tried to do something about himself. There are a lot of people who have things wrong with 'em an...and they don't even try to help themselves."

"There are many different kinds of breakdowns, too. You don't always go off your rocker," I said. I should have reminded him about how *he* reacted to *my* breakdown, but I didn't.

Ray continued, "But can you imagine a person who condemns you for tryin'...you know, if your hand hurts or whatever hurts you, you try to see somebody who can do something about it." Ray was very upset. He couldn't get over it. "Uh...that really turned me off. Well, alright then, I won't vote for McGovern and I'm *not* a Nixon man, so I gotta be true to myself. I'm not going to bastardize my conscience by voting for somebody just to be voting. Hell, I don't like either one of them. I'll tell you one thing, babe, in the latter fifties and early part of the sixties, every Civil Rights bill that was introduced, McGovern voted *against*!"

I told him I wished I hadn't voted for him. I should have been like him and not voted.

I remember the things Ray said to me when I mentioned going to group therapy. He said, "You don't need that, babe. Just get hold of yourself. You're a smart woman, Marci." When I review those remarks in my mind, they sound irksome. Smart had nothing to do with my mental and emotional status.

We got off that subject, thank God!

Then Ray asked me what I disliked about Catholicism. My answer was that there were many reasons. One reason was when I was trying so hard to become Catholic because my husband wanted me to (certainly not because he was a good church-going Catholic, but because his family was), I was rejected because I had been divorced. To me, that was bullshit. I also thought both of the priests who baptized my kids reeked of alcohol, and seemed whoozie. I didn't like that!

Ray said he understood my feelings.

Today, years later, I have even less respect for the Catholic religion because of priest pedophilia and the church covering it up. Because of the hypocrisy I see in *all* religions, I am a non-religious person, and do not ascribe to any denomination. I have my own belief. I keep it to myself, and I *do* live it. I try not to be a hypocrite.

29
Singing Christmas Songs
❦

I finally let Ray come back a few days before Christmas, 1972. Talk about a happy man. He said he was delirious. He thought he would never be here again.

He was delighted to see Lisa and Mitzi, too. When we arrived home from the airport, we all gathered in the living room to catch up on everybody's activities for the last two months. Then we went downstairs to sing Christmas songs. Ray played the piano while Lisa and I sang *Rudolph the Red Nosed Reindeer.*

Ray said, "You gonna sing, Mitzi?"

Lisa suggested *Silent Night* and *I'm Dreaming of a White Christmas.*

I chimed in, "Oh, yeah. Those are good."

Mitzi said, "We sing that at school."

Ray was playing, "*I'm Dreaming of a White Christmas.*" We were singing again, and Ray played, but didn't sing.

I said, "That was gooooood."

Ray agreed, "It *was* good. What else you wanna sing?"

Mitzi said, "*Silver Bells and Dashing Snow,*" Ray laughed, "You mean Jingle Bells, Mitz?"

I said, "I like those songs." Ray played and we sang at the top of our lungs.

"You're not singing, Ray," I said. He kept right on playing so Mitzi and I started singing again. All of a sudden, Lisa kicked in with gusto. Mitzi got louder, too. So cute. (Ray was wearing his "Mona Lisa" smile).

He asked, "How's that? Okay?"

"Good," I said.

Mitzi said, "Now let's sing *Silent Night*."

Ray started playing *Silent Night*.

I said, "Come on, Ray. Sing."

"I don't know it. I've never sung it before. I always had to play it," Ray told us.

Mitzi said, "We sang it in our choir and I didn't know the words either, but I learned them."

"That's good," Ray said.

Lisa said, "Now play, *Silver Bells*, Ray."

He said, "I don't know *Silver Bells*, honey."

I said, "Play *Winter Wonderland*. You know that one, don't you?"

Lisa said, "I don't."

Ray started playing it. We were singing away and Ray stopped–he didn't know the middle part. I sang the melody, "In the meadow we will build a snowman."

Ray said, "What?" Then he got it and sang, "Walking in a winter wonderland," just those few lyrics with us. He still was uncertain and asked me to sing it again. He played and I sang the song by myself. Ray kept playing the part he didn't know until he *did* know it.

When the phone rang, I told Lisa to answer it and tell them I was busy. She said it was someone selling something. Tell them I said, "No thanks." Ray was noodling on the piano.

Mitzi said, "Good. Now we can sing a song from my school."

I asked Ray what the song was that he always harmonized with everyone.

Lisa said, "Why, mom? Do you wanna sing with him?"

"I don't know which one it is, babe," said Ray.

Mitzi said, "It's the song with tear drops in your eyes."

I started humming the song. For some reason, I could never remember it.

"That's *Cryin' Time*," Ray said. "Mitzi, you were right."

"Oh, yeah. That's it," I said. "Will you sing it?"

"No," he said.

"Why?" I asked.

220

"'Cause I won't," He started playing it. "You sing it."

"I don't know the words," I said.

"You do. That's the song you and I just sang recently," he insisted.

"No, it's not," I persisted.

"Yes, it is," he said.

Lisa said, "You can sing it, Ray."

"Course I can. I sing it every night. That's why I don't wanna sing it now, honey," he told her.

I started humming it, then he started playing and said, "Go ahead, Marci. Sing it."

I sang, "I can tell by the way your hold me darlin'," and I added my little soul.

Ray said, "Oh, yeah!" I was still singing when he said, "I like that little thing you put in there." So I did it again. "Alright!! Now go on, baby," he said.

We were all laughing. I said, "That's my Ray Charles."

"Sing it. Awww, you're doin' it. Go on, awww baby."

Ray was urging me on. "That's you. That ain't me. That's you, honey. Swear to God. 'Fraid or not." That was a saying carried over from his childhood.

Lisa said, "Ray, sing this one." We couldn't figure out which one she wanted. He asked me if I knew the words to *Till There Was You*. Then he began playing it.

I said I recognized the song, but I didn't know the words. I hummed until I got to the "Till There Was You" part. I did know that part. I asked him if he liked that song.

"Yeah. I've got it recorded," he answered.

The words starting coming to me and I began singing the song.

He said, "That's right. You got it." He was singing too, and he got some of the words wrong.

I asked him what if that happened when he was recording.

"Well, I can record over it if I mess up. I don't have a band. The band is recorded first. Then I can play around with it, till it's the way I want it," he explained.

I loved that he sang, *Till There Was You* to me. I asked him to play *My Man* and reminded him that he had asked me to learn the words to it a long time ago.

"Yeah, but I don't know it," he said. "It's funny. I like it and I don't know it."

I started singing it and he picked up the melody and played it. "That's nice," he said. "Sing it again."

Mitzi said, "Mama, that's the song you sing a lot."

Ray asked, "What's the next verse?"

I sang, "Oh, he's not much for looks. He's no hero out of books. He's my man." He caught on and played. I was still singing. Then he got stuck again and started playing with one finger.

"My timing isn't good," I said.

"You don't pat your foot for rhythm, babe. Your rhythm is always there." He beat out the rhythm for me. Then he played and hummed the tune without any words and we sang it together. He said, "Nice. Very nice."

"Well, that's just to prove to you I *can* sing that song," I bragged. "You said I couldn't."

"I never said that," Ray said shocked.

"You sure as hell did. On the phone, you said, 'If there's anything I have to say regarding that song, it's that you can't sing it.'"

Ray stammered, "Well...I...I"

"That made me mad, so I practiced."

Ray laughed, "You practiced that?" He was still laughing.

"No, I didn't," I said.

Lisa said, "You've been singing that song since you saw it in a Barbra Streisand movie."

I said I had been singing it since Ray told me about it.

"Mama," Lisa asked. "Can we open one of our Christmas presents?"

I said. "No. Not now." As I am writing this, I am thinking how good my little girls were. Ray thought so, too.

Lisa and Mitzi said simultaneously, "Mama, Ray's playing another song."

"Is that another one that you are recording?" I asked.

"Yeah. *Life is Long*, except I don't know it yet." He started to sing it, then he said, "There's some strange songs I recorded. Remember the song The Everly Brothers did?" I didn't recognize it. Then he said, "There's another song, *Louise*. Do you remember that song?"

I elbowed him hard. "Now you know better than to ask me that. You know what I'm talking about, just slide on by that one."

He laughed at me and said, "Awww. Come on, babe."

He forgot that I knew his first love's name was Louise.

This entire conversation was recorded on tape. When we were finished singing, we would listen to ourselves. Ray got a kick out of it, all of us laughing, talking, singing and having such a fun time.

When we wrapped up our recording session, we came upstairs for dinner. Ray and the girls ate White Castle burgers which I had picked up earlier. I didn't have any, but everyone else loved them. The four of us spent the evening watching television, and then it was bath time and bedtime for my little six and eight year old girls.

After I kissed Lisa and Mitzi goodnight, I joined Ray in the bedroom. He told me over and over how happy he was to be with me. He caressed and kissed me all night, and we had the next day to ourselves. My kids were in school and I took the day off from work. We lounged from the bed to the couch all day.

As I look back, it reminds me of his song, *All I Wanna Do is Lay Around and Love on You*. That song wasn't even a thought in Ray's mind in 1972. But it certainly does reflect the way we were. It was on the album, "Do I Ever Cross Your Mind," which was released in 1984.

The next morning, after dropping my kids off at school, I drove Ray to the airport, put him on the plane, said my usual tearful goodbyes and drove to work.

My emotions were like a roller coaster. Soaring to the moon, then hitting rock bottom. That state of mind was taking its toll on me. Christmas was a week away, and I was busy baking, shopping, wrapping gifts and preparing for Christmas with my family. That helped me get through the emotional highs and lows. Henry was here for the kids Christmas. Ray hated that and couldn't understand why he had to be here.

I said, "Well, you aren't here, so don't worry about it. When you can be here, then he won't."

"Well...uh...okay, babe," was his response. He damn sure wasn't about to fix it. He was trying to have his cake and eat it too, in typical Ray fashion. It didn't work.

There were many phone conversations. He was back the early part of January bearing a gift. It was a promotional album titled "Through the Eyes of Love."

I played it immediately and found it to be a lovely album. I listened intently to every song, as I always did. I was completely absorbed in Ray's beautiful love songs. To make it even more special, that wonderful, magical singer was snuggled next to me on the couch as I listened to them.

That album was the last album with Ray's Tangerine Record label. It must have been painful for him. I didn't know about the end of the Tangerine label at the time, and wouldn't until 2004. There was something else I wouldn't discover until 2004, thanks to that informative book *Man and Music.*

I always checked to see which songs Ray wrote. Suddenly I stiffened, and my blood curdled. I asked, "Are you writing songs with your wife now?"

"What?!" Ray said as he sat straight up.

"Are you writing songs with your wife?" I asked.

"No," Ray responded. "Who told you that?"

"Well, her name is on the back of this album," I said.

"No, her name is not on that album...you see that's how people..."

I interrupted, "Well, who is Ruth Robinson?"

Ray said ache was a very good word for it and it described his awful feelings as well. I told him I knew all about aching, but told him that you just had to learn to live with those kinds of feelings and make the best of it.

He asked me how I was feeling and I assured him I was feeling okay. I wondered why he thought I wasn't feeling well.

"No...I had a feeling that...you've been weighing awfully heavy on me, baby."

I said for him to give it a couple of days and it would go away.

"Well that's not...You know the main thing, hon, is that what strikes me is how heavy you can weigh on me, you know, where I can really feel your presence. You can say, well in a couple of days it will go away, and maybe it will. I just know what it's been with me. And I thought it would be fair for me to tell you. You're weighing heavy on me. Now you know. So okay, sweetheart tha...that's the way it is." (This last part was in his normal voice. The other parts were in his, "I'm pitiful, I'm hurt, I'm sad, I'm sorry and You can fix it" voice). He added that he thought his feeling was some form of depression or something.

"It's just a thought, Ray," I said.

"I don't think it's that. If you wanna say that, you have every right to, Marci. But I must tell you I disagree, because you don't weigh heavily on somebody's mind like that and it's just a thought. Maybe you didn't understand me (how could I not have understood him when he pounded it into my head for an hour or longer). No it's not, 'no just a thought.' If it were, I think I could probably cast it aside. It's far more than a thought, babe. I said you weigh very heavy, real heavy, and...and there's no way I can dramatize this to you. I mean I don't know the right words to tell you the way I really feel. It's far more than a thought, Marci, much more!"

"It'll go away," I said.

"Well it ain't went away in two weeks. I told you, you were weighing on me, very heavy, for at least a couple of weeks. For

"That's a writer," he said as he lit a cigarette and paced back and forth. "I'm not the only person in...in the world with the name Robinson, baby. There's Joe Robinson, Frank Robinson, Robinson's a very common name. Ruth Robinson happens to be a writer.

"You see, that's how people can get hang-ups about things like that..." he started laughing a nervous but cynical laugh. "That's very funny, uh...okay, that's just crazy." He was acting just plain shitty, "That's really cute. I bet you thought of that all by your own little self, didn't you?"

"I sure did," I answered, just as cocky.

"It's just amazing how you could think of that," Ray said.

I said it was the title of the song that got to me, *I Can Make It Through the Days, but Oh Those Lonely Nights.* It was on the album, "Through the Eyes of Love," released in late 1972 or early 1973 and written by Ray Charles, Ruth Robinson and Dee Irvin.

Ray was agitated. He said, "So you put two and two together and say, 'Hey, that must be his wife.' Oh! Man! Wow! See, I would have said, 'Well, Jesus Christ, there's a jillion people with the name Robinson.'"

"Well, of course I know that, Ray. But it just struck me as strange that the album said Ruth *Robinson.*"

"Well, I'm sorry, babe. That's the child's name. That's really something, the way you think."

"I'm jealous, Ray. I'm jealous of something I can't do anything about."

"No, you're jealous of things you don't know about, honey."

He was certainly right about that. Ruth Robinson worked at RPM and was one of Ray's women. He must have been surprised at how close I came to the real truth. I was right being jealous. I had just given her the wrong position. She wasn't his wife, but Ruth Robinson was *far* more than just a writer.

Since I was already pissed off, I continued complaining, "I don't care. I don't like you being married. It makes me nothing but a slut."

"Oh, I don't...I don't *ever* want to hear you say that again," That *really* upset him.

I said, "Well, God! What do you think I am? I'm nothing."

"Did you hear what I said." Ray was pacing back and forth, his forehead was furrowed. He put one cigarette out and lit another. "Let me put it this way. Do me a favor...and I mean I'm really gonna ask you to do this favor. Don't *ever* let me hear you say that again. If you're gonna say it, don't *ever* say it where I can hear it. You know...I...I really don't like that, Marci. That's *not* the way I think of you and you're *not* that. And I don't like it."

"Well, that's how I feel, Ray," I kept on.

"Anyway, I hope you understood me. I'd appreciate it," he reiterated.

"I understand you, but it doesn't change my feelings," I said.

"Okay, babe, if you want to think that, all I'm asking of you is *don't* say it to me or where I can hear it. I really don't like it."

I just couldn't stop nagging. "Why didn't you call me Christmas Day?"

"I did," he said, "and it was impossible."

That certainly didn't satisfy me. I said, "Well, I got four other long-distance calls."

"Well, I've got news for you. There's no way in hell you could get a call from anywhere in the State of California. I think if anybody could have gotten through, I could have. Every circuit was busy. I even tried one last time before I left for work and I still couldn't get through."

"You could have called on Tuesday and said you tried to call me all day Christmas." Christmas must have been on a Monday.

Ray threw his hands up, "Oooooh, Marci! I...what can I say, babe?"

I finally shut up. I know he was grateful, finally, for some peace of mind.

৵৶

He told me that he got the statues I sent, that were made from nuts and bolts, and that he loved them. He did not get my poems. I wonder if someone else in his office intercepted them... hmmmm. They were written in Braille, but I read in the book *Man and Music* that someone else had learned to write Braille also...a certain *writer*.

I had read in a magazine that Ray's friend Quincy Jones was dating Peggy Lipton of Mod Squad fame. When I read it to Ray, he said, "Who?" He had no idea who Peggy Lipton was.

Ray was very concerned when in 1974, Q, as he referred to Quincy, was stricken with a brain aneurysm. When he recovered, Ray breathed a sigh of relief. Quincy, as everyone knows, was Ray's best friend. He told me many times and said publicly that Quincy was as close to a brother that he would ever have.

Later, when Quincy and Peggy were married, I asked Ray if he knew who she was. He said, "Yeah, but I don't know her well."

When Lisa and Mitzi got home from school and had a snack, we went downstairs to listen while they practiced piano lessons. Ray always told them how good they sounded. When they finished, Ray played, *Cryin' Time* for us to harmonize as usual. But this time, I asked him to sing the melody. He said, "Okay, but you won't sing harmony."

"Yes, I will," I said. "I can harmonize with you."

"Oh, you can, huh?" he said.

I said, "Don't you sing, Lisa. You'll throw me off."

"I'm not singing," Lisa said, irritated at me.

Ray hit the key with one finger to indicate my part, and said, "You sing this part, honey."

Because I had harmonized with my family and in church all my life, I knew I could do it. I said, very haughtily, "I *know* how to sing, Ray."

"Oh. Oh. Oh. 'Scuse me," he said making fun of me, and started singing the melody. I started and sang the wrong part.

"WRONG!" Ray said.

Lisa and Mitzi were laughing so hard. I started singing again, and still couldn't get it.

"Wrong!" Ray said again and pounded on the note he wanted me to sing. I still couldn't get it.

In frustration, but happy frustration, he said, "Sing me something else. I won't tell you what to sing, babe."

Finally, I got my part.

"Right," he said. "Now *that's* what I want."

We sang it really well. Ray said, "That's good, honey."

"See, I know how to harmonize," I said, still giggling.

My girls laughingly said, "Mom, what was wrong? You sing that song all the time."

"I don't know," I said. "I think Brother Ray made me nervous."

We listened to Lisa play *Love Story* and to Mitzi play *Reuben Reuben* and *Hello Dolly*. Then, we went upstairs and had dinner–pot roast with vegetables and warm dinner rolls. I have this singing and piano session recorded, too. I'm so happy. Now, thirty-six years later, I can still hear Ray and my little girls happily playing and singing at our old studio upright.

The kids had their television time and then bedtime. Add to that a little magic for me and my sweetheart, and all in all, it was a very good night. The next morning, we were all up early getting ready to face a bitterly cold day...in my bitterly cold volkswagen!

Volkswagens in the 70's didn't have heaters–they were engine heated. I went out 20 minutes before time to leave and put a brick on the gas pedal to get the car warm for my kids. I did that every morning. I'm lucky I didn't burn up my engine. But the car was toasty!

After I dropped my kids at school, I took Ray to the airport, got him on his plane and it was bye-bye sweetheart...again.

It goes without saying, I was getting sick of putting him on a plane that was always taking him away from me. Oh, well. I consoled myself with wonderful fresh memories again, and went to work feeling powerless to ever have what I wanted more than anything, Ray Charles Robinson.

30
More Lengthy Discussions
❧

In 1973, my girls and I were still riding horses, but we also added piano and dance lessons to our routine. I was a busy mom, working, driving my kids to their lessons and to school, painting our house inside and out and sewing recital costumes.

Now that was a feat that always surprised me. How I ever got those costumes finished, I'll never know. I'm not a seamstress. I can alter things but patterns baffle me. Many mornings at 2:00 o'clock, I would still be sewing and worrying how the costumes would turn out. Finally, when I turned them right side out, they would miraculously be okay and I would absolutely not know how that happened. The same thing happened with their Halloween costumes, but somehow I muddled through. It was either hire a seamstress or do it myself, and having very little money, the choice was simple.

Ray was always good at encouraging me to handle things. "See, honey, you can do anything you set your mind to," he said many times. God forbid he would say, "Is there anything I can do to help you?" Nope! That wasn't him. He said he wasn't the Bank of America, and what money he gave me was at his own discretion.

I would have loved for him to help with my household bills, but that looked like too much commitment to Ray. He wanted the convenience but not the commitment. He wanted *me* to be committed to him, but not vice versa.

Time was taking its toll on me and I was complaining more than ever. Ray said he almost dreaded talking to me because it was a constant drilling, but I couldn't help it. I wasn't happy so I continued to complain, not always, but enough, he said, on one of our more pleasant conversations. When he called this time, as usual, we began talking about what we had done since our last phone call.

I asked him if he had done some writing for Carol Burnett's show and he told me, "No, I just do arrangements for things that I'm doing."

"Well, what do you do for other people?" I said.

He said he didn't write for anyone else, only himself.

"But I see your name on things," I said.

"Well th...there are things I've written that people have to get my permission to use."

"Oh, that's why," I said. Then I asked what he was going to do for the rest of the day.

He said he was going to the drug store and then he was going to do some work on the material for the film they shot in Israel.

"Oh," I exclaimed, "will we see it here in the U.S?" (I finally saw it in 2006, two years after Ray died).

He continued, "Yes, providing we even do it. We shot the film but now we've got to see what we've got. I saw a couple of the rushes but I don't really know if it's good or bad."

He said it was a documentary of music and the way he saw the Middle East when he was there.

I knew from his conversation that he loved the Israeli children, but the highlight of the trip was his visit with former Prime Minister David Ben-Gurion. He was elated to have had that once in a lifetime opportunity. Ben-Gurion died that same year, 1973, so Ray's visit with him literally *was* a once in a lifetime experience.

Ray toured the Holy Land on foot with Bob Taylor leading the way. He touched the Wailing Wall and he also knelt and touched the fourteen point Star of Bethlehem. He felt an inherent bond with Jewish people. He told me that they were as persecuted as African Americans and that he felt a kinship with them.

৯৶৫

Speaking of kinship, the next time he was here, my brother Don brought his wife to meet him. Ray was always happy to see Don and he liked his wife, too.

A few nights after he arrived, we decided to go to the Red Lobster for dinner. Don's mother-in-law was a server there. I had asked her ahead of time to reserve two booths for us, even though the Red Lobster didn't take reservations. But because it was Ray Charles, they did. When we arrived, my friends Don and Colleen Eaker were already there so they could meet Ray. I had arranged this meeting secretly because I had invited so many people to my house to meet Ray, I thought he might one day just say, "No, babe. No more." He never did.

When we walked into the restaurant, everyone stopped eating and stared open-mouthed at Ray. It wasn't very likely that a person would see Ray Charles stroll into a family restaurant on South Lindbergh in St. Louis, Missouri and have dinner.

I introduced Ray to Don and Colleen. He was fully aware of what I had done and laughed about it. I had wanted them to meet for some time. I knew Ray and Don would like each other and they hit if off immediately. We all had a great time...that is, except for Lisa. She ordered oysters rockefeller and didn't like them, so Ray let her order something else.

We had such a nice time. I could tell that Ray liked Don and Colleen. He seemed comfortable with them, and on the way home he confirmed my feeling that he enjoyed their company.

Colleen asked Ray what his favorite pie was and he told her blackberry. She said she would make him one if we promised to come to her house for dinner when he came back. He promised, and I knew then that he really liked them. Ray wasn't a socializer.

In 1968 his favorite pie was apple with melted cheese. I was surprised when he said blackberry. That's mine too!

Ray was here for two nights, then it was back to the airport again. I was finding it harder and harder to deal with my undulant emotions, so I started complaining again. He called it drilling and nagging. He didn't fix the situation so I drilled and nagged. As I write and look back, I don't know what I expected him to do...except be single. But then what? I would never have moved. Dynamite couldn't have moved me from this house. This was, and is, my security. So that was it. That was all Ray and I had–a love affair with me here and him on the West Coast.

I didn't think rationally in the 70's. Now I have a clearer understanding of the way things were. I would never have moved anywhere with Ray because of the 1969 move to L.A. that broke my heart. It also taught me a lifelong lesson–I would never, ever put myself in such a vulnerable position again if I could help it. I would always be in control of my own well-being. I'm seventy-two now and I still feel the same way.

I learned some valuable lessons because of Ray. I learned how to pull myself out of quicksand and move forward, how to be firm in my decisions and not be swayed (even by Ray), and how to switch my brain channel. Ray said, "When you find yourself unhappy, honey, change the channel." That's what I did.

I know that he regretted telling me that because he taught me how to switch him off and somebody else on, and eventually, I did just that. But at that time, I was still drilling and nagging.

I called him and left a message that I wanted to stop seeing him. Very soon he called. He wasn't saying much, just making some throat clearing, growling and grumbling sounds.

I said, "You called me, but you're not talking Ray."

"Well, I don't really have anything to tell you, baby. I um...wanted to talk to you. I um...mostly wanted to hear you...so I...I...um that's about it. And you know, since you've struck me down I can't...there's not much I can say." Then he said, "So I can't see you no more?"

I told him no, that I couldn't do it anymore.

"Okay. Okay. I had to ask, Marci. 'Cause I had to know."

"You just want to visit–run back and forth. If you really wanted me it would be different, but you don't."

"Well, that's what you say, Marci. So I mean…"

"I know it. I've lived it, Ray."

"Okay…alright…whatever you say, baby."

"Maybe I wouldn't fit into your life anyway. All the people you know, your associates, are show business people, and I don't know anything about them."

"You know, Marci, its strange the kind of picture you have of me. I can see it now. Glamorous. You use words like that. I guess you really think that's the kind of life I live." He did a cynical laugh, "That's funny. You're just as wrong about that as you were about Ruth Robinson. I don't live that kind of life, I'm sorry to inform you, very simple, very plain. Don't live in Hollywood. Don't live in Beverly Hills."

"No," I said, "You live in a huge $300,000 house (which was a *lot* of money in the 70s!). That's not so plain and simple. Gosh, when you're here you must feel like you're in prison."

"Aaah, honey. It makes no difference to me what a house is like. I don't need no house. You know, an apartment would be fine. The house is for the younguns and it's not so much the house. It's the area, the space that they have to play…and where I live at is just everyday people, the houses around there are just regular houses."

"Okay Ray, whatever."

"You know, babe, there's something about this time of year that seems to depress an awful lot of people."

"It's not the time of year, Ray. It's the situation. You know damn well what's wrong with me. We don't spend enough time together. You're not my ole' man, like you call yourself. I would never tell anyone that. It's embarrassing. I can't even think that."

"Well, I don't know who you're tryin' to please, the people or yourself." That always agitated Ray, me mentioning other people and their opinion of our relationship. I really didn't talk to anyone about it. I just said it to him.

"Anyway, when you want to come here you can. I'm always here for you."

"Naw, naw, what you meant to say is, 'Once upon a time that might have been.' But you've clipped my wings now. You know I...I don't like it, babe."

"Well, I've clipped mine too. I can't stand knowing there's never gonna be any change."

"Marci, I'd like to know, babe, how in the world you know all these things, and I don't."

"Ray, you have things the way you want them. I'm just extra curricular and maybe one of many extra curriculars, I don't know." (I certainly was getting close to the truth and I didn't even know it).

"Awww, man...okay," he said.

I continued to rail–accusing him of never being with me on the holidays. (He always came right before, which was thoughtful and nice, but it wasn't enough for me). He couldn't be with me because he was where all married men were–at home with their wives. But he informed me that he worked on holidays and was never home, which I knew because he would always call me.

I brought up an old girlfriend of his from twenty-five years earlier. He said it was a terrible mistake that he mentioned it to me.

I said, "You'll have to find yourself a woman who will just sit back and let you do whatever you like. I won't." After I read the book *Man and Music,* I realized he already had a couple of those.

What has always puzzled me is why he listened to me drill and nag as he called it. I wonder why he didn't tell me to go to hell and hang up. He never did.

And I didn't let up. "I'm sure there are women who will be exactly what you want, someone who'll be a puppet for you."

He said, "Uh, why are you tellin' me what I want? I would know what I want better than you. I don't need you to tell me. I know what I want. I know it well."

I shot back, "Yeah, you want a good shot of Marci when you get damned good and ready!"

"Oh Boy! Oh Boy!! Ooookay, babe. What's the point in me calling you, we just go 'round and 'round and the venom flows."

"Well we don't have to discuss you and me again–EVER!," I said.

"I'd like to know what we're going to discuss then. I love you, Marci, and I...I don't know...if you feel that keeping us separated is gonna do it. Maybe you're right. I dunno. But I don't like it at all. You know I want to see you and I think you well know how I...well no, I guess you don't know how I feel, but I had a much better shot at getting something done before you shut the door. It's just maybe I wasn't able to do it that year or the next year. You know, babe, it must have taken...I don't know how many years before I was able to...you know, make enough money to keep from starving to death. So one could easily say, well shit, I can't continue this kind of thing and...and, give it up. But the thing is, I think anything that I want...uh...I...I might not be able to have what I want, the way I want it, but I think that if I'm sincere in what I'm doing and if I work at it, and work at it good, then at least my percentage of achieving my aims and my goals are far better.

"If I shut the door and close out the thing that I want...or the person that...I...I want, I think it's very difficult to uh...you know...achieve anything once you have closed off everything... shut out the person that you dig, the person that you love. Then obviously, what you're really saying is, okay, I'm just gonna put death to this and that's it. Finished. Over. Complete.

"I do think it's fair for you to do what you want to do, as well as for me to do what I want. But you can't just uh...uh...maneuver people around like they're pawns on a chess board. You know, honey, it's impossible to do that...but time will take care of many, many things if you have the patience for it. You can't uh...drive people up a wall and figure you're gonna get what you want done just because you want it. It does take a little diplomacy and uh...a little patience."

I explained that we were at an impasse. I told him I wasn't trying to pressure him into something, and I wasn't just keeping on until I got what I wanted. I said that I couldn't make him do anything, and that if he didn't want me there was nothing I could do.

Ray wasn't nearly as abrupt with me. When I said things like that, he would get frustrated. "Well...it's...it's not a question of not wanting you, babe. I mean...there's no point in putting it that way. And...and...er...uh I do...I do want you. It's just that the way that you...that I figure you want things done ...uh...just can't be done that readily or that quickly."

I thought it had been long enough. I told him that I had a lot of willpower and a lot of strength, and I could make myself do almost anything if I pushed myself. I didn't want to have to push myself.

I said, "I'm here. I've done my part. That's all I have to do. The rest is up to you. I know things are more difficult for you. Gosh. You've got so much, and it seems that you have your life planned out so beautifully, I...I...just can't see why you would even want to mess it up."

Ray tried to say things to me in a non-confrontational way.

"Okay, you know you may be right about a lot of things dear, but I...I think your concept...of my life and the way things are with me and the way I live is totally incorrect."

I realized later that my perception of his lifestyle was wrong. His wife wasn't the threat to me. A million other women were!

Ray had two agendas. He either wanted to be secluded somewhere with a woman or working. That's it. But lucky for me, I didn't know about the other women at the time.

There was a period of silence in our conversation. Then he asked me if I were a hundred percent sure I wasn't going to see him again.

I said that I didn't know but that I wanted to be, because I wanted to find somebody who would love me.

"I love you, plain and simple," he quickly and firmly responded.

I began to cry and tell him how it hurt me when he went away and left me.

"Alright, baby. I...I don't want to upset you...I don't mean to hurt you, sweetheart."

When Ray spoke to me so sweet and softly like that, he almost had me again. He was an expert at reigning me back in. But each time I tried to stop seeing him, it was getting harder for him because I was getting more determined.

I said that we could still communicate, but not be so emotionally involved with one another.

He didn't agree with that solution. He said that his conversations had to do with us. That he learned long ago that he couldn't always have everything he wanted, the way he wanted it. Sometimes he had had to accept something even though he didn't like it, but because he felt so strongly about it, he accepted it.

He said that life was evil and good and that if he felt very strongly about something, he would have to overcome whatever the wrong portion may be.

He told me there were many examples that he could relate to me about really caring for someone. If I were married, for example, that would not stop him from loving me. He might not like the fact, but he would consider which situation was the strongest for him.

He explained, "My situation may be bad but if I...in other words, if I love you and you're mine, I feel like a hungry man, I guess, it's the only way I can put it. If you're hungry and...and if you're offered bread, you don't demand steak if you're hungry. That's it. You can understand that, babe, right? Okay, so if you love someone, really love them...I mean in spite of the fact that there may be obstacles, I mean we can't always live our lives and set up our own deals, our own little specifics and say, 'Well look unless it's my way, it's nuthin.'"

Ray was working his magic on me. The more I listened to his reasoning, the more unsure I became if I was being fair to him. Never mind me.

He continued, "You told me, and you're perfectly right, you have your own feelings and I respect them, whether I agree with you or not. I definitely respect them. And the question is… that as far as I'm concerned, I'm not so sure…as a matter of fact…I'm positive as far as I'm concerned that…uh anything I care about, that I love, I can't imagine there comin' a time when I would tell myself, 'Well look, if it can't be my way–the way I want it, I just won't have no part of it.' I don't know if I could …"

"Ray, I knew I wouldn't stand a chance with your semantics. You always phrase words so that I look terrible and uncaring."

"Please allow me to apologize, Marci. That's not my intent, hon. I'm sorry."

"The way you phrase it sounds like I just don't love you enough to cope, but you're the one who doesn't do anything about our situation."

Ray said I was taking the defensive; that I had missed the whole point and he was sorry. He didn't mean to make me feel bad.

I said again that I thought it was wrong. I was disgusted with myself and because he was married, I felt like a slut. That I deserved a more important position than I had with him and I was gonna get it. I didn't like being the other woman, (Ha! What a joke that was!) and that I would write him a letter (I had taught myself Braille in 1969) and say everything I wanted to say so that he couldn't back talk me. "You can't say one word. You can either read it or throw it away."

"Babe, I wasn't trying to back talk you."

"We can be platonic Ray, so if you want to call, you can."

"Really and truly, honey, what for? I'm not a hypocrite. I'm not two-faced with myself. I mean…I can't act like you're my sister. Then I'm sure 'nuff lyin'. I can't be that way, babe. Besides, what are we gonna talk about? All I wanna talk about is us, just us. That's it. Finished."

We argued and argued. Me accusing and him defending himself and trying to keep me calm. He said he didn't need to get his head smashed in every time I opened my mouth. My response to that was, "Well then, get a divorce."

Finally I yelled, "Listen. If you want to be married so bad, then stay married and just don't call me. SHIT!"

He was trying to say something, "Marci, listen," but he couldn't because I was angrily yelling. He said, "Bye, Marci. Bye-bye baby."

I hung up on him and refused to talk to him. I would hang up on him every time he called. After about a month, some time in early December, I answered the phone and heard a desperate sounding Ray saying, "Marci...don't hang up baby... Please... just listen to me, honey."

A few days later, we were all, to quote Ray's song, "Together Again," playing the upright piano and singing Christmas songs.

31
Dinner at Don and Colleen's

❧

Ray and I talked on the phone a lot during the first part of 1974, but we didn't see much of each other during that time. These sporadic visits weren't making me very happy. I had made myself stop complaining so much, however, even though I'm a firm believer in "the squeaky wheel gets the grease."

So I thought, *I'll stop drilling and complaining just to see if things do get better, like Ray promised.* They didn't.

Ray had been in New Orleans and that always made me nervous. Because of Henry's hatred toward him, he wouldn't have thought twice about having him hurt–or worse.

Henry called and told me, "Your boyfriend's in town and some of the band members are coming to my club–and Ray Charles is coming, too."

I called the Roosevelt Hotel where I knew Ray was staying and left a message. I called right back and told them to cancel the call. I didn't want to scare him and I was pretty sure that he wouldn't go.

When I told Ray, he said, "Honey, you know I don't go out to clubs...you can almost bet your life on it. When I'm in a club you can be sure–I'd say 99% sure–that I'm workin'. Did you think I was gonna have some problems?"

I told him I always worried when he played New Orleans. Then I asked why he hadn't called after he left New Orleans.

His response was "Well, I guess it's negligence or something and uh...I felt kind of embarrassed on top of it."

I asked how he was doing.

He said, "Basically...I'm...I'm...I guess I'm a lot better now than I was before you called."

"Have you been ill, Ray?

"Well, no I...haven't been ill, Marci, not physically ill, but you know how you run into all kinds of stomach blocks and pitfalls...stuff that bugs you to death, things that play on your brain, nerves and everything else? So uh...when they told me you were on the phone uh...that did a lot to cheer me up. You know, babe, just you being on the phone."

"Well, you could have been cheered up before. I've been calling and calling. I finally quit and wrote you a letter. Did you get it?"

"Well, honey, I'm on a jet a lot right now so I wasn't able to get your calls and no, I didn't get the letter."

I really wondered about him not getting my letters–so many didn't get to him. I wondered if somehow I was being sabotaged. But who would be sabotaging me–and why? (I later suspected that Ruth Robinson intercepted my letters to Ray. I became even more suspicious after I read Lydon's book. I knew she had worked for Ray, but after I read the book, I found out that Ray had an affair with her for years.)

Ray said he had to go to the Union Court and bullshit–that he had had a lot of trouble. The union fined him, and he fought it and lost. If Ray thought he was right, he would fight for his belief even if there was no chance of him winning.

He wanted to see me, but my mom and I were going to take Lisa and Mitzi on a road trip to Silver Dollar City in Branson, Missouri. Branson wasn't the showbiz hot spot in 1974 like it is today. Ray eventually played "The Grand Palace" in Branson, but that was in the mid-'80s.

Lisa, Mitzi, Mom and I had such fun on our trip. We left early in the morning in my little V.W., packed to the brim with food and drinks for a picnic lunch. Our motel wasn't the greatest, but it had a pool. The weather was cold for June and the water was ice cold. The kids could take it, but I couldn't.

The next day we went all around Silver Dollar City. We went through Marvel Cave, and then the kids took a helicopter ride that thrilled them to death.

From there we went to my hometown in Southeast Missouri. We showed my kids the small house where I was born and Grannie's house where I lived until I was eight or nine. Then it was back home to St. Louis.

Before we left, Ray told me that he had two days off on the 20th and 21st–Thursday and Friday, and wanted to spend the time with us if I would let him. He always said it like that, sounding like a pitiful little boy.

I said yes I would love for him to come. I would be home on the 14th, but that I would be working on Thursday and Friday.

Ray said, "Uh oh."

"It's still alright if you don't mind staying by yourself 'til I get home. I know that's nothing new for you, or maybe I can cancel. I'll try."

"Well, babe. It wouldn't bother me to stay alone, you know that."

I told Ray I would be home from work by 1:30 p.m.

"Well, that would be groovy, Marci. That's fine, if it's fine with you?"

Ray said he would either be in Virginia or Augusta, Georgia. He wasn't sure which.

I asked if he would take a taxi or wait at the airport for me to pick him up. He said he would time his flight to arrive after I got off work. Then he said, "Oh, I forgot–you need to pick up the younguns."

He forgot that my kids were out of school for the summer and probably would go to New Orleans for eight weeks. I hated that, but I've always felt they should spend time with Henry and their relatives. I have never regretted it.

Some time earlier, Ray had sent me a Polaroid camera, and he asked me if it still worked. I told him it did and that I would have plenty of film when he got here. He liked taking pictures of us.

He said he'd make sure I heard from him the week before he came here just in case something unexpected came up. (He was worrying about Henry picking up Lisa and Mitzi).

He told me to enjoy myself in Silver Dollar City, and tell Lisa and Mitzi he called and said hello to them.

Lisa and Mitzi did go see their dad in New Orleans as planned. When Ray got here, we called Don and Colleen Eaker and they invited us to their home for dinner and that blackberry pie Colleen promised Ray.

We arrived in the early evening at Don and Colleens split level house. I took Ray up the stairs. They greeted each other and Colleen got a hug from Ray. Then I took him through the house to show him where the bathroom, living room, and other rooms were. They were amazed at how easily Ray adapted to his surroundings.

Out of the blue, Ray asked Don what he thought about cremation as opposed to in-ground burial. Ray knew I had donated my body to science. We had just discussed it on the drive to their house. After Don's initial shock, the question prompted an intense nose to nose conversation between Don and Ray–and that closeness remained throughout my relationship with Ray, some twenty-three years.

When Colleen served her delicious blackberry pie, Don said, "Sorry to say I think it's the worst one she ever made." Colleen thought so too, but Ray and I thought it was wonderful. After dessert, they broke out a bottle of Tia Maria liqueur that a friend had brought them from the Virgin Islands. When we finished our after-dinner drinks, we moved to the living room for more coffee, conversation and picture taking.

As I mentioned before, Don was a wonderful artist. He made beautiful wood table-top sculptures that he entered in art shows. Some won awards, and since those special pieces were not for sale, he still had them. When Don showed them to Ray, he was mesmerized. He lightly touched every one of them, but one in particular, the diving bird, he kept going back to, saying, "Don, let me see that one again."

Finally, he said, "Don, we're just gonna have to clear the air. You're either gonna have to sell me this sculpture or you're gonna have to make me one just like it. You just tell Marci how much it is, and give it to her and she'll see that I get it." Don, Colleen and their son Kerry had a little private discussion and decided to give it to him. Ray was ecstatic. He couldn't believe that they just gave him one of their award-winning art pieces.

Don said Ray told him later that he hand carried his precious bird sculpture to Los Angeles. I had wrapped it in lots of newspaper, placed it in a canvas bag and Ray carried it on the plane himself. When he got to his office on West Washington Blvd., he placed the diving bird in the glass case where he kept his special mementos.

Don snapped a lot of photos of Ray and me that night. One was of Ray looking at his newly acquired art piece and there were a few of me wearing the necklace that Don made from Ray's turquoise tie bar. Ray loved that necklace–just the fact that Don could make something so beautiful out of a simple tie bar fascinated him. It was Ray who suggested I wear it that night and I'm so glad I did. That picture is all I have left of my beautiful necklace. Some damned thief has it now.

There's one photo of me getting up from the couch and Ray is holding my wrist, trying to stop me. He said, "Marci, just sit down and keep your body still for a minute, baby." Ray often touched my hand or arm softly with a slightly possessive but gentle, "I'm so glad you're mine" touch.

Don and Colleen loved Ray with absolutely no reservation. Don said it was just fantastic having known Ray. He said he was so comfortable to be with. He wasn't Ray Charles–musician, celebrity. He was a guy who was interested in what *you* thought–what *you* were doing. Ray felt the same about Don. Years later he told me, "You know, babe, I still have that diving bird that Don Eaker gave me." It was very precious to him.

Don always felt comfortable talking to Ray. He said Ray would answer honestly almost anything that you asked him...his current events or even his childhood.

Don asked Ray once what he remembered when he was sighted as a kid of five or six. Ray said, "The sky is blue, the grass is green. My mother's head scarf and her apron were red."

Those were colors that he recalled, but he didn't know colors like chartreuse or hot pink–he never saw them.

I knew that he remembered his mother's long black hair. He loved her hair. Maybe that was one of the reasons he never wanted me to cut mine.

Not too long ago, Don and I were reminiscing about some of the things we did with Ray and the many conversations he had with him. Don remembered one particular discussion about Volkswagens and how Ray loved them. He told Don about the time he drove one on a military base where he was doing a show. He was driving and his passenger was telling him where to turn when an M.P. stopped him. Ray told him that he was appearing on base at the theatre and Don said, "He probably invited him to the show," and the military cop said, "Oh, well carry on Mr. Charles." The M.P. probably didn't even know that Ray was blind. If he did, he probably didn't believe it after seeing him driving around the base.

Don also talked about the time Ray rode his scooter down the street in New York City for a television show. We all saw him. Of course the streets were blocked off.

Ray told me that he sometimes rode the scooter on a track, following the sound of someone in front of him. He was so amazing. No wonder I loved him so.

Don said he remembered the SX-70 Polaroid camera that Ray bought for me. Don thought it was because "it did something" and Ray liked that. It was a hi-tech camera and very expensive for that era and for a Polaroid. It wasn't just an ordinary Polaroid camera–it was top of the line. Streamlined. It made a buzzing sound when the picture came out. Because it was a mechanical device, it was something Ray could relate to. He could operate it and he liked that.

Then Don mentioned the Frank Oma coffee mugs from Sepulva, Oklahoma that he and Colleen surprised us with. Ray's cup had ridges on it and mine was smooth. For some

245

reason, those cups were so special to Ray and me. We always used them. In fact, when we got home from our dinner visit with Don and Colleen that night, we had our coffee in those mugs, along with another piece of her delicious blackberry pie.

After our dessert, Ray decided he wanted to shower. When I handed him one of my brand new thick wash clothes, he said, "Babe, I need a hand towel. I can't wash with that. It's too small. I'm a man, honey."

I think he felt a lot bigger than he was. Even now, that memory makes me smile.

We had the house to ourselves until it was time for him to leave. We made good use of it. We walked around in the nude, lolled around in bed, bathed, ate and did some other things that you can't do when kids are around.

He was here for a couple of days that time. The next day, Friday, when I got home from work, I found Ray snoozing on the couch. After I showered, we had plenty of time to play our word games, watch Ray's game shows on television and talk. That's what usually got us into trouble–the talking–and this time was no exception.

"Ray, do you think it's alright? I mean, me being with you while you're married?"

"Ooooh, babe, are you gonna ruin our last day together?"

"Well, read St. Matthew and see what's gonna happen to us. I sure don't want to burn forever."

"Oh, I don't believe nuthin like that in the first place," Ray responded.

"Well, you read the Bible. Don't you believe it?"

Ray said, "I didn't read nowhere in the Bible where it said you were gonna...uh...burn forever."

"It says you're going to eternal fire, Ray. What does that mean?"

"Babe, I never saw that all the bad people in the world were going to an eternal fire."

My strict religious upbringing with Grannie, Aunt Reth and Uncle Leland, and studying the Bible endlessly, enabled me to be a good devil's advocate.

Ray said he had read the Bible all the way through and he never saw that. I told him he was like everyone else. He saw what he wanted to see.

He said he wasn't a scholar. He just read it and either accepted it or he didn't. He said that someone once asked him if he believed in the Virgin Mary, and he said he did 'cause the Bible said so, even though people asked "How can that be?" Ray said when you start analyzing the why's and where's and trying to reason with it, you get all kinds of different religions–Methodist, Baptist, Catholic, etc., because people make the Bible say what they want it to say.

I thought he did a good job of that too.

I said, "Well, what it says is clear and it says it right here, 'Everlasting fire.' It's eternal, Ray." Ray kept on arguing that he didn't see anything like that, even after I read it to him.

He said, "I don't think when God comes, He's gonna take a handful of people and let them live in serene dignity and the rest of us are gonna burn like hell...I'm sorry, honey. I just don't think he means..."

"Ray, you know damn well what he means. If you're doing something wrong, and you know it, you should stop it."

"Well, first of all Marci...I don't...I mean I can't say that I know it's wrong to love you."

I threw up my hands and said, "Oh My God, Ray!" Then I started laughing at him. "You know you aren't supposed to be married and have another woman."

"Well, I don't know," Ray said, "As I was reading the Bible, I saw where David did and Solomon did."

"Ray, that didn't make it right. David was wrong."

Ray was fighting me with words and not winning. He continued, "But David was one of God's most fav...you know, you read about the Star of David and all the Psalms of David. He was a top man."

I retorted, "Yes, and David lost his baby and had nothing but hell. He had to beg for forgiveness for what he did. Oh

Well! Maybe David was so involved he didn't know what he was doing."

"Bullshit," Ray said, "Ain't no way he could be king of a whole empire and not know what he was doin'."

"Well, that's the same way I feel about you, Ray."

"Right. I knew it'd hafta come back to me somehow."

I snuggled next to him, kissed him and loved him and we spent the afternoon making love, playing word games and drinking coffee from our Frank Oma mugs.

The next morning it was back to the airport for one more goodbye.

32
Cheating
❧❧

Ray called and asked me to call Don and Colleen to see if we could take them out to dinner when he came back. They were so excited and said to tell him that of course they would be delighted. Ray did not want to go to a casual restaurant–he wanted a very nice place, so I decided on Al Baker's. I knew Al and his wife, Mary, and their restaurant was one of the nicest in St. Louis.

I called and told Al that Ray and I and another couple were coming for dinner. He said we would be able to be seated immediately even though they didn't take reservations.

Don and Colleen picked us up in their cute little orange wood paneled V.W. station wagon. Colleen and I rode in the back seat, and Ray, as always, was in the front seat with Don. We valet parked the car, and Ray took my arm as we entered the restaurant. We were warmly greeted by Al and Mary. We chatted with them and then Al took us to the dining room and seated us immediately, as promised.

The piano bar was brimming with customers waiting for dinner so it was obvious to us that Al had been very gracious to Ray. Ray was impressed with the restaurant. The food was superb and the service was excellent. Our waiter was standing by in the shadows ready to light our cigarettes, pick up a dropped napkin, or do any other service that we might require. If Don raised his hand, a waiter appeared like magic, but he was never intrusive.

Al Bakers truly was an elegant restaurant. It's gone now. The building was razed and a new building occupies the site. I have wonderful memories, though, and not just of Ray. Lisa and Mitzi were both, on separate occasions, invited to be a guest bartender there. Knowing how to tend bar wasn't the criteria–being pretty was. Those were fun times.

When we finished with dinner, we went to the piano bar for a drink. The entertainer introduced Ray and asked if he would like to play a song. Ray politely declined, saying, "I would much rather hear you play." The piano player then honored Ray with his own rendition of "Georgia." Ray graciously thanked him.

Then the piano player said, "Ray, I don't know if you'll remember this, but I opened for you about three years ago,"and he named the place. Ray said that he did remember and he named two of the songs the man played.

Don said he was amazed. He said he guessed Ray picked up on the man's voice, and maybe his piano style, and that Ray was so kind to him.

We had such a nice time together–it was really a memorable evening and we were all in a great mood. On the way home, Colleen and I began to tease each other as we often did. She and I jokingly began calling each other "little bitch," which we had done before and had always done in fun. Once Don and Colleen had brought me a tee shirt from one of their trips that said, "I'm Not Just a Bitch, I'm The Bitch and I'm Miss Bitch to You." I kept that tee shirt for years just to remind myself who I really was.

After we said goodnight and they thanked Ray for a wonderful evening, we came in the house to get ready for bed. He brushed his teeth and got ready for bed while I poured us some coffee. Then I took my turn in the bathroom.

Ray was sitting on the side of the bed, smoking a cigarette and sipping coffee when I got into bed. I was getting comfortable when he abruptly said, "Marci, you have to call Colleen and apologize as soon as we wake up."

"Why?" I asked shocked to death.

"Because, honey, you must never, and I mean never, talk to your friend like you did tonight. That's wrong."

"She did it too," I said defending myself.

"I don't care. You have to apologize and don't do it again," he admonished.

I told him I would apologize, but that she would think I was crazy. He still insisted.

The next morning as I went to get our coffee and breakfast roll, he reminded me that I needed to call my friend.

Sure enough, when I apologized to Colleen, she laughed and asked why I thought I needed to apologize. I explained that Ray didn't like crass behavior from me and asked me never to act that way again. I promised him I wouldn't.

She said in her cute Texas accent, "Okay then, I won't either." But we continued joking around with the silly name calling over the years, we just didn't do it around "Brother Ray!"

Towards the end of 1974, I met a man who I was attracted to enough to date. I told Ray that I was seeing him. He was upset and asked me to meet him in Evansville, Indiana. I agreed, and he made the arrangements for me to come. Within a day or so, I was in Indiana with Ray. It's amazing how quickly he could make a decision when he was about to lose something that he wasn't quite ready to give up.

He said he didn't like me being with another man and asked me not to. I said that if he made some changes, I wouldn't–that I wasn't that involved yet, but that I could be because I liked this man. Of course, Ray being Ray, didn't make any promises to me.

During 1974, I went on a few more trips with Ray, but I was also seeing the other man.

Finally, on our last trip, I said, "Ray, I'm not doing this anymore."

He was shocked. "What are you tellin' me, Marci?"

I told him I had made a decision to be with someone else. I said, "This is painful. It's the same as it was in 1969. We've gotten nowhere. We're stagnant."

"Oooh, babe," he said sadly. "How long have you been see...never mind, don't tell me. Wow! Okay, baby. Can you at least tell me what happened?"

"Nothing, Ray. That's the problem. Nothing's happened and never will. You're still married."

"That's what you say, Marci. That's not me talking. Honey, tell me...can I...is there any way...anything I can do?"

"No, there's nothing you can do, Ray."

We held each other. I was crying. He was crying...and I left. His valet drove me to the airport. I boarded a plane and came home to St. Louis.

I was just as sad that day as I was when I drove down the freeway from L.A. to San Clemente, crying my heart out. That was 1969...this was 1974. Five years had passed and it was time for me to make a change, even though my heart couldn't bear to leave Ray.

He broke my heart in September of 1969, and broke off a little bit more here and there along the way. Even after all these years, it's never mended. It is functional, and I get by, but I've learned to live with a broken heart. Only occasionally does it flare up and become unbearable, and when that happens, I seclude myself and the tears flow. I suppose it's a cleansing of the soul process. Afterwards, I'm able to go on with my daily living—seemingly unscathed on the outside—but certainly damaged on the inside.

I started dating Patrick, (not his real name, but anyone who knew me then would know who he was). I most certainly will not pay homage to this man, however, and as I move along in my story, it will become understandable why I feel this way.

The first six months of our relationship was rocky, but as time went on, and we became more involved, we went out a lot and had fun together. We went to church, out to dinner, clubbing, and to other fun places. We even went to Don and Colleen's little tattoo shop where Patrick put his foot down about me getting a tattoo. I did get a period tattooed over a mole on my face, however, but that was the extent of it.

Patrick, my kids and I drove to Colorado for a vacation. We took camping gear and cooked our meals in different city parks. We went up on Pike's Peak, and I was terrified during the bus ride up the steep mountains. Patrick smoked and nearly fainted, but Lisa and Mitzi, as typical kids, were undaunted,

Driving in the City of Colorado Springs, I spotted a theatre with a billboard that said, "Currently Playing – Ray Charles and his Raeletts." As soon as I got to our motel I called the theatre. I didn't catch Ray, but I caught myself a whole lot of trouble. The call was on the bill when we checked out, and Patrick was livid. We got through it, though, and went on to Aspen, checked out the town, had lunch and drove through the high priced areas where the beautiful homes were. (We were trying to find movie stars' houses.)

My girls were still taking their summer vacations with their Dad. He took them everywhere–Disneyland, the beach, and one other special place that my kids referred to only as "The Island."

I've been told that the Island was a Mafia hideout, owned by the Mafia, but how true that is, I don't know. I do know, however, that it was across Lake Ponchatraine, off the beaten path and in a swamp area. It was surrounded by a wide body of water. When their car reached the water's edge, they would blink the car lights a certain amount of times, blow the horn in a signal fashion and someone would come in a canoe to get them. Lisa and Mitzi's cousins, Melissa and Maria, were always with them when they visited. They loved it.

There were two real houses on the island and three cabins. My kids and their dad stayed in a cabin that had an outside cold water shower.

Their dad bought them whatever water toys they wanted. (Well actually, he bought them anything they wanted.) And of course, Henry stocked himself with plenty of booze and marijuana. Mitzi said she and Lisa just thought they were rolling cigarettes.

When my kids were younger they would go on hikes in the dark and someone would put a sheet on and scare them. They played in the water, also, and chased the wild pigs that lived on the island. The last time the girls visited, there were wild boars there instead of the pigs. They said the boars were big, and had tusks and hairy faces. They chased my girls and scared them.

When Darlene left Henry, my kids never went back to the island, but they still went to New Orleans. They considered New Orleans home–and they still do. Even though Henry isn't there anymore, his spirit still is. Henry Soto was Mr. New Orleans. He loved that city. All New Orleanians feel that way. New Orleans is a special place for them. I once told my elderly sister-in-law that New Orleans was cold at Christmas time, and her reply, in typical New Orleanian style, was, "But Aad ratha be cold in New O'leans than any otha city in the world!" That was the general feeling of everyone who lived there.

Back to Ray. It was early September of 1975. I hadn't seen Ray for several months when I got a call from him telling me that he would be performing in St. Louis at Stegtons Restaurant on the 13th and 14th. He asked if I would please just come and talk to him–nothing else, he said, just talk–that it would mean so much to him just knowing I was there. I told him I couldn't go because I was still dating the other man. Ray and I were both sad. I still loved him so much. Even though I still loved him, there was no way I could be out three or four hours in the evening. That was out of the question.

He called when he got in town and asked me again to come. "No," I said. "I can't come." He was disappointed and sounded sad. Reluctantly, he told me he understood and that he would sing a song for me.

Don and Colleen went to the first show by invitation from Ray. I told them that Ray said he was going to do a song for me, and for them to listen closely and tell me if he did.

Their seats were great. They were escorted up to the front row, directly behind the piano and Ray. They practically had it to themselves–only one other couple at the other end–but the rest of the seats in the ballroom were filled.

These are Don's words verbatim describing the show:

"The band played a few songs. Then Ray came on. When he passed us I said, "Ray, we're right down here." He nodded and then probably did two-thirds of his program. Then he said, 'I ordinarily don't do dedications, but I have a dear friend here in St. Louis who couldn't be here for the show and I'd like to dedicate this song to her.' And uh...there were about a thousand people there and you could hear a pin drop when he started singing, "I Can't Stop Loving You."

Colleen said, "And boy, everyone was glued to him."

Don continued saying, "Before it was over, he was wiping his eyes. You literally could hear a pin drop. I mean, he had control over that audience."

Colleen said, "They must have been wondering who he was singing about...and we knew."

Don said, "Oh, at the end of that song he thanked the band and the Raeletts. Then he said, 'The only thing I can think of to say is, Don Eaker'...then he started singing, "Let's Go Get Stoned," and that was the end of the show. It was interesting. He did kind of dedicate two songs–one to Marci and one to me."

After the show, Ray invited them to his motel in Earth City for some coffee and conversation. The next morning, Don called and told me about the song dedication, how serious Ray was and that he cried as he sang to me.

Soon after I spoke to Don, Ray called. He asked me to come see him. I said I couldn't but he pleaded with me. He was good at that. He said, "Babe, I won't touch you. I'll behave myself. I just wanna be in the same room with you."

Finally, I agreed. I just wanted to touch him and smell his aroma. It had been a year or more since I had seen him.

We were so happy to be in each other's company. We sat on the side of the bed and talked. I touched his face and kissed him.

He pulled me next to him and, of course, the inevitable happened. I shouldn't have allowed that. Not only was I in a relationship but I didn't have any protection. I had been taken off birth control pills for medical reasons, so I left myself vulnerable to getting pregnant. When I expressed my fears to Ray, his response was, "It'll be okay, babe and maybe it wouldn't be such a bad thing."

I didn't feel that way.

We had another sad good-bye. He asked if I could come to the show that night, but I couldn't. He just nodded sagely as if he understood. But stark pain twisted his features, despair held his face. Dear God, this man could reach into my soul. Misery washed over me as I walked away from him, thinking I may never see him again.

Many years later, I was told by the owner of Stegtons that in the wee hours after the last show, Ray sat alone having his solitary dinner. Archie, the chef, was flattered to be cooking for Ray Charles so he didn't mind staying late. Sorrow panged my heart as the picture of Ray, sitting alone, flashed through my mind. I regretted that I hadn't been there with him.

He called before he left to say good-bye and tell me that I had made him so happy. By the end of October, *I* wasn't so happy. I realized I was pregnant.

My boyfriend Patrick, couldn't have children, so I knew who the father was.

"Oh My God! What will I do?" I panicked at first. Then I made a decision and acted on it immediately. I had an abortion at Regency Park Clinic performed by Dr. Escondido.

Within two weeks I was okay. I didn't even tell Ray–there was no reason to. I definitely wasn't having a baby. I struggled raising my girls and couldn't imagine having another child. I never ever wanted kids with different fathers. I've never regretted my decision.

Years later, I told him. He said, "Don't you think I had a right to know that?" I answered one word, "No." He laughed and said, "You don't mince words do you, babe?"

Now after reading Michael Lydon's book, I'm sure I made the right decision. Who knows–Ray might have gone to court to prove he wasn't the father, and even if he hadn't done that, it seems like the women who had a baby with Ray got the axe. Honestly, the heartbreak that I would have had to endure wouldn't have been worth a million dollars.

There was no gold at the end of the rainbow for me. Like his song, "Sunshine" (another one of my favorite songs) says, "But I don't mind. My pot of gold is my peaceful life and wonderful family."

The next year, my boyfriend, daughters and I went to Mexico City for three days. We saw the Moon and Sun Pyramids at Chitzen Itza. Mitzi climbed all the way to the top of the Sun, which was the tallest pyramid. She looked like a speck.

Patrick had gotten angry at me during breakfast and had gone back to our hotel. My girls and I were talking to other people on one of our tours and he must have gotten jealous. We were glad he wasn't with us. We had so much fun, and with him not there, there was no tension.

We went by bus to Tasco, where we visited a silver mine and bought silver jewelry, then continued on to Acapulco the next day. It was there, in that beautiful town, that I had the biggest scare of my entire life! I almost lost my precious Lisa. I had gone to the bathroom for just a minute, and that quickly, the waves pulled her out to sea. The beach patrol boat rescued her and when she got out, the waves got her again! She was pulled back into the boat. All the time Mitzi was yelling "Lisa!!! Lisa!!" but she couldn't help her.

When I got back to the beach my kids weren't there. I was worried when I saw a woman being pulled out of the ocean by the beach patrol and I panicked. I ran to both pools, then up at least ten flights of stairs to our room. Thank God! They were there! Then they told me what had happened. We wrapped our arms around each other, fell to our knees, crying and praying, so grateful everyone was alright. Needless to say, they didn't get in the ocean again. It was the scariest thing that had ever happened to me. The thought that I could have been bringing my precious baby Lisa's body home was heart wrenching. I've spent a lot of time in my life contemplating that whole incident, and I will be eternally grateful for the happy ending to that story.

We were back home again, and soon the phone rang. Ray was calling to see why I hadn't been answering the phone. I told him I had just returned from Mexico.

He said, "Oh, wow! Colorado last year and Mexico this year. You're traveling a lot aren't you?"

"Well, Ray, remember you had promised to take me, but never got around to it."

His response surprised me.

He said, "Yeah, I should have done that. I think about that and...I feel guilty...you know, about the whole thing."

"Why do you feel guilty, Ray?" I asked.

"I...I...just had to say that. Now I've said it and I'll shut up...but...I...I think I would have died if I hadn't said that."

He was so dramatic!

That's how hard it was for Ray to ever admit that he was wrong or that he wished he had handled something differently. He really hated me being with another man and not seeing him at all. But I felt like he created that problem for himself. I just couldn't sit idly by and let him walk on me, no matter how my heart ached. I had to think of my future, and I knew that I had no real future with Ray.

33
Free Like the Birds

Even though I was not seeing Ray during this time, he still called me often. Once when he called, he casually mentioned that he could be in St. Louis if I wanted him to be. I told him I couldn't because I was getting ready for a trip to Florida. I wouldn't have agreed to see him anyway, it was just too difficult, but he certainly never gave up trying.

Patrick had bought a new Lincoln Continental and my mom and I drove it to Florida, stopping off in New Orleans to pick up my kids who were there visiting their father. While there, we visited with Henry and all of my in-laws and then Lisa, Mitzi, Mom and I continued on to Miami Beach.

We stayed five days. One day, we flew to Grand Bahama. Mom didn't go—she was afraid to fly over "The Devil's Triangle." The girls and I had such fun! We shopped at the International Square, where there was every kind of shop imaginable, and then took a bus to the beach. All too soon our time was up and we had to get to the airport for our flight back to Miami. We had a few more days of sunning on the beach in Miami, then it was time for the long drive back to St. Louis.

Ray continued to call at least once a week or every other week. On one of the calls, he said he would be in St. Louis performing at the Chase Club and wondered if I could come to the show. I told him I didn't think so, but it just happened that I was able to go. Don and Colleen picked me up. Ray knew they were coming, but he didn't think I would be there.

As his valet walked him down the aisle toward the stage, and he passed by me, I stood and said, "Hi, sweetheart!" Those were his favorite words from me, and he was so surprised.

He stopped and turned, facing the direction of my voice. Then he said, "I heard that. I heard you, babe."

The show was its usual perfection. Close to the end, he said, "This is for you, babe," and he sang "Am I Blue." Some of the words to that song go like this, "There was a time, I was the only one, and now I am, the sad and lonely one."

I was emotional when Don, Colleen and I went backstage to see him. I held on to him–kissed and hugged him–but all too soon I had to leave so that I would be home when Patrick came by. Ray was reluctant to let me go, but I had to get home.

He called the next day to thank me for coming to the show and to plead with me to come to The Chase to see him before he left. He said that he would catch a later flight if I could come. But I didn't go. Ray was sad.

I'd cheated on Patrick once, and it was painful as hell. I didn't want to do it again. Besides, I had a man who treated me well and took care of me, and I took to that like a duck to water.

Now the kids and I had money to do things. We had a great Christmas. Finally, I had someone to help me when my car wouldn't start, and help me with all the little things. In general, life was so much easier.

Patrick and I got engaged, and that really upset Ray. He said he was distraught. He asked when I was getting married and I told him I didn't know.

In my heart, I knew I really didn't want to get married. Something wasn't right, but I couldn't figure out what. One thing that really bothered me was that I thought Patrick was over-sexed. I hated that. One little kiss would ignite a flame in him that could only be quenched in the bedroom. I enjoyed making love, but this was just too much.

Don and Colleen liked Patrick, but didn't feel the same way about him as they felt about Ray. They loved Ray. They did get along with Patrick, though. In fact, after Don and Colleen moved to Wichita Falls, Texas, we drove down to visit them.

Our visits to Don and Colleen were another thing that upset Ray. He wanted to know why I would take some other man to Don and Colleen's home. Funny, it was as if Ray thought I didn't live unless he was in my life. I had only seen him twice in three years, but he still had an impact on me like no other man ever did–or ever will.

Patrick and I left Texas with a special traveler in the back seat–a beautiful Afghan hound dog. Don gave him to me. His name was Vladimir. Don neglected to tell us that he would bite and that a rolled up newspaper just pissed him off. So after he bit Lisa, Mitzi and me and got us whipped into shape, he lived the rest of his life ruling the roost with his not *royal*, but *loyal*, subjects, the Soto girls.

Ray called to tell me that he was playing at Stegtons again and could I please come. My answer was the same as always, "No, sweetheart, I can't come." By this time, Don and Colleen were living in Texas so they wouldn't be there either.

Ray said, "You know, honey, this place in St. Charles is a helluva nice place. You know...I mean who would ever think of St. Charles. But really and truly, I hafta tell you, honey...the food is not just cooked. It's done very well. And it's near a town called Earth City or some such. Who would ever think...most folks would think, 'I'm going to St. Louis,' but you gotta know about this place to come out here. I must say from an entertainer's standpoint, it's very nice." Then he paused for a moment and finally he quietly said, "Marci, will I ever see you again?"

I told him that I had finally made a decision that had taken me seven years to make, because he was always there to interrupt, but that I intended to stick with it.

He said, "Well, now I've heard you and I guess as long as I can find you, I'll never stop trying."

"I know, but Ray, I have to have a life. I can't just be frozen until you come around or call me. I can't live like that any more."

"Babe, I guess the only way I'll stop trying to be with you is if I can't find you and nobody knows where you are. If that happens, I'll just be shut out, but that's the only way."

"You have to accept it, Ray. You have to. You have your memories and your dreams."

"It's not the same, babe. You know Marci, I'll tell you something...I...I never know if we'll see one another again. That's why every minute that I'm with you, in my mind, I treat it as though it were the last time. Honest to God I do. Everything is magnified. Everything. Everything we do is magnified. I didn't take it lightly, babe."

"I didn't either, Ray. You're my true love. I just can't live like I did before–there was just too much anticipation and anxiety."

I told him that sometimes I liked to be alone, that I didn't want Patrick to be there. But then I felt like a horse's ass when I was aloof to him.

"Oooh, Marci...you're something. You really are. God knows you are and damn it, I want to see you. Anyway uh...yeah you amaze me. You're truly different...God knows that's true. You are a different woman. I guess that's another reason why I dig you, babe. You're unique and I like that."

I asked in what way. He chuckled and said, "You can say some of the cutest things. And uh...and I like it, you know. I also like to read things in many ways. And I've been able to watch you...you know. Now you're very seasoned, just like I like a woman–which shows you again what time can do."

I told him that at one time, I thought I couldn't live unless I had a part of him with me–that all I ever felt I had was a small part of him. At one time, I thought all of this was my fault. Because I instigated our initial meeting, I felt that I had to take what I got. I told him that he taught me himself how to live without him, just by the sheer absence of him.

He responded with, "I dunno, babe. You know what I think about now, is...if I thought I could just...just...be happy without...but, you see, I can't...can't separate myself from my music."

"I know that, Ray." I was shocked that he even thought something like that, much less said it. "I would *never* expect you to separate yourself from your music. The first thing I fell in love with was your music."

"I realize that, Marci, but I also know 'cause I've been through it now, that it's hard to expect a woman, and particularly when she begins to get older, to adjust to my lifestyle."

He knew he couldn't control himself in connection with his music–there was too much temptation on the road for him to experiment with. He knew that I wouldn't be able to cope with the absence, let alone all of the other distractions that I didn't have a clue about until after his death.

Ray went on to explain that in order for me to get a better picture of his life, "See," he said, "think of it this way. Music is not separate from me. It's not something that I do to make a living. It's something that's a part of me. It's like someone saying, 'I'm gonna separate you from your liver.' It can't be done."

Ironically, twenty-seven years after that, he would be dead of liver disease–at least that's what he told me his illness was when I spoke to him for the last time in 2004.

After all of the music conversation, he said something that surprised me to death. These are his words verbatim:

"Marci...I...I guess...I suppose...I dunno...I've been having some problems."

"Like what?" I worried.

"Oooh, ain't nuthun," he said.

"Don't do that to me, Ray. Tell me please..." His next comment knocked me for a loop.

He said, "Well...I...I...frankly...er...uh like the birds. I guess I'm...I'm free like the birds out there."

"What?!" That's all I could say.

"Yeah, babe. It's pretty much over," he said.

Those were the words I had been wanting to hear for so long–and now it was too late for me. I was committed to someone else.

"Why did you wait so long?" I asked. "Now it's too late for me."

"Well uh...I haven't waited. You know like I said...it...it's a funny thing about the clock, babe. It's that clock, really, you know time solves a lot of things."

We talked about me being forty years old. He said he couldn't get me past thirty, and that's how I would always be to him–his petite thirty year old baby.

Thank goodness he can't see me now. I'm seventy-two years old and not so petite.

I asked if there was another woman involved. He said no. He said that the negotiations had been going on for about two months and that he told his children the truth about his divorce.

I asked if it would be in the news. He said he didn't think so. I don't remember reading about it, or seeing it on television. And with Ray, just like everything else in his past, it was over and never mentioned again.

He continued calling me from different cities, wanting me to let him come to see me. One time he said he would be in Memphis, Tennessee and would have some days off after his gig and he would like to spend those days in St. Louis if I would see him. He said if I would give him just one hour, he would take it. That one hour would be worth it to him.

I said, "No, if all you wanted was a one hour rendezvous with me, you should have left me in New Orleans. That's all I expected then. But you wanted more, and it turned into nothing. I don't want to mess up what I have."

Ray said, "I know, babe...I guess it's some form of sacrifice or something...that's a poor word, I s'pose. But many times for something sweet, it always seems to cost a little something."

"Yes," I said, "but if Patrick found out I even talked to you, that would be it. I don't want to lose him because I know *you* don't want to take care of me. But *he* does. I'd be a damn fool to do something like that."

"Well, let me put it this way," Ray coaxed, "I feel that I am sound enough in my mind and if I think that things are right, I don't feel that someone can find out something like that if I really don't want them to...uh...unless somebody says, 'Hey, listen–I'm gonna get a tailman, just to tail Ray Charles everywhere he goes and if he goes to the toilet, let me know. But short of that, there's just too many ways to get the job done!'"

"Ohhh! My God Ray! Nooo!"

"I didn't mean...I'm just saying...tellin' you a fact, merely telling you I wanna see you. Now you can say, 'Well I don't give a shit what you want and I definitely don't wanna see you.' Alright, honey, you know how you feel. You know what you wanna do."

He continued, "I can only tell you what I'm feeling, and I know that what you're thinking is absolutely one hundred percent opposite of what I'm thinking. I think I've got sense enough to understand that."

Again I told him that I wanted more than he could offer me, which was no security whatsoever. "I'm not condemning you for it. I'm just telling you what I know."

He said, "No, that's what you say. I didn't say that."

"Well you tell me something different then!" I said.

"That ain't gonna do no good 'cause you'd say, "I don't wanna hear that shit.' You know I know you–no matter how I try to prove it." He was right. I would have said that.

Ray abruptly changed the subject, as he was prone to do if he thought I might get agitated. He asked how my brother was, I said he was okay.

"Well, I...I...always like to ask. I really like Don. As a matter of fact, I always remember the first time I...I met him. He picked me up at the airport. That was around the first of 1969."

I said, "Yes, he did and took you back."

Ray said, "Now I hafta tell you something abou...about that. This is just a little side note. I remember it well, 'cause I, you know when I first came to see you in St. Louis, I had fear. I... you know...I didn't know what the hell was gonna happen, how he was gonna take to me...I mean, after all, you are the man's sister. And uh...oh I was thinking everything, ya know, 'cause I just didn't know."

I said, "I didn't know you had thoughts like that." I was surprised.

"Oh sure," Ray continued, "you know. Yeah, I had thoughts like that. But then once he started talking to me, you know, and making jokes about you, I felt better. But I hafta tell you, I was very worried at first.

"Oh, Ray, you didn't have to be afraid."

"It's one thing, babe, for you to have felt one way, but it's another thing when it comes down to how your brother might have felt. It could have been totally the opposite of the way it was. You know, he could have been very uptight about us and...."

"I'm sorry you had to go through that," I said.

He continued, "So I figured I don't know how this is gonna go. But after Don started...started joking and carrying on about you, I said, Oh it's gonna be alright. I'm not gonna get into no trouble."

Ray must have been dying to be with me–or very brave–or crazy as hell. He was so nervous, and I had no idea. As I look at that situation now, I can see where he would be afraid. I didn't think how apprehensive he would feel as a black man coming to the Midwest to meet the brother of his white girlfriend. I wish I had been more reassuring to him, but I didn't have a clue how fearful he felt.

After he told me about his fears, he said, "Now, what am I gonna do...now you tell me this Marci, what am I going to do uh...uh...you know...when...when it comes time for me to hear, "Oh, hi sweetheart!" Now what am I gonna do for that? I mean who's...you know?"

I finished his question, "Who's gonna say that to you?"

"That's right."

"Well," I suggested, "Maybe you can teach somebody."

"Huh! Oh shit! Ain't nobody gonna say that like you do, Marci. You know that. I mean, honey, that's you!"

"You haven't seen me in a few years Ray, but if you remember, I wasn't always sweet."

"Yeah, but honey, those are the things I...I must remember about you. I like to remember what feels good to me, what sounds good to me. Like, you know, if I touch you and uh...put my arms around you and...and feel your heart beat close to mine. That's what I like to think about. That's very good for me. Or to hear you say, "Hi, sweetheart," those are the special things about you that I love."

I asked what he thought would have happened if we had spent more time together, really lived together, would we still have the feelings we have?

His response was, "Yeah. Of course. I think it would be even better now 'cause you've settled down a lot. Far more than I ever wanted you to in the beginning. I think the only thing, Marci...that led us astray was really...I...I felt...I really felt like I...was...uh...I don't know the right word...I felt...like... uh insecure."

I said, "In other words, you're telling me that all along you felt that way. So I messed it up from the very beginning and it was too late right then."

"No! No! No!" he tried to straighten out what he said, but he never did convince me.

When I relisten to what he said now, I can understand why he felt that way. He never knew if I would leave him or not. I could leave him anywhere–any moment–at the drop of a hat if he said something that would make me get frustrated and fed up. I guess that was because *I* was also insecure.

❧

Ray remembered every conversation we had, and was always concerned about my family. No wonder I loved him so. He always asked about the kids. He said, "Last time I talked to you, Lisa was having knee problems and had to stop dancing."

I told him that Lisa had Osgood Schlatter's disease. It's when the quadriceps muscle pulls through the knee and away from the shin bone. It is quite painful and is usually caused by a growth spurt.

When he asked what the girls were doing, I told him, "Well they're still taking piano. They had a recital but Lisa has such stage fright that she actually shakes and gets sick, so I didn't let her go. Because she didn't go, Mitzi didn't go either."

"Their instructor told me that she was so disappointed because they are her two most progressive students–Lisa was number one and Mitzi was number two."

Ray said, "Alllrrright!!"

Then he said, "Well, babe. I guess I'd better get off. Are you sure I can't...can't see you just once more?"

"Oh Ray, once more...always once more. I don't think so..."

"You remember," he whispered softly into the phone, "I love you, baby".

I was never convinced of that, but I do know that we could never totally be apart. Ray and I had sort of a sad love affair. We wanted so badly to be together, but were too afraid of one another to really make it work.

34
The Betrayal

This chaper is the hardest one for me to write. What happened during this time is devastating still, even though it happened so many years ago. It's something I will never be able to forget. It has made me so sick I have thrown up several times throughout the years, and has angered me to the point of wanting to do bodily damage—or worse!

There are no words to express the agony I have suffered over this incident. There is no forgiveness in my heart for the person who committed this act—and there never will be. Frankly, I haven't forgiven myself for being so unaware of what was happening, and I've spent my life trying to make up for it.

Remember when I commented to Ray about what a wonderful thing I had with Patrick? At the time, I believed it. It wasn't true. Not true at all.

This is what happened.

Patrick had spent the night with me, as he had done many times before. But this night was different. When he left for work at 5:00 o'clock in the morning, Lisa immediately appeared at my bedside, visibly shaken. I asked what was wrong, thinking she just got scared by a noise or something. I told her to get in bed with me.

"No, Mom! Listen!" she said, very emotional, "I woke up and Patrick was bending over my bed, lifting my cover. When he realized I was awake, he left and came back upstairs. I waited till the clock went off and he left for work to come up here."

I got up, held her and tried to calm her down. Oh my God! I couldn't believe what I was hearing. I asked her if anything strange had happened before and she said no.

I was in shock and angry as hell.

We had been dating for three years! I was in disbelief and I couldn't wait to confront him. At three o'clock in the afternoon, he came to my house. The first thing I said was, "What the hell were you doing in Lisa's room last night?"

He very calmly said, "I heard a noise and I went down to check. Then I covered her up."

"Well, you woke her and scared the hell out of her. Don't you ever do that again!"

When my kids got home from school, he apologized to Lisa for frightening her and he explained what he was doing. She seemed to accept his explanation, but later she said it still made her nervous when she saw his car in the driveway. I told him that he couldn't spend the night again until we all became more comfortable, if ever.

I explained the situation to everyone I was close to. I asked my brother, my mother, Don and Colleen–all of them said "No, I don't think Patrick would have had bad intentions."

So time went on and Patrick would come here to eat and sometimes he would stop by after work. But I wasn't okay. Something was eating away at me and I couldn't help it. I became irritable towards him and I just didn't want him around.

My mom said, "You'd better get Patrick out of your life, Marci. I don't know if you realize it, but you leave the table as soon as he sits down. You can't stand him."

I said, "I know, mom. I have that sick feeling inside of me that's telling me he's guilty." But I couldn't just break up with him and let it go. I felt compelled to make him pay–even at the discomfort of my children.

Finally I convinced him to take a polygraph. I told him that the kid's dad told me that any good liar could pass it, and Patrick believed me. Actually, no one told me that. I just wanted him to take it and I would have said whatever it took to get him to.

We went to Wells Fargo. I sat in the waiting room until he was finished. I could tell by the look on Patrick's face that it didn't turn out as he expected. The man who administered the test called me into his office and showed me the questions, Patrick's answers and the results. It wasn't good. Patrick was guilty, but in my heart, I already knew it. Even if he would have passed the polygraph, I would have known better.

I brought the paper with the results home with me to file and keep in case I needed it at a later date. I still have it.

As soon as I returned home, my kids and I discussed what we were going to do. Christmas was only a few days away, and they really wanted this to be a normal Christmas with all our relatives here enjoying the holiday. They didn't want any upheaval, so together we decided that we would have Christmas as normal as possible and afterwards he would be gone forever.

Even though we found out about Patrick before he had a chance to really do anything worse, I still feel enormous guilt. I guess I always will.

He really was a terrible man. I was cleaning downstairs shortly after he left and noticed that he had gone downstairs and unlocked a window before he left. It had to have been purposely unlocked. It didn't just happen–we were really careful about making sure our doors and windows were secure.

A few months later, I heard a noise beside the house, and a car idling on the other side of the street. I opened the door and a big man, his size, went running fast through my front yard to the car and left. The next morning I checked for footprints in the snow. Sure enough, there were big footprints by our windows.

I called the police but they couldn't do anything without proof. I didn't put much credence in them anyway. I knew that I would have to handle anything that happened myself–and I knew that I could. I had a loaded, registered pistol and I knew how to use it, and I was not afraid to do so.

Nine years later, I got a call from a panicked Lisa, "Mom, Patrick's here!" She was tending bar at Bogart's Club and had to serve him. I called right back and asked for him. I said, "Get your ass out of there now! I never want my daughter to look up and see your face looming at her again! I still have that paperwork from the polygraph test and I'll be at Chrysler in the morning to show your boss. If you ever see Lisa again, you take your ass the other way."

He said he didn't know she worked there and wouldn't go in there again.

I said, "No matter where you go, until you die, if you see her you leave!"

Fortunately, I never had to follow through with my threat. Patrick was smart enough to know I wasn't bluffing and Lisa never saw him again.

Years after that incident, I got an envelope with the return address of his former apartment on it. I opened it, and Lisa's drivers' license, that she thought she had lost, was in it with a note that said, "I found this in a ceiling light fixture."

Patrick had stolen her drivers' license! What a creepy perverted pedophile he was–and still is. They don't ever stop. They need to be dead. It makes me furious that there are so many missing and murdered children, and inevitably they're always surrounded by those contemptible, malicious perverts.

I have a solution. Don't put them on death row for forty years–actually put them to sleep. There would be a definite change in their behavior if they knew, *for sure*, they would *die* if they molested a juvenile. They would be afraid. But it has to be a proven fact that it would happen. If, indeed, it ever happens, the rest of the perpetrators would think before unleashing their careless and malicious desires. I did *not* say sick desires. I think of *cancer* or a *heart attack* when I say sick. Desires are just *that*. Mean, cruel pedophelia or predatory desires.

I feel *that* way about all abusers–animal, elderly, spousal, mentally handicapped–all of them. I wish I could be in charge of punishment for all of them. There would be no contest. I would be the best punisher ever. I would do to them what they did to their victims. Having been molested by an uncle at age 4, I know that the mental scars remain forever. The vision of me having my panties removed and sat up on a horse feeding trough in our barn still crosses my mind...and I'm seventy-two years old.

৵৵৵

So here I was again back to square one. All alone with two little girls–and scared to death once again.

Having my children to care for instilled in me an innate drive to persevere. Blessed with my mother's strong constitution, I knew that I could do it. We would be okay–but most of all, we'd be safe.

Ray's book, *Brother Ray* came out in 1977, but I hadn't read it yet because I couldn't have it in the house while Patrick and I were together. Naturally, I was very curious about it.

When I finally read it, overall I found it to be well written. But I didn't know the Ray in that book. My Ray didn't curse much or get so specific about sex and a woman's anatomy.

I enjoyed reading all of it, with the exception of the chapter on women. I especially hated the part that said something about "a hen house with many chickens and one rooster." When I read that, my ears were steaming.

Oh my God! I couldn't believe that my quiet, sweet man could say something so Goddamned cocky and stupid.

I had to call him. "Well," I said. "I just read about the many chickens and only one rooster! So who the hell are you–Mister Cock-a-Doddle-Do?"

His dreaded response was, "Ohhhh, Marci! Babe, that was twenty years ago. That's some twenty-year-old shit, Marci." That became his mantra over the years and a phrase that I have heard more times than I can count.

The irony with the chicken and rooster statement was that I had always considered the old children's book, *The Little Red Hen,* my biography. I felt like I was the worker, and no one lifted a finger to help me.

I told Ray that I had broken up with my boyfriend, but I didn't see him until a few months later. I was going out, dating and having fun, and I wasn't really eager to have Ray breaking my heart again. Besides, I was reading and re-reading his book and trying to sort through my emotions about the kind of man the character in the book portrayed. That character certainly was someone I didn't know. There was one exception, however, the way he treated women. I recognized the pattern. The same careless abandonment that happened when he invited me to live in Californaia was the same thing he had done to some of those women.

My initial reaction was shock and then anger. *Well, Brother Ray! As far as I'm concerned, that was some over-and-done-with shit, and it wasn't happening to me again! Absolutely not!*

Although I was not seeing Ray, I was frequently talking to him on the phone. I continued asking him questions about the book. It always irritated him when I made a remark about something he had written.

It seemed to me as if he were trying to burn some of the women–one in particular. He said she would have come out better off money-wise had she not taken him to court. Who was he kidding? He would not have given her more money and she knew it. She did the right thing. I could identify with the way she felt, in fact, that's another reason I never wanted a child with him. I knew how frugal he was.

As I read the beginning of his book, I was saddened by his early life–his little boy years, his adolescent years and all the way through his pre-adult years. I had never known anyone who'd had such a miserable life so full of heartbreak. It just never seemed to end.

I asked why I wasn't in the book. His answer was, "Well babe, you were with someone else at the time. That might not have gone over too well. And honey, those people in the book were long before I met you."

What he didn't tell me was that a whole new harem of "those people" had accumulated about the time he met me. I was an unwitting member of that harem, which, of course, I found out about in Lydon's book after Ray's death.

As I read on and discovered how many children he had, I

called and asked him if he thought God whispered in his ear, "Brother Ray, I want you to multiply and fill the earth."

He laughed, but he knew that I was giving him a dig.

Later, I discovered that he had disseminated his seed all over the world. Ray was a worldwide baby-maker.

Maybe that comes from having been so alone all his life, and perhaps wanting to leave something of his biological self for posterity. He had already given the world his legendary music. I guess it wasn't enough for him. I felt that he was thoughtless, careless, selfish and certainly irresponsible. But he didn't stop. He continued right on making babies, but not with me. Thank God!

He called to say he would be performing at the Barn Dinner Theatre and would the kids and I please come and bring any friends who wanted to come. What he really wanted was to be in my house, on that lumpy Goodwill bed again.

He said I didn't need to pick him up at the airport. He had his driver with him, but he didn't know how to tell him where I lived. I said I would meet him at the exit off I-270 and Big Bend and they could follow me home. When I asked what the rental car would be, he said a blue green "pony ac." That's how he pronounced Pontiac.

They followed me home. The first thing his driver said when he entered my house was how pretty it was.

Ray said, "She's a good decorator." I don't know why he said that. How would he know either way? He commented often about objects that he would pick up and look at, and he always noticed how clean I kept my house.

We were happy to be together. Ray said, "It's like old times," and it was. It was wonderful.

The next evening was his concert. I drove Ray and me to the Barn Dinner Theatre and got us lost.

"Oh my God, Ray!" I cried, "I'm so lost. What am I gonna do?"

He tried to calm me, "Its' okay, honey. The band will warm up the audience. Obviously, nuthin can happen without me.

Just pull over and read your directions again. We'll be alright, baby."

I did and we made it on time. I got all nervous for nothing– but that's just me. He was fine. He was always very patient with me.

Band members were certainly not allowed to be late and Ray, being the perfectionist that he was, very diligently obeyed the rules of the road. But, obviously, when you're Mr. Super Cocka-Doodle-Doo, you can do whatever the hell you wanna do.

Of course, everyone loved the show and afterwards we came home and gave the Goodwill mattress a whirl. Ray left early the next morning. I didn't have to drive him–his driver came in the rented "pony ac." I'm not sure what this man's function was. He might have been something more to Ray–maybe a friend. Who- ever he was, he was the man whose phone number Ray gave me, telling me that if I ever needed him and couldn't reach him, this man could locate him for me. I never used that number.

In May, Ray was here again for Mother's Day weekend. What a fun time that evening was, laughing and talking and playing the piano. Lisa was sixteen and Mitzi was fourteen. Ray hadn't heard them play the piano since they were little girls.

Lisa wasn't taking lessons anymore. It was a shame because she played well. She told me years ago, and I told Ray, that she was going to get a hatchet and chop up all the pianos she could find. That's how much she disliked piano lessons.

Ray said, "Wow, Lis –," that's what he called her, "You're gonna put me out of business."

Mitzi liked playing the piano so she played a song called, "Blue Boogie" and one more Boogie song.

He was shocked. "Mitz...Mitz. I didn't know you could do that!!! Wow! I don't know what to do. Wow! Honey, that's very good."

Mitzi said, "Your turn."

Ray laughed and said, "You couldn't wait to say that, could you? I love that, Mitz. I really do."

Everyone was laughing and having fun.

I said, "Now you hafta top that, Ray."

"Wow. Oh no. There's no way I can top that, honey. No, no. That's an impossibility," Ray said as he started picking out the notes to Mitzi's Blue Boogie.

I recognized the tune, "Oh, he's playing Blue Boogie."

He had never heard that song before, and he just played the hell out of it. We were jumping, dancing, snapping our fingers and clapping–really getting into the rhythm. He took Mitzi's little song and made it his own, like he did every piece of music he came into contact with.

When that song was over, he started playing Silver Bells. He said, "I'll bet you can't recognize it 'cause it's the wrong time of year."

Mitzi said, "I know it."

"What is it, Mitzi?" Ray said.

"City Sidewalks and I know how to play it."

"Yeah, okay, baby," he said.

I asked him to play "Sunshine."

"How does it go?" he asked.

I hummed the melody for him.

"Oh, I can't play that," then he started playing and singing it. But he had forgotten the words.

"I love that song," I said as I started singing the words.

He joined me, struggling with the words. We got through it. The words were coming back to him as we got further into the song–with my help. That was just one more lovely soulful song by the Genius...and he truly was.

Ray and I harmonized on "Cryin' Time" as we always did, but I started off singing the wrong part!!

"You got to sing the top part, honey. You can't sing my part." With one finger, he pounded the key that he wanted me to sing.

"Okay, I have it," I said as we harmonized. I said I thought we sounded pretty good. He agreed saying, "Everything we do together is good, babe."

He was completing an album, and sang a new song that he was presently working on. He said it was the last song on the album.

"You like it?" he asked.

"Yeah, I like that. I'm ready for that one," I answered.

Every time we played the old upright and sang together, we had such a good time. We were rockin' that night.

Thank God, I have that whole wonderful time on tape.

We almost didn't though, because I couldn't get the tape recorder to work. "I can't get this damn thing to work," I told him. Here–you look at it Ray." I handed it to him.

"Honey, I don't know how to fix it. Did you check the batteries?" he said, handing it back to me.

"Oh," I said. "I'll go get them."

It worked, and now I have a priceless tape of the most memorable Mother's Day ever! Nearly thirty years later, I can listen to, relive, and picture in my mind that day with the three people I loved most–Lisa, Mitzi and Ray. What a joyous moment to have captured on tape for me to relive, at the flick of a button, and to be with me forever.

35
A New Used Car

∂◦∂

A few months after Mother's Day, I called Ray. We talked for a while–just about things in general.

He asked, "Has Lisa left yet for work?"

"No," I answered.

"What time does she go," he questioned.

"She said she's going in at three," I said. "It's different every day."

"Oh," he said. "You mean she doesn't have the same time every day?"

"No," I said.

"That's strange," he said. "So, whatever time she goes in today, it won't necessarily be the same tomorrow, you're saying?"

"Right," I said. *God! What was taking him so long to get this?*

Lisa said she was leaving, and asked who I was talking to. I told her Ray.

"Oh. Hi, Ray," she said as she ran out the door.

"She's just now leaving?" Ray asked.

"Yeah, she's gotta go to school for something."

"Oh," he said, "And she's gonna come back home before she goes to work? My goodness, honey, isn't it almost...What is it–around two-thirty?"

"Ray, she has to be at work at five."

"Oh, I thought you said three."

"I did say three, but she had to be at school at three and work at five."

Ray said, "Well what time...school oughta be getting out about three, won't it?"

"Honey, school's out now. Mitzi will be home soon." I don't know why he was so interested in what was going on here, but he always was. He would stay on the phone and ask questions until he was satisfied.

Finally, I got around to asking him what I really called for–would he be willing to help me get a different car.

His answer to that question was, "Well, at the moment I don't have six thousand dollars I can give you. That's about what it costs now."

"Ray, I was thinking about a used car. My car's completely torn up. It just won't run. Thank God Lisa has one."

"Say what?!" Oh boy–that statement perked his ears up. "Lisa's got a car?" he asked.

"Yes, Ray. She has a nineteen seventy Nova. She needed it to get to work."

Here we go. "Well, how'd you manage that?"

"I didn't manage it, honey. Her dad's girlfriend gave it to her."

"Oh, really." That seemed to surprise him and soften him a bit. Maybe it embarrassed him too.

I repeated that I had to do something–that I had been having so much trouble with my car. It had stalled on the interstate and I was on the side of the road until some stranger helped me. There were no cell phones at that time. "It's been doing this for a month."

"Well have you...been look...lookin' around to see what's possible or..."

"Oh yes, and I know I can't get one for under $3,000. I don't know what I can get for my car. I went Monday to look at used cars, so I know about what it will cost. But Ray, no matter, I have to do it."

"Well, I think that I'll be able to help you. I don't know what I can come up with." *Oh Please!* "However, you know the guy who lives next door, I would advise you to...isn't he a mechanic?"

"He can't do anything. He's not very knowledgeable."

"Well Marci, I was gonna suggest that you take him with you when you look at a car. Sometimes, babe, you can spend a lot of money and don't get nuthin."

I started to talk, "I...I know but..." I couldn't finish. He continued talking.

"I know, babe. I'm just tryin'...tryin' to help you get a reliable opinion on it."

I was getting so aggravated, "Ray! Stop! I'm hanging up! You know, after twelve years I think you should want to help me. You've never had to help me, not really, with the exception of grocery money and a few hundred dollars here and there. I've been a damned cheap date for twelve years."

"I told you, Marci, that I'd be able to help you...you know to...to get the car. But I can only wait till you tell me what it is that you come up with and I'll tell you what I can do."

I was yelling into the phone. "I don't want you to. I don't even want to be bothered with it anymore. Just don't call me anymore. Ever!" Then I beat the cradle with the phone about five times, and tried my damndest to break his eardrums!

After I hung up the phone (miraculously, it didn't break), I just fell on my bed and cried. It hurt me, terribly, that Ray had such a hard time helping me–even just a tiny bit.

He was here shortly after that and he did give me some money for my car. That stinginess made me sick.

As I re-read this transcript, I realize that he was willing to help me, but as always, I had absolutely no patience. I would get pissed off and slam the phone down before God could get the news!

36
Surprise, Surprise, Surprise

I finally thought of something that would get Ray where he would hurt the most, and even that wouldn't be enough as far as I was concerned. When Ray called, I asked if he lived with a woman named Norma. His answer was, "No. I know somebody named Norma but she doesn't share my roof."

"Well, I don't believe you. Your son told me all about you and her!"

"Oh, come on Marci. Do you think I believe my son would say those things? Don't you know that he knows you're my woman? And don't you know that I know who told you that shit and they're just trying to cause me trouble?"

"No, Ray. You're wrong. Bobby did tell me. He also told me that he lived there for a while with Norma's daughter, down the hall from you and her."

"That's some more bullshit and you can't ever convince me that Bob told you that shit. He knows that's a lie. There ain't no Goddamned Norma!"

Ray thought Ed Langford told me everything, but he really didn't. His son Bobby really did, much to Ray's disbelief.

During that time, it was difficult for me to be civil to Ray. But it took a few visits before I got my chance to get even with his ass. I stopped mentioning Norma. I wanted him to be re- laxed with me. I had a plan. Finally the time came. He got a room at the Holiday Inn, close to my house, so I wouldn't have to cook and wash dishes, he said.

Sometimes Ray had with him all the money from the gig that he had just done. He didn't always have it with him when he came to see me, but this time he did. I knew I had to bide my time, shut up about Norma, make him happy and wait for the right moment.

Finally the moment came. The red T.W.A. zippered money pouch was stuffed to the brim with one hundred dollar bills. Ray had put the pouch in his baggage in the closet just across from the bathroom. (I have pictures of us during this visit and of Ray unpacking in front of the closet where the T.W.A. money pouch was. What a memory!!).

He would be here two nights, so I relaxed with him the first day and night. However, I did sneak in the pouch to count the money just to make sure there was enough there to suit my purpose.

The next day, I went to the bank and got a bunch of one dollar bills. I also stopped by my house to pick up some blackberry pie—his favorite.

Ray hated for me to go anywhere. He wanted me with him every second. Normally I didn't leave him because I wanted to be with him every second too.

I waited until he went to sleep. I could always tell when he was actually sleeping, because he made some horrible clicking, gagging sounds like he was choking to death. So when I knew he was asleep, I exchanged the one hundred dollar bills for the one dollar bills. Then I stuffed the hundreds into my purse and set about making Ray Charles Robinson ecstatic. He experienced eroticism with me that evening. That was new to him. And why not–he had paid me quite well–and I felt damned good about it!

I certainly didn't feel like I was "robbing the blind." I felt like he was getting ready to do something he should have done years earlier–pay off my house!

If Ray was paying for Norma to ride around in a Mercedes, then the least he could do was pay for my house (and buy me a Goddamned mattress without lumps)–which he did– albeit unknowingly!

The balance of what I owed on my house was not nearly as expensive as a new Mercedes, so he still got off cheap. I only took enough to pay the balance on my house and buy a new bedroom suite. He's lucky! He could have bought me a new Jaguar. There was enough money there.

I didn't have to drive him to the airport, this time. His valet was with him. We kissed good-bye and he said he would call me in a couple of days.

I left the motel and went straight to a girlfriend's house to leave the money. I wanted Ray to be in L.A. before he counted his money. After a couple of days, I picked up the money, went to the loan company and paid my house off.

Now my deed was free and clear. I felt so good. I felt like a weight was lifted from my shoulders. Now, I reasoned, if something happened to me, my girls would have a home paid for.

That night Lisa, Mitzi and I went shopping for a new bedroom suite, which I bought at Sears along with a queen sized mattress and boxed springs.

We all got new coats and some sunglasses. Then we treated ourselves to dinner at Bonanza. (I wasn't extravagant–it could have been Al Bakers again!)

A week later, I was sleeping on my wonderful new mattress– no more backaches. It was about time!

The funny thing was, I never got a call from Ray. He said he would call in a day or so. A week went by, no call. A month went by, no call. *Hmmmm, I wonder if he's mad?* (Giggle). I didn't call him either.

I knew he wasn't through with me forever. But frankly, I didn't give a damn if he was mad, or through with me, or whatever the hell he was. I took just enough money to pay my house off and buy a bedroom suite, (and just those couple incidentals) not a cent more.

I've never disclosed how much it was to anyone. Only Ray and I knew that. But there was plenty of hundred dollar bills left in his T.W.A. pouch, along with lots of checks...and lots and lots of one dollar bills (giggle).

I missed him something awful, but I wasn't about to call him. I knew that he would eventually call me.

Sure enough, one day he called and said, "Marci, baby, you've been mad at me for a long time."

I told him no, that he was the one who had been mad. Then I told him that I had paid my house off.

His response was, "I know, babe. That's fair."

I knew that he understood and thought it was okay, and that he would never mention it to me again.

I said, "Ray, now we own a house together, but I'll just hold the title." He laughed and said, "Alright, honey."

He sure did enjoy sleeping on that new mattress! We used to sleep on a lumpy, full-sized Goodwill mattress, and now we had one that was new and firm and Queen-sized.

I couldn't resist reminding him that he had finally fulfilled a promise that he had made to me in 1969–move the kids and me to Los Angeles and buy us a house.

And I was right. He never mentioned it again.

He continued to bring his gig money with him in the T.W.A. pouch. For twenty-two years, I never bothered it again, and he knew I wouldn't...that is...unless....

He was just very careful what kind of information I found out from then on.

During 1981, 1982 and 1983, Ray was here sporadically. He was having a slow time with album sales. I met him a few times when he was on the road, and he was here when he could be. Basically though, I had come to accept the fact that Ray and I were completely different people, and I acted accordingly.

If I met someone that I wanted to date, I did. Ray hated it and couldn't bear to hear it, but unlike him, I kept no secrets–much to his distress.

Times were few and far between that I found anyone who appealed to me. Ray Charles was a hard act to follow, not only because he was Ray Charles, but because I still loved him so much. I did find someone, occasionally, but it never lasted. Ray was the only one I ever wanted forever.

Sometime in the early eighties, Lisa moved into her own apartment, so it was just Mitzi and me. It seemed like in no time, she was gone too, and then it was only me. I missed them terribly, and nearly drove them crazy calling them. I was truly an empty nester.

We bought another house, Lisa moved there from her apartment, and later Mitzi moved in with her. We did a lot of work on it. We even added partitions and made more rooms, got some pretty carpet, tiled the kitchen floor and painted. Later we added a deck. It was so cute.

We thought it was smarter to own than to rent. So we pooled our money for the down payment and bought it. My girls were thrilled living in their own home at ages eighteen and twenty.

They were very good workers, having worked since age fourteen, when I had to get them a work permit in order to get a job. My girls always had a job.

They also won their share of beauty contests. Mitzi was Miss Fantasy. Lisa, later won a Cher look-alike contest and an all expense paid trip to L.A.

Lisa and Mitzi both did some television commercials–Mitzi's were for Fantasy Coachworks. She held their title for two years, so she was a busy girl.

They also did a commercial for Channel Three Cable T.V. which was so cute. It was a skit where they talked to each other over a pretend lunch at a pretend restaurant.

Lisa got the hysterical giggles and they couldn't shoot for a while because she couldn't stop laughing. Mitzi was sitting across the table looking at her with that look like - God! Lisa! She eventually got control of herself. I have a video of that whole scenario and I still crack-up when I watch it.

Ray was excited when I told him about Mitzi being "Miss Fantasy." He said, "Tell Mitzi I'm voting for her."

Then he asked a lot of questions about their commercials. He said, "I know you're proud of them, honey!" Yes I was, and always have been, no matter what they did. I was their biggest fan, and they were each other's biggest fans.

One day, my cousin Jeraldine Smith called me and said,

"Marci, there's a good deal in Sunday's paper for a trip to Honolulu. I wish you, Lisa and Mitzi could go. You'll never get it this reasonable again." Jerry had been everywhere.

I had made a very poor investment with an individual. (I won't go into what it was, but Mary Ann was here at the time and had warned me against it.) But true to my nature, I didn't listen.

I turned the matter over to the authorities and told my kids that if I got my money back, we would go to Hawaii. Being so persistent and angry as hell, I got my money back. So, on December 2, 1984 we boarded a plane for Hawaii and had the best time in the world.

The night before we left, Jerry and her daughter Connie came over with a bottle of wine for a bon voyage party. Thanks to Jerry's persistence about us going, we learned that we could afford to travel, and since I knew that I could never afford college for my girls, I thought traveling would be educational for them. I wrote a detailed account about all of our trips. It's wonderful to review those stories and recapture all of the fun we had together.

Right before we left for Hawaii, Ray called and invited me to meet him in Dallas, Texas. I knew Don and Colleen would be there, but I would be in Hawaii! When I found out who I missed by not going to Dallas, I was sooo disappointed.

Don and Colleen got a huge surprise, meeting another favorite of theirs, Willie Nelson! They went to the show at "Grannies" and after the show, Don, Colleen and their friends Harold and Judith went backstage.

Ray was busy but asked where they were staying. Don told him across the street from where he was staying. So Ray invited them to come to his suite about noon the next day for coffee and conversation. They went to his hotel at noon and called to let him know they were there. He was visiting with Ray Price at the time, discussing doing an album together.

So while they were in the lobby, waiting for Ray to signal them to come up, Willie Nelson walked in with his wife Connie.

Don mustered up all his nerve and walked over and asked Willie what he was doing there. He said he was there to see Ray Charles. Don said he was there to see Ray also. Then Willie and Connie went on up to Ray's suite.

Soon the desk clerk told them that Mr. Ray Charles requested they go on up to his suite. Don knocked and Willie answered the door. Then Ray came over and introduced Don to Willie as "one of his dearest friends." Don said that it was the highlight of his life, to be introduced like that.

Colleen, Judith and Harold waited in the hall while Don was in the room. Don said, "I told them 'I don't know if my old heart can take being in the same room with my two main men.'" He said they were both so gracious and nice.

Then Don excused himself and he, Colleen and their friends went back down to the lobby until Ray and Willie were through talking business. Soon they saw Willie and Connie walk through the lobby. Don walked over to the top of the stairway and looked down. He saw Willie get into a limo that had the windows all blacked out. He and his wife stayed in it for a while as Don stood and watched. Pretty soon, Willie got out. He walked directly up the stairs to Don and said, "Ray said if I saw you to tell you to come on up."

He turned to leave and Don asked if he could take a picture of him with his friend Judith. He graciously complied. Don said Willie was such a great guy, and such a gentleman, and that he was walking on air after meeting him and being with Ray.

I asked Don what kind of visit he had with his buddy, (meaning Ray.) He said they had a great visit and Ray was so attentive and gracious to his friends. "You know, just his usual easy mannered self."

They stayed for a long time and drank coffee and chatted and Ray was kind and relaxed with everyone.

Don said, "Well he was just a great guy."

Colleen said she was crazy about Ray. She always said she had a crush on him. She remembers the time she saw him in his orange boxers. It was backstage and Ray told them to come on in. "Colleen won't mind me in my shorts." Colleen said of course she didn't.

Needless to say, I was pretty sad that I didn't go on that trip to Texas. I screwed myself. I could have been sitting right there with my sweetheart, having coffee and visiting with Ray Price and Willie Nelson!

The next time Ray called, I told him how sorry I was that I missed Willie Nelson. He said, "Awww, you'll meet him sometime," but I never did, much to my regret.

⁓⸰

It was now wintertime, and Ray and I were on the phone.

"I thought you were having so much ice and cold weather that...uh...when you breathed out it would turn into icicles."

"We were, but today we're having a scorcher." I said, "It's forty degrees."

"Oh," he said. "It's a scor...you're having a heat wave, a forty degree heat wave!"

When our weather made the national news, Ray knew it wasn't just cold, it was really cold. Usually he called to see if we were okay. I told him that if I ever won the lottery, I would get out of here–maybe go south.

He said he thought the Midwest would be too religious for us to have the lottery here. He was right. (Who knew that years later, Missouri would have a its own variety of lotteries and casinos.) I had to go to Illinois to get the tickets. He said, "Well, you have as much chance of winning as anyone. It's one of those things that never happens to some people, but..."

"Well, look at you Ray. Now there's a situation that's unbelievable, but it happened to me."

He said, "Yeah, it did Marci. It sure did." I could hear the delight in his voice.

He asked about Lisa and Mitzi. Then he wanted to know what I was doing when he called. I told him I was doing Jane Fonda exercises. He wanted to know why the hell I was doing all these exercises all of a sudden.

I said, "Well, my age I guess. I don't want to go to pot."

He told me at length how he felt about age, exercise, etc.

"Without a doubt, I'm obviously older than you. So therefore, if age had anything to do with it, wouldn't you think I'd be fat and sloppy?" (He was about 54 years old.) I don't think it's necessarily a matter of age. I think it's how you conduct your eating habits."

He said he found that the older you get, you're doing less strenuous things. Let me put it this way: ya see when you were a kid, you were running, jumping, climbin' trees and doing all kinds of stuff that kept you active. Then when you get older, you get a desk job, don't walk anywhere. You drive your car. You have a more relaxful (I don't know if this is a word, but it was what he said.) lifestyle. You don't walk or run no more, but you don't change your eating habits and as a result, you gain weight."

He went on to say, "What do you think I do...to...I mean you...know what I do."

I said, "Nothing, but your vocal cords."

He said, "I work hard when I'm on stage, but other than that–nothing."

I said, "I hate to do these exercises, but I don't want to get ugly."

His response to that remark was, "Well, you ain't never gonna be that, even at your...your worst, Marci, 'cause that's not possible."

I was never very diligent at exercising, so Jane Fonda ran her course pretty quickly.

37
The Prison Sentence
❦

I had sort of cooled it with Ray. I talked to him, but I wouldn't let him come here. I did that periodically when I felt my emotions slipping away.

Don and Colleen were living in Killeen, Texas at this time. They called to tell me that Ray was on a television special, but I didn't even watch it.

When I told Ray, he said, "I don't blame you, Marci. You know I...I just turn me off, too. When I come on the radio or television I turn it off, so I don't feel bad (if someone else does).

"Ray, I wasn't trying to make you feel bad."

"Well, honey, I'm just letting you know that uh...I...I ain't got no hang-ups over me either, so I do the same thing."

I said, "Well, I listen to you now. I'm back in control enough to where I can handle it. Sometimes I can't. So I don't even try–don't put myself through it.

"Anyway, Colleen was having one of her Ray Charles love attacks and she would call and say, 'I just love him. I love that Ray. Look how handsome he is.' All of this in her cute Texas drawl."

Ray said, "Well it's nice somebody loves me, honey. That makes up for all the love you cancelled on me."

"Umm, Ray, I'm afraid it's not the same kind of love."

"I know that, Marci, but hey, these days any kinda love's better than none."

"I never said I didn't love you. I've never said that or felt that way. I just had to stop it for awhile–think about things–sort of regroup. I think I've put things into perspective in my mind, and now I'm able to communicate with you again."

"I hope so, honey. It's very disturbing not to see you or talk to you. Very disturbing. But one thing I never wanna do is make an ass of myself and bug you. Only because I don't like that either. So, you know, you put your feelings out there, and I don't care how strong they are, you have to respect the rights of others. And if you really care about them, it's even more reason to do that.

"I'm one of those kind of people, babe, that I just hope and hope. You know how you hope and wish and maybe if my prayers are right, or my feeling is correct, maybe one day....you know how you just hope for that one day?

"And, honey, when I tell you I'm totally thrilled, pleased and happy and all the right words that go along with what I'm trying to say to you, that I heard from you, it does an awful lot for me. You know it really makes me feel good inside...I...you know Marci...it relieves me to be honest with you. You know how it is when you want to hear from somebody...but yet you know you can't. It's like a person being in prison–you know how you wanna get out but can't?

"It's a helluva thing when you're in prison, if you know all you gotta do is open the door and walk out, that's one thing. But it's different when you're in there and you can't walk out."

I wondered how this prison parable related to him not being able to see me.

Later he told me that David, his middle son, was in prison, and why. He asked me never to discuss it and I promised that I wouldn't.

He continued on with his frustration about me cutting him off. "It's...ah...different...if you know, you can pick up the phone and say, "Hi, babe. How you feeling?" and just listen to your voice. The difference is when, you know, you're forbidden. And so it's nice, babe, to know you got a reprieve, or at least a probation, you know, giving you a little taste of freedom. Like hearing your voice is giving me a little taste of happiness, you know, same thing. That's why I can relate to it."

I said that I didn't put him on probation. I just protected

myself. I didn't like the situation and couldn't cope before, but that now possibly I could.

He made a sort of growling sound and then, out of the blue, asked me, "Are you gonna cook supper?"

I said, "No."

"Why not?"

"I don't want to."

He was quiet for a couple of seconds, then he started laughing his head off, really just cracking up. When he regained his control, he said, "That's why I love you Marci. There's no way in the world that I can not love you. I don't give a damn what you say, there's no way. Try as I might, there's just no way I can get you out of my system. Just things like that, "Are you gonna cook supper? No. Why? 'Cause I don't want to." See if you could get more people in the world to be straight ahead like that, you wouldn't have near the bullshit that you have today. And that's the truth." He was still laughing. "I really like that, truly, the world just needs more people like you, honey—be a better place to live—wouldn't hafta worry about the bullshit."

I asked, "What were you expecting me to say?"

"Well you know, babe, I thought we were gonna make a conversation out of it. But once you said, 'I don't want to,' that stopped it right there."

Then he said, "If you'll let me call you, at least I'll do that, and let you know what's happening with me."

I agreed that that would be nice.

He said, "I haven't seen you in five years."

"Oh Ray, you saw me a month or so ago."

"Well," he said, "that's the way it feels to me. As a matter of fact, the guy at the airport asked me, 'Where's that little lady who comes out here to get you all the time?'"

"Oh, Ray, please," I said in disbelief.

"No, the man did ask me that. I swear it on my mother's grave." He said, "Don't you remember, you all were going the wrong way when we were remodeling the airport and I helped you.'"

"Oh yes," I said, "I remember that. That's amazing that he remembered that incident." I guess it's really not that amazing since it was Ray Charles. That alone would be enough to tweek his memory.

Ray said he was doing a Christmas album, the first in his career. This was 1984. He also told me he was doing a country music thing called, "Ray Charles and Friends."

"The one with George Jones is out now," he said. "It's called, 'I Didn't See a Thing.'"

"I haven't heard it," I said.

"You're not gonna find it on a soul station. It's country, so keep that in mind."

I said, "Just send me the album when you finish it."

"It's Midway–your street–right? Is it 300?"

"Ray, you sent Mitzi an album, remember? When I was having a shitty spell and said I didn't want it. She heard me and said into the phone, 'I do Ray,' so you sent it to her." (I still have that package addressed to Mitzi.)

"I know. I know, and I know the address, honey, and almost had it right. If I'd of thought a minute, I would have had the street number."

I said, "Well you did have the street number."

"I know you, honey. I know you very well."

"I know you do."

"I know everything about you, Marci, including your toes." He loved to tell me that.

I giggled and said, "I know. Keep that to yourself."

He went on, "And I love you. On that note, I'll ring off. Tell the kids I said hi, and oh, how's your brother?"

I said, "He's going to Tahiti. He won a trip for two."

"Oh. Wow! How's your Mom and Dad?"

"Everyone's okay, Ray."

"Okay. Well I just thought I'd check on the family. One of these days you're gonna have to get down and write a book on your family. I'll tell you, it will be a best seller. I swear to God."

Well Brother Ray, here it is!

༄࿐

The next time Ray called, we discussed the making of, "We Are the World, We Are the Children."

Later, sitting in my living room over coffee, Ray told me he had been "roaming around up in Canada," and when he got my call it made his day–and that he was very happy that I liked the little song, "We Are the World."

"Oh Ray, I just love it. I bought four albums. I sent one to each of my friends and asked them to buy one for their friends, then maybe bunches of people will buy them."

"Honey, I think that's very nice. I'm pleased about that." He had that sweet smile on his face.

He told me about making, "We Are the World." He said he had to be back in L.A. the next day to do his solo part. I asked if everyone had a solo.

He said, "Oh, yeah. Most of the people did theirs Monday night, because they all had somewhere to be. Quincy (Quincy Jones) told me he was in the studio from Monday night till about 9 a.m. Tuesday morning. He said I could do mine any time 'cause I live in Los Angeles and Tina (Tina Turner) could, too, because she lives there."

I asked if Quincy was the one who got it off the ground.

He said yes, along with some others–that no one person could do it alone.

"When Quincy called me about it, you know Quincy and I have been friends since we were children, naturally I said, 'Well Quincy, you have to be crazy to ask me that, of course I will.'"

He said every one of the artists was happy to be a part of that historical event. We discussed how horrible it was that the devastation in Africa ever got to that point. Ray said, "You know, babe, all these countries that have uh...massive amounts of money and they just...it's kind of hard to forgive when they've spent not millions but billions on all kinds of weaponry, bombs and missiles and stuff. And yet, when you look at the world where they've spent all of this money, then you look around and you see this. Our priorities are mixed up."

He really was concerned about the neglect from the governments of the world.

He said, "A lot of us don't know what's going on behind the scenes, but these governments do know."

I said, "Ray, I was so happy to see your face (on television) right up there in the middle of all of those V.I.P.'s."

He laughed as he said, "Well I'll tell you something funny about seeing my face among the V.I.P.'s. I was talkin' to the guy who was handling the photo shots for *Life Magazine*. I said, "Why in the hell don't you guys let me sit...'cause I had some coffee I was drinkin' and I figured I didn't wanna be on T.V. looking like I had a drink in my hand 'cause man, that ain't gonna look too good. But he said, 'Hell, don't worry bout it, everybody else's got drinks.' So I said, "Okay.""

I guess his "coffee" was his Bols gin and coffee. I didn't know too much about that drink back then, other than he drank it to hone his vocal chords before going on stage.

Ray was so happy to be involved with that project. He said, "Entertainers are the worst people in the world to get together, but they did, and all at one time. That's an amazing feat."

"Ray, I didn't see Willie's (Willie Nelson) face. Was he there?

"Oh, believe me, honey. Willie was there. He wouldn't have missed that."

I said, "It must have been fun."

"That's what was so nice. You see, because the first hour–we started at ten o'clock–Quincy just threw his hands up, 'cause he couldn't do nuthin. Everybody's 'round talkin' and tellin' lies and bullshitting. You know, babe, we're all workin' at different places so we rarely see each other. So it's natural when you get that many artists together who know, love and respect each other, there's gonna be time spent visiting."

I could tell how happy he was. He just couldn't stop telling me about it, and I loved hearing it.

I asked, "Does all the money for the sales of this album go to help Ethiopia?"

He said most of it did and that they thought it would reach sales of fifty or sixty million dollars. He personally thought more like thirty or forty million. He said there were no overhead costs, so approximately 85% would go to the people, which was great because with most charities the recipients only got 40% if they were lucky. The rest went to administrative costs.

We finally got tired of talking and went to bed. He had to be back in L.A. the next day to do his solo part on the album, and this time I was taking him to the airport.

The next time he called he was in Atlanta, Georgia, doing something for Maxwell House–promotional stuff for the officials, not for the public. He said he would be doing about eight concerts in different cities–South Carolina, then Texas, then Newark, New Jersey and back to L.A.

Ray traveled far too much for me. I was a homebody, and I still love to be at home. I love vacations, but I wouldn't have wanted to travel like Ray did.

Ironically, in nearly thirty years, we never took an actual vacation together. We meant to, but honestly I don't know what we would have done. I don't sit in my hotel room much. When I traveled with my kids, we were on the move. Our trips were not just fun excursions. They were that too, but they were also adventurous and educational.

In the Caribbean, and sometimes in Mexico, we would hire a driver and see everything, not just the beaches. The drivers seemed to like us because invariably, they would take us home with them.

In Jamaica, we went high into the mountains. Our driver's brother had the tiniest grocery store we had ever seen. We bought a soda, and then we were taken next door to his sparsely furnished home. His wife was ironing while the men were in the back room drinking and playing cards. In the back yard, we saw a nude little girl, who looked to be about six years old, bathing in a wash tub.

We felt pretty uncomfortable. No doubt, they did too, with us parading through their private domain. My kids were scared.

"We thought they were going to kill us, rob us and throw our bodies in the forest," they remembered. Thank God nothing happened. We would not do that nowadays.

When Lisa and I went to Barbados for her thirtieth birthday, we got a very formal driver, uniformed in a starched white shirt, tie and black jacket. He drove us all over Barbados.

One evening, we went to a night club to celebrate her birthday. I asked the trio to play some Ray Charles tunes. The leader said, "Oh, he's my favorite musician." I said, "Mine too!" and showed him a picture of Ray and me. He asked if he could keep it, and of course I said yes.

Mitzi and I went on a seven-island cruise two years later for her thirtieth birthday. Barbados was one of our ports of call. We hired a driver and, of course, he took us home with him. He had a very small house, minimally furnished, but his wife graciously served us a beer. So there Mitzi and I sat in some stranger's house in Barbados, having a beer and looking at one another like, "Can you believe this?"

In Mazatlan, Mexico, Lisa and I wanted to see where their famous big, beautiful furniture was made, so our driver, who was Lisa's age and in love with her, drove us far off the beaten track to a small town. We saw the furniture shop, and it was no big deal. On the way back, the Federales had the road blocked. They were in uniform and were wielding big machine guns. They searched the car, scared the shit out of us, and then let us go. We never did find out what they were looking for.

Another time, in Puerto Vallarta, Mitzi and I heard of a place forty-five minutes away by car where you could buy silver at bargain prices and where we could go inside people's homes and see how they really lived. We found a driver and took off.

He drove like a maniac, but luckily, we got to our destination in one piece. He said he had been up late and had a hangover. Great!

He got us there alive after he scared the shit out of us. We didn't find any bargains and there were no homes to nose into, but at least we got a sensible driver back to Puerto Vallarta.

In Italy, we took tours because we didn't want to miss all of their wonderful culture. We saw as much as our bodies could stand. Lots of walking. It was amazing.

In France, we saw the Louvre, the D'OrSay, museums and Monmartre. We took taxi's there. We were scared to drive in Paris, but we rented a car in Nice and Lisa and Mitzi drove me and Henry's widow Sandra, who met us in Paris, all over the south of France–Cannes, Monte Carlo and St. Tropez.

When we were in a hotel in Nice, overlooking the Mediterranean, the first thing my two lovely daughters did was to become very European–they sunbathed topless on the beach. I didn't tell Ray about that. He would have been a fuddy-duddy about it.

When Mitzi and I visited Tortola on our cruise, we found a Rastafarian named Rocky. We climbed into his rickety van, (with no passenger-side doors) and headed for a rain forest high up in the hills. We went into a restaurant. It was morning but Mitzi and I had a rum drink...or two...(but who's counting?).

The rain forest was wonderful and we truly enjoyed Rocky's outlook on life. I asked if he resented the wealthy people taking over so much of Tortola.

He said, "No. My view is the same as theirs." We were stopped on a high hill looking at the magnificent view of the ocean. "We all see the same thing. All of this is free to me."

Mitzi liked Rocky's philosophical view of life. She later sent him a book called, "Beachcombing at Miramar." The book is about a rich man's quest for an authentic life. We thought Rocky already had it.

We headed on down to a very famous place by the ocean called "Bomba's Love Shack." What an experience. Unbelievable! It was filled with ladies underwear and bras. They were hanging everywhere and signed by the former owners. The place literally was a shack, with sand floors and seemingly thrown together with aged lumber. Huge sailboats docked there and young people from around the world invaded Bomba's. We were told that the crowds rocked the shack.

Bomba gave us a concoction of something strong and intoxicating, and then convinced Mitzi to leave her panties. She went to the restroom and brought them back all signed and ready to hang. They have been seen and reported to us by friends who also visited Bomba's.

He tried to get me to leave mine, but since I didn't wear undies, I couldn't. He insisted I prove that to him. Absolutely not, Bomba!

I didn't tell *that* to Ray either.

We learned a lot on our special trips–some good, some not so good. But we wouldn't trade any of our experiences for anything in the world. We always had such great adventures.

After thinking about all of the things we did on our trips, especially the amount of walking, I doubt if Ray would have enjoyed a vacation with me. Although he walked a lot when he went to Israel and he felt everything when he went to the interesting ancient sites, I still didn't think he would have enjoyed our jaunts.

✑✑

I've digressed again. I thought I had nothing to write about, but I find that I can't stop. Maybe I have too much to say.

The next time Ray called, he asked if I ever did any drawings anymore. He said he thought I was good at it and wondered if I had kept it up.

I said that I had. Lisa wanted some drawings and paintings to hang on her walls, so I did a few. We also starting doing miniature paintings on fingernails which we had seen when we went to Hawaii.

Ray said, "Oh wow! I never heard of that."

"Me either." I said, "and I thought it would be a breeze to do them, but it was really hard."

He said, "Babe, anything you do in this world is hard till you get the hang of it."

"Mitzi painted some on her friend's fingernails. She was actually better than me."

300

Ray wondered if we still rode horses. I said, "No, not as much. My kid's sort of traded horses for boys and cars. But Lisa still rides occasionally. You know, she has always loved horses."

He said, "I love you. Gotta go, honey. I'll see you in a week or so."

38
Struggling to Get Back Together

This era is from 1983 through the early nineties.

The album *We Are the World* was number one on the charts for a while. *Seven Spanish Angels* with Ray and Willie Nelson reached number one on the country charts and Columbia released a video of them.

Ray told me "We Didn't See a Thing," with George Jones reached number one on the charts, also.

I know how good this made Ray feel after a long slump in record sales. He also had been having problems with his ears, and that had him very worried. The fear of losing his hearing was devastating to Ray. He said he thought being deaf would be much worse than being blind. He was ready for a break and his hit records definitely came at the right time.

Ray had discussed his ear problem with me, and told me what the doctor had done to fix it. Ironically, I had had the same procedure done in1968, just before I met him.

He told me that when he talked, he heard his voice echo. I knew exactly what he meant. I told him that my own voice was magnified in my head. He said, "Yeah, yeah that's right."

My doctor put tubes in my eardrums. He said it was a simple procedure and that I could drive myself home. Wrong! I got up from the recovery table and just fainted away. I went to the floor. Henry had to come and drive me home, telling me all the way how fucking stupid I was to let somebody put holes in my eardrums. I must say that was one time that I agreed with him.

I never could adjust to the tubes and had them removed.

Then the doctor took me off birth control pills and I recovered.

"Oh wow, babe. You never told me about that."

"Well, I only thought about it when you had the same problem!"

Ray said he didn't have any surgery problems and was sorry that I had such a bad experience.

That's not the only bad experience that I've had with doctors and surgeries. My body doesn't respond well to either one. I still try to follow their direction, but I usually just ride it out and eventually hope that whatever's bothering me will go away.

One surgery in particular went horribly wrong.

In the early nineties, I had a brow lift at a local hospital. Ray was surprised that I had this done in the first place. He said I didn't need it. How would he know?

The doctor promised me that he would be the one doing my surgery, but I don't believe that he did it. His assistant, a resident, was sniffling and seemed sick the day of my surgery. When I asked her if she was sick, she said no that she felt fine. My intuition told me that I should not proceed with the surgery, but I went ahead anyway. That choice was a big mistake.

Whoever did the surgery severed a nerve that paralyzed the left side of my forehead. It was a botched job. The hospital administration refused to refund my $3,000 that had taken me so long to save.

We are led to believe by the medical profession that it's easy to sue a doctor. Not true. Eight attorneys refused my case. They couldn't prove negligence and it was elective surgery. Jurors don't respect plastic surgery.

That's bullshit. It was surgery and the doctor was a Board Certified Plastic Surgeon. He should have been held responsible, and so should the hospital!

I've taped my left brow up for years. It's unpleasant and unfortunate, but we all live with mistakes caused by "so-called" professionals! To me, after you maim someone for life, the very least you can do is be sympathetic and refund their money. They did neither.

When I told Ray about this, I said, "Here's a little information about me. I didn't take it lying down." He chuckled and said, "Honest, babe?"

Mitzi went with me for a follow up appointment with the doctor. I was upset, of course–who wouldn't be? I listened to him tell me the nerve would come back in six months. Was he kidding? Even I knew better than that–and I'm not a doctor!

Then I heard Mitzi say to the nurse, "Don't roll your eyes at my mom!" That sent me over the edge. I told them how unprofessional and under-qualified they were, and we left.

"But I wasn't finished with them!" I said to Ray. He just sat with a smile on his face, waiting for me to finish my story. He knew me so he knew I wasn't finished with them.

I bought an A-frame stand and put posters on both sides of it and on both sides of my car that said, "This facility paralyzed my face. Beware of these doctors."

I passed out flyers saying the same thing. I did that every day after work for a week. I put flyers on every parked car, even in their garage, but when I put them inside the building in the restrooms, they prosecuted me.

My attorney-cousin, Gerald Simmons, handled it for me, but I was forbidden to come on their premises again.

Try to imagine how little I cared.

I've jumped ahead. Now back to the late eighties.

୨∼ର

Ray had been in Atlanta, Georgia doing something for Coca Cola. I asked if it was a commercial. He said, "It's something for their archives. You know, I've been doing Coca Cola for years."

"I know," I said, "You and Aretha (Aretha Franklin)."

He said, "Even before that, I did some commercials that won awards. Anyway, they've been down here to do this special thing for me." I never did find out what it was. I guess they put him in their archives.

When he called from Atlanta, he asked if it were a gruesome idea if he came to see me, just for one night.

"No," I said, "but my house is a wreck and I'm working two jobs, so I'll be gone all day."

He said, "I know you, so I know your house is not a wreck."

But it was. I had finally taken out the Goodwill carpet and had new carpet installed, thanks to a friend in the carpet business.

I said, "All the furniture is in the living room. You'll have to maneuver your way around it."

When he arrived, at least I had gotten the bed set up, so we had a place to sleep. We had one night and until late the next day. It was nice. We had many times like that. When he left, he said he would call me in a day or two.

Ray called several days later and said, "After I left you, I called you the next day and talked to Mitzi." (He had said we would talk in a *day or two.)*

"I know Ray. She told me, but it's been two weeks since you left."

"Then," he said, "the following week, I called you every day - Every day at four, five o'clock - not before that because you were at work. Every day...Every Day!!!! I gave you the benefit of the doubt, but didn't nobody answer the phone. As a matter of fact, I'm sorry I didn't get Lisa's phone number or Mitzi's phone number in case that sort of thing happened, but I didn't...I didn't think that way.

"But I called you every day, Marci. That's the truth. Every day...five...four because I couldn't get you to answer."

"Why didn't you call in the middle of the night, Ray?"

"No, because I know you work every day."

"You've done it before."

"All I'm....sweetheart, I'm not makin' any excuses. I'm tryin' to be very sincere. When I get offa' work Marci, it's one, two o'clock in the...well, you know how I work, I don't hafta tell you that."

"Ray, sweetheart, I appreciate your concern, but it seems to me like this was important enough to awaken me!"

I was upset if he didn't keep his word so I guess he was desperately trying to prove to me that he tried. He didn't always keep his word.

He continued, "Well....okay Marci. See I looked at it ass-backwards–but I'm only tellin you what I sincerely thought. If it was bad judgment, I'm sorry 'bout that. I called myself tryin' to be considerate, thinkin' you hafta get up at seven o'-clock in the morning.

If I call you at two, you ain't gonna get back to sleep 'till four. I know how I feel when I'm awakened in the middle of the night."

"But, Ray, think about it. I may have gotten more sleep than I did not hearing from you at all. I just thought it was the same old story."

"Marci I...I'm tellin you the Gospel. If you look at your schedule...you'll know what you were doing."

"God, Ray, I don't have any idea what I was doing at four or five o'clock last week."

"Well, babe, you told me...you said to call you...you said you got home around two-thirty and I called you every day and you weren't home. So I don't know where you were.

"And last week I called you…let's see...we got back from Mexico on Monday and I called you Tuesday and Thursday of last week and you didn't answer the phone."

"Well, honey, sometimes I'm not here at that time you know? You'll just have to try different times of the day or night."

"Marci, let me put it to you this way, really and truly, I struggle very very hard to try to get us back together like we used to be. If you would just say to me, 'Look I don't care what time of night or day you call me...' then I'll do that, babe. It's six-thirty where I am. It should be about five-thirty in St. Louis and this is the time I called..."

Then the phone cut off. He said, "Marci...hello?" I couldn't get him on the line. I kept on clicking the phone, trying to get him, but I couldn't. He thought I was trying to hang up on him.

I could hear him say, "Marci? Marci? Hello? Do you have just five minutes that I can talk to you?"

We got reconnected and I told him that I had been gone all day long lately because I was out delivering fliers, trying to advertise my house cleaning business.

Ray said, "Oh, that's good. I'm glad to hear you've been busy. That's great."

"Well, I'm not making money. I'm just busy."

"Oh, you're not making any money?"

"No, I'm trying to arrange to make money," I said.

He laughed, but I didn't think it was humorous. I thought he should have been more forthcoming with some financial assistance. We had been seeing each other for about seventeen years and Ray was still just as stingy as ever. I was getting sick of it.

He said, "Let me ask you this, would you think...although I would never, and believe me you can trust me on it, I would never, ever, ever use her number unless it was a die hard emergency."

"Lisa?" I asked. "Oh my gosh, Ray, you can call them any time you want. Mitzi and Lisa live together."

"Well, let me get a pen," Ray said. "Okay, I wrote Lisa and Mitzi's phone number is 314-###-####. I appreciate it and I...I put it in my book and as I said to you, it is sacred."

"Ray, you know they would love to hear from you. They love you."

"Well, I got it now and I love them too. It's strange how children grow up. I remember when they were itty bitty things."

"God yes," I said, "I've got pictures of them when they were tiny sitting beside you on the couch, and of Lisa on my bed with you, eating a peanut butter sandwich, watching T.V. while you were sleeping."

"I love it. Oh, wow! That's great! That is marvelous. Can they relate to that?"

"Yes, they remember everything, Ray, and wouldn't take anything for their wonderful memories."

"I'm so glad they're doing great, babe. I am very happy about that. I'm so pleased."

We talked about Don and Colleen coming to Missouri. He asked if I would see them. I told him I didn't know. It was according to how much time they had. I also said I told them what a jerk he was but now that he had called, I would call and tell them different.

He said, "Oh my God, you're something, Marci!"

I said, "I got a little cute something for you...just a little thing that you'll like, for your birthday, but I was mad at you so I didn't send it. I will now."

Ray said, "Oh please do."

"It's a little bitty nothing but it's something that you'll like," I said. It was a little Baby Grand piano that played, "Let Me Call You Sweetheart" when the lid was lifted. "Hi, sweetheart" was his favorite sound from me.

"No...it...it's a whole lot to me, baby. Anything...ju...just your sound means everything to me."

Ray said he was going to be in Iowa in the next couple of days. He had an off day and asked if he could come here.

"Yeah," I said, "that would be good. Do you want to stay here?"

"Well...I...I...wanna be where it's pretty comfortable for you, babe, and I don't want you to hafta think about doing anything, so maybe we'll stay at the hotel and you can just sit back and order things and don't hafta wash the dishes and you can just talk to me."

"I was gonna do that anyway," I said.

Ray said, "I would like that. I really would. As a matter of fact, how's that place we stayed before...Frontenac or..."

"Oh, the Breckenridge? Yeah it's nice," I said.

"Well if you like that place, honey, why don't you go ahead and get it. Book a room for David Simmons, too." He was Ray's valet.

Ray came on Wednesday. He had told me before that he wanted to talk to me about us getting back like we once were. Whatever the hell that was! I was looking forward to that talk.

Well, it didn't happen. He said he thought that we talked last time he was here.

We had a terrible argument...the worst one we ever had. He jumped straight up off the bed and yelled, "Marci, I'm an old man. I can't take this!!!"

I had asked him about Norma and he blew up. "I didn't come here to discuss no Goddamned Norma!" he said angrily. "I'm not gonna spend this time talking about that–I didn't come all this way to argue!"

I said, "You still don't feel like you owe me an explanation?"

"Marci, I said I'm not gonna argue." Then he said, "Case closed–boom!" and he clapped his hands together hard.

I jumped up and said, "I'm not staying in this room another minute!" I opened and slammed the door about three times and left. I really wanted to walk over and slap the hell out of him, but I left instead. Frankly, I've always been a little sorry I didn't smack him.

The last thing I heard him say as I was walking down the corridor to the elevator was, "That's your problem, Marci! You always run away!"

I yelled back, "Oh shut the fu%$ up!" and kept walking.

Angry, hurt and disappointed, I cried all the way home in the rain.

I didn't hear from him for a long time. I missed him as always, but I wouldn't call him either.

Then it started again–with the phone calls. "Marci, babe, please don't hang up. I miss you, honey and I love you."

I hung up on him several times, but I finally gave in and listened.

He said, "Listen, honey. I'll do whatever it takes for us to get back together. I truly know that we can make it work. I know that we love each other." Then he said something to me that he had never said in all the years. "Marci, I'm sorry for everything, for all those years of neglect. I know I haven't treated you good, babe. Give me a chance to show you that it can be right."

"Okay," I said, with renewed hope. I made reservations for us at the Breckenridge...and here we go again.

This was the middle of October, 1987. He asked me to try to get there earlier than I did before so we could spend more time together. The last time he arrived at three and I didn't get there until six.

I had just gotten home from a trip to Las Vegas for Mitzi's twenty-first birthday and was eager to tell him about it. We had such a good time–my girls and I–as we always did.

Ray called me when he arrived and I went directly to the hotel. I stopped at the bar and ordered a shot of Amaretto, something I never do. I guess I was preparing myself for the inevitable–another nasty argument.

Sure enough, I asked questions about our future, which is what I thought he came back for. He said I was drilling him. Then he said, "Are you drunk?"

"No!!! I'm not drunk, Ray! I had a shot of Amaretto to prepare me for this bullshit. I'm damned glad I did, and I'm not putting up with this shit!"and I left.

I heard him say, "Marci, I've come a long way to be with you."

When I got home I realized that I had forgotten to give him a little stuffed heart that played, "Let Me Call You Sweetheart," when you squeezed it–and I had dabbed my signature perfume on it–White Shoulders...which he loved–so it had my aroma on it.

He liked things that allowed him to use the four senses that he had left. So this little heart, he could touch, hear and it smelled like me and the "Sweetheart thing" was something special between Ray and I.

I decided to drive it to his hotel and have it delivered to his room.

The hotel desk clerk said she would deliver it immediately.

I came home and waited for a call, but an hour later, still no call.

The desk clerk said it had been put in Mr. Charles room, but that he was out.

I was so mad! Where the hell was he? He never leaves his room.

Would you please ring his room? I asked. Then I heard a sleepy sounding, "Yeah?"

I said, "Did you get my gift?"

"No," he said.

"Well, they said they put it in your room."

He said, "Babe, I've been here all night and nobody brought a gift."

I said, "They told me you were out."

"Oh, boy!" he said, "See how rumors get started? I've been here all night. Wait a minute, I'll go across the hall. They probably gave it to David (his valet)."

Yes they had. David had gone out and the hotel people mistakenly put it in his room.

I had written a note in braille with the little heart that said, 'This is a replica of the one you broke."

He loved that. He said, 'Oh, babe–how sweet!"

He wanted me to come back, but I knew we wouldn't get anywhere this time so I said no. I thought he needed to rethink our situation.

I had a restless night. He called before he left. I said I didn't see any hope for us.

He said that he was sorry to hear that I had given up on us. We said, "I love you" and he left.

39
Tell Me What You Want
୬৶৩

Soon there was another phone call–and another debate over who was right and who was wrong. I thought Ray had an uncanny ability to talk a lot and say nothing!

I told him I was sorry that he had come so far to see me on his last visit and that I disappointed him. Sounding sad and pitiful (a Ray Charles special effect), he said, "It's alright, Marci."

Then I said, "I also wanted to tell you that if I had known things were gonna be the way they were, I could have prevented you from making that uneventful trip."

"I didn't….I still don't know what you meant by, "if things were gonna be this way, Marci. I told you that in the beginning, and I still don't know what you meant by that. I truly...when you said, "if things were gonna be this way." I ain't figured that out yet, but if you're satisfied that I know what you were talkin' about, then there's nuthin I can do."

"Well, maybe you don't know Ray. I'll just ask you. What did you plan for me? What does my future hold with you? What did you come back for? Where am I in your life?"

"Marci, it's the whole thing that I explained to you when I was there. (No, he did not!) I thought we...you know, once we...we got together, we would deal ourselves whatever, as I explained to you when I was there. I said, 'Marci, you tell me the things that you want–that will make you happy,' 'cause, I mean my...my intent was for us to...you know to...to try to make something of ourselves and I told you that when I was there.

"You know, Marci, I don't always know...I mean I...I'm not

psychic. I don't have the intuition that some people think I oughta have...you oughta think like this and you oughta know this or that. I don't have none of that. But what I said to you was 'Look, babe, you know I want us to be together and since I don't really know ev...everything like the way you want...if you tell me things and...and show me how you wa...want things to be, then I'll...I'll certainly come as close to that as I can.'

"I mean, you know my....my work, but anything other than that, that's all that matters. Now I can't tell you anymore than that, babe."

"Well honestly, Ray, this is the first time I've heard all of this."

"Well babe, that's what I was tryin' to explain to you, but you didn't believe me." He was getting frustrated.

I wasn't making matters any easier for him. I was trying to remind him of what he said. "Ray, you said we had already talked about this, but we hadn't." He misunderstood me. He thought I was throwing up our past, and he got very very agitated.

"Look, Marci, I know how I used to be. All I can tell you is, you know, life goes on. I used to shoot heroin, too. But what does that mean? I used to piss in the bed, but what does that mean? There's a lotta things I used to do. But, you know, I can't...I can't...what I'm talkin about is how things are now.

"That's what I can deal with and that's what I was tryin' to tell you. I explained all this when we talked before–we must have talked 'bout three-four hours about this."

I yelled, "Oh my God! We did not talk three or four hours. We got nothing straightened out–Nothing!!!"

Ray said, "But...but...well I'll be dogged, babe."

"No, Ray. I didn't tell you a damned thing about the way I wanted things to be, and you didn't tell me anything about what it was gonna be like."

"Yea...Marci I told you exactly what I'm tellin you now. If you don't remember you just don't remember. I...I...I'm not backin' up off a nuthin. I said exactly what I'm saying to you now.

"I told you where I was and I explained that the reason I want us to be togeth...first of all I told you what I felt for you...how I felt about...that's why I want us to get back together. And you said, 'What does that mean, Ray?'"

"Well," I asked, "What does it mean? Does it mean you're gonna come in and out of town a few more times, and then see what we can build up to? After nineteen years we're gonna build up into something...uh...start all over? I'm too old for that. I don't even want to do that. I don't have the God-damned time for that anymore."

"Well...uh...okay, honey. You don't hafta convince me of anything. You're tellin' me watcha *don't* want, and you this and you that. But you ain't said what you *would* like.

"You know, all you're tellin' me is you don't want *this* and you don't want *that*. I ain't havin' *this* and I ain't havin' *that*. (He's mimicking me.) What is it that you expect me to do? What is it that you *do* want?"

"One thing I want to know is why is it, when I say something to you and I get emotional, why do you accuse me of being drunk? Why? Ray, I stopped at the hotel bar and got one shot of Amaretto. Do you know why? Because I knew if we were going to talk about money it would be a big ordeal. I was nervous. One shot Ray. I was hardly drunk and you have never even seen me drunk. Ever!!!"

"Look, sweetheart. If we hadn't had this talk the last time I was there, I wouldn't have been so put out–shocked."

"Shocked?" I said exasperated.

"We...we went through all of this so it was like you were starting in on me all over again."

"Starting in on you? When I talk to you about something why do you always wangle it around to where I'm starting in on you or bitching, when all of my life that I've been with you has been at your convenience. That's what I've been–a convenience. I've been at your beckon call. I've done everything in the world that you've ever wanted me to do.

"If you told me to come to California, that's what I did. If you told me to come to the Breckenridge, that's what I did. Whatever you told me to do, that's what I did. Now I'm asking you, what are *you* gonna do?

"Before, nothing ever happened–nothing. I had to come back from California and start all over–by myself. Where were you? You weren't with me. I've been on my own."

"Uh....Marci. If you wanna talk to me about what went on twenty years ago th…that's fine, but I said to you…, you've already gone through all the negatives that you can possibly go through. I asked you, what it is that you would like as opposed to...."

"I told you–I want security. If you want to be in my life, then you be the head of my house. You be mine. You worry about what happens to me. You don't worry about what every Goddamned woman's doing in the world, and about Norma, and moving somebody else in with you, Ray, while I'm sitting here."

Six years ago I found out there possibly was a Norma. And I never forgot. He thought I did. He was surprised to hear that I didn't after all this time.

He said, "Okay. Fine. If that's what you think I'm doing, you can think anything you want, Marci."

"I know what you do, Ray."

"No, you don't know, Marci."

"Yes I do," I argued.

"No you don't know, and I ain't gonna defend shit, and that's a lie, and I ain't livin with no Goddamned body and cut the bullshit and don't tell me 'bout stuff you don't know watcha talkin 'bout."

I said, "I'm not sure if you are now–but you did."

Ray never cursed much. I cursed more than he ever did. But he was very angry and cursing a lot.

"Hey, look Marci!!! Fuck what I used to do! I'm not gonna keep sayin' the same thing over to you. I don't give a Goddamn what I used to do. If we're gonna base the shit on that, then it ain't ever gonna be a fuckin' thing. I'm talkin 'bout what I was interested in tryin' to do now. Not what I've done…I've done a whole lotta shit in my lifetime, babe – whole lotta shit. Probably more that most people."

"Yes," I said, "And a whole lotta that shit was done to me."

He said, "I don't want to hear about that. What I've done is what I've done and I can't take it back."

"Everything that deals with you, Ray, is supposed to be forgotten and forgiven, no matter how severe it was."

"Okay, Marci. I'm not gonna live my life through the past and all the shit that I've done and keep repenting and shit. I don't do that, babe."

I said, "Well you don't have to."

This conversation had Ray so frustrated he angrily retorted, "That's right. I don't have that..I ain't…they'd hafta kill me first." I guess so I could get a clear understanding he repeated, "I don't do that, babe.

"Marci, everybody makes mistakes. I've done a lotta wrong shit in my time. But I don't see no reason why I gotta just keep on reliving and rehashing it. What the fuck does that do? You know, babe–that don't do nuthin for nobody, including you."

I was surprised as I wrote this conversation, at how much Ray cursed. He rarely cursed and he really used lots of curse words this time. Obviously he was very upset.

I asked what I was supposed to do then? Just chalk it all off, like it never happened?

Ray said, "No, babe. What…watcha do is, I mean at least the way I think anyway…you know all of us have..have had bad things happen to us, babe, but you know life goes on. You pick yourself up and start anew. You don't…"

This made me livid. "Ray!! I've done that!!!"

He continued, "You don't keep harping about…"

"When you discarded me, I picked myself up and I brushed myself off and I went on, with or without you, Ray."

He said again, "So what are you harping about what all I did…all the shit I used to do." He couldn't hear me because he was hell bent on saying his piece.

"I'm telling you that I'll still do it Ray. All the shit you used to do are things you've done to me. So I don't know where I stand? Where are we going now? What are we doing–the same old thing?"

"Well, baby," Ray said, "If I don't try to do something, ain't nuthin gonna get done. Don't you understand that, babe? I can't keep livin' in the fuckin' past. I can't accomplish nuthin that way. But if I'm tryin to do something, aaah that's different."

"I don't know what you're trying to do Ray."

He was disgusted. "Well then, it doesn't matter, Marci. Hey, look...I'm...I'm...believe me, I didn't mean to trouble you or anything. I...I had my feelings and I tried. That's all I was trying to do."

"That's all I can do, babe. I don't know how to take it any further. All I know is to try do something and if you get shot down, you get shot down. That's all. And I understand that, too. I've been shot down before."

I just couldn't let my guard down. I was very apprehensive. I said, "I don't think that you're capable of truly caring for me, Ray."

"Well you don't hafta believe it, babe. That's up to you. If you don't think I'm capable, that's you. That's in your own mind. You hafta deal with it."

I didn't make a decision then. I couldn't. Mitzi, Lisa and I were leaving for Los Angeles soon with six women who Mitzi worked with at Blondie's Hair Salon. They were going for a Vidal Sassoon hair cutting class, and I planned to do a lot of thinking about Ray's conversation.

The class didn't occupy much time, so we had lots of free time. But there was absolutely no time for contemplation. We were there for nine days of fun, fun, fun. There was just no time to think about Ray.

We went everywhere. We snuck through someone's property to their private beach in Malibu. No one noticed. Then on to Patrick's Restaurant–a quaint little place housed in a brightly colored lime green building that looked exactly like a mobile home. I think it was. It was located on Pacific Coast Highway in Malibu, prime location just across from the ocean.

We were on our way inside when we saw Dabney Coleman (*Nine to Five*) and a lady friend. They had just come from horseback riding and stopped at Patrick's for lunch. We took a picture with their permission.

We had lunch, then went back for breakfast the next day and Patrick, himself, showed us where Arnold Schwartzenegger's special table was and Sylvester Stalone's.

We had our picture taken with Patrick, who was a slight elderly man with lots of personality.

We thanked him and left.

We visited Universal Studios where Lisa was chosen to fly above us in an astronaut suit. All we could see was her little face.

Another day we went to the Equestrian place to meet Alex Cord, actor (*The Brotherhood* with Kirk Douglas, *Stagecoach*, etc.) and father of Mary Ann's daughter, Toni.

He was exercising his horse in the coral. We waved to him and watched, seated on bleachers, for over an hour. Finally we stood and motioned for him to come over. We visited for an hour or so, and left for lunch without Alex. I like him, and have stayed in touch sporadically through the years.

Next we went to Cher's house in the Canyon and took pictures and tried to duck her security camera.

The next day we all went to San Diego and stayed at the Sheridan on the Harbor, then on to Tijuana the next day. We bought all sorts of things to drag back home on the plane.

While I was in L.A., I called Ray and left a message that we would like to tour his studio. I got a message from our hotel desk clerk to call Mr. Ray Charles at his hotel in St. Louis, Missouri.

What?!!! St. Louis??!

I called and asked him to call me back so he could pay the bill.

He wanted to know what I was doing in Los Angeles and why I didn't tell him.

I giggled and said, "I don't tell you everything, Ray." Then I said, "I didn't think about it–I knew I would call you while I was here."

He said, "As you know, babe, I rarely know my itinerary, so I didn't know I would be in St. Louis and when I found out, I couldn't get you to answer the phone...again. So I called Lisa and Mitzi's number and nobody answered there either. Now I know why."

I came home to St. Louis and Ray went to his next job.

In no time he called, struggling to get us back together again but I was still struggling with the past.

He said, "I feel if you're gonna do anything in this world, I mean, if you want to, you can take it a step further...and say okay...what's wrong with us trying to see what we can do about this..if we both want to. He emphasized, "If we both want to. But if we're both gonna keep talking about what we did wrong or...what I did wrong–I mean, that's a piece of shit, cause ain't nuthin never gonna happen with that, you know, never."

"So you might as well just say, Look, we're wasting each other's time, it's...it's crazy, absolutely stupid....nuthins ever gonna happen."

"Well, Ray, what do you suggest? Do you want to reintroduce ourselves to one another and just start like we never knew each other and we didn't have a history and nothing ever happened? Then we'll just start all over–right? Courting and dating, you coming to see me, buying me dinner, is that what you're suggesting?"

Sort of exasperated he said "Well, Marci, uh, you know, let's not be absurd...I mean...uh..."

"Well, you tell me how it's gonna be, Ray."

"Uh...uh...I think you well know what I'm...what I'm sayin to you, Marci."

"No, I don't. You need to spit it out, tell me...you have a way of twisting things. If you tell me so that I can understand it...and you want me to understand, maybe I will."

He started beating around the bush, not getting to the point. He said, "Well would you...would you admit that that depends on whether you want to understand what I'm tellin you? Would you at least acknowledge that much of this conversation?"

I said, "I'll admit to this, Ray. I'm a bright enough person that if you tell me something straight forward, without beating around the bush about a whole damned bunch of things, I think I'm smart enough to understand it. So far you haven't said anything to me."

He was sort of grumbling and saying okay in a low growl. Then he said, "Well, I haven't said the things you want to hear. I've said everything that I can possibly think of to say to you, Marci, really and truly..."

I asked what he thought I wanted to hear.

He disregarded me and continued, "So I don't know what you want me to do, you know, I mean I've said everything I can possibly say to you and that's all I can do. And obviously you don't understand me or it's not enough."

"Well maybe it's not enough," I said.

He continued as if I hadn't said one word. "I don't know which it is, but you see when you don't know, you don't know. And I'm completely ignorant of it."

I tried to squeeze in a sentence. "When you tell me..." (Uh oh, here he goes again,) but I know one thing...I do know this. I know I've told you everything I know how to tell you, Marci."

Again I tried, "Well...(*Okay Marci. You're not gonna get* to participate in this conversation).

"And I've told you as sincere as I can be," he went on talking over me. Now whether...unfortunately for me that's not...you don't accept that. So that's it. That's all there is to it."

Finally when I got a chance to say something, I said, "When you tell me that you want to start over and get back together, what does it mean to you? How? I mean, tell me what it means to you. What does getting back together mean to you? And what does starting over mean to you?"

His answer to my question was: "It means wh...whatever we want it to mean, Marci. It's up to the two of us once we...you know. It's up to us to work out whatever the logistics of it or the situation is that's gonna happen between us. Because we do have...you know...you have a life and I have a life, you know, so all we hafta do is work out how we intend to deal with...with our particular situation and stuff...(in a frustrated voice) to me...I mean looks like to me that's just simple. You know...I mean maybe it's not. I could completely be out in left field, but it seems to me that if...if the two of us were sincere about each other...if we really want to be with each other, uh, obviously you can't say that it's regular, because it is...uh it is different because of the way that my situation is...the way my...my work goes, but...but that not withstanding everything else we ought be able to iron out between us. You know, sit down and talk about whatever it is. I don't know that just seems to me to be logical. But I don't know about all this goin' back and talk...and just making a conversation of what all I used to do and what all went down an...because th...that don't mean nuthin, babe. I mean for me, whatever it was, if it was wrong, I'm sorry for it. I apologize, but that's all I can say. But that's in the past, and for all intents and purposes, is dead."

I asked, "Well, what else do I have to base anything on? I mean how do I know what'll hap...?"

He's so frustrated. "Well, baby, you don't know. Don't you understand that?"

"I don't know. You're right about that," I said.

He said again, "That's the whole...that's the point. You don't know."

In a sort of whimpering voice, I said, "Well how scared do you think I am?"

He's telling me again, that I have to trust him, "What's terrible, you know, babe, is there's nobody in this world that I know of that can look into the future or even look into somebody else really, far as that goes. There no such human being. You got to feel...if you're gonna be with somebody, babe, you hafta learn to trust them and that's something that..."

He was disappointed when I said, "No, I'm too afraid of you."

"Well, babe. If you can't do that then we...we're in trouble!!!"

"I can't...I can't do it," I said, "I'm scared to death of you."

Ray said, "Hey, for whatever reason, you can say it's being afraid if you wanna...if that's your...you know, reasoning, fine. You know, but I'm...it...you know it comes down to that, baby. I don't care who it is. If you were God. If you don't trust it, it ain't gonna happen and I mean that's the way...that's the bottom line. (He said "line" in a high pitched voice and it sounded so funny). So you know it...uh really I mean, you know, I mean I know where you're comin from and I uh...respect that...but that's what it comes down to."

I responded, "Let me tell you something and I know it's gonna make you mad when I say I used to, but I did use to trust you, Ray. All the time I trusted you. At the beginning I trusted you for thirteen years and waited and waited and waited..."

He did not want to hear this, "Okay...Okay...Hey babe...Okay. Fine. Okay that..."

He tried to interrupt but I finished what I was saying. "And what happened? Nothing."

He said, "I understand."

I continued talking, "Do you think that...wait a minute, Ray. Do you think that I can just...lay my heart out again? Do you think I can do that? No...I'm scared to." Then I began crying uncontrollably and said, "I can't do it."

Here was his next attempt at convincing me. "Alright, babe...Alright...Hey...I'm just saying…...that...that you know babe, that...that was my point. I'm saying that we hafta start somewhere but if you don't wanna start, you don't wanna start. I'm just saying that you gotta...basically if we feel...if we think we're in tune with each other and if we think we half way care about each other...you...you know then as far as your trust in me is concerned, you're gonna hafta sort of wean yourself to the point of saying, 'Maybe I don't trust him totally but I…I gotta start somewhere.' But if you're gonna keep the attitude of saying, 'Well, I ain't never gonna trus…cause I know what happened eighteen years ago…' I know what happened twenty…well if…if it's gonna be like that, they ain't nothing gonna…so all I'm saying, babe, is you cannot get something outta nothing. I don't give a damn who he or she is, it's impossible to do it. Believe me. So that's all I'm saying, Marci–believe me–no more, no less. You know, I know that sometimes things can happen and you may…feel…and stuff you know, but if you're gonna get invol…then you hafta allow yourself, certainly at least a small amount of space to…to grow."

But I kept talking in past tense and irritating him. "I did…God I gave it my all."

"I'm not talking 'bout what you did, Marci. Now here we go back to what I just said. Okay…Okay…Okay."

"Ray!!! I gave it my life practically. From the time I was thirty years old. Now I'm fifty. What am I supposed to do? All I've got is that to go on. I mean, Goddamn. What happened to me?"

"Okay, babe," he said softly.

I felt like I wanted to get said, what I wanted to. "I came to you. I did everything…what am I supposed to do–believe you again when…when look what you did to me before?"

"Naw, you ain't s'posed to do that, babe. If you don't wanna."

"If I don't wanna. Oh! I don't wanna hear that. I can't…do it Ray. Look what happened to me. How would you feel?"

The American Standard Dictionary's interpretation of the word "rhetoric" is "the art of using language effectively and persuasively." I'm here to say that Ray Charles Robinson was a master of this art, and even if you were a person who could stay focused, he could still confuse you. He answered my question as follows.

"I'll tell you something. I'll tell you…if you really…you ask me a question. How would I feel? I'll tell you how I feel,

Marci. If the shoe was on the other foot, and let's say that if I was in your position and the whole thing had went down with me like it went down with you, okay. I'm trying to be reasonable about the whole thing, then I would have to say to myself, first of all, let me first check me. Do I really care for the man to start with? That's number one. Now I know in my mind, in the past, what has happened so we won't get into that, but do I trust him, and do I feel that I care about the man? Does he mean anything to me at all? That's number one. Number two–do I think that I mean anything to him? (*Oh God!*) That's the second thing. Number three, third and not last, you know, how do I feel? Can I trust him? Can I be…well I don't really trust him cause he's done this to me. Well, if I care about him and I think he cares about me–number one and number two, then I hafta tell myself, I'm gonna hafta try to give myself a chance to try to trust him again. I'm gonna hafta do it cause that's the only way. Why? Because I care for him, number one–and number two–I think he cares for me. And I think it could work so I hafta try. That's all you can do. Now whether or not I know it's gonna work or wheth…uh uh ain't nobody got no guarantees on nuthin on this earth period. But if you believe that it's something, not so much in the person but do you believe in what you're getting into, and if you think it's possible, that's what it comes down to, babe. But if you wanna sell yourself short, and say well, you know, I mean, I know this happened, and I know…and I understand what you're sayin'. And I'm not completely a fool. I understand what you mean by what happened to somebody in the past. But what I'm saying is with the circumstances being what they are, you hafta… in my view…uh what I would do is I'd hafta say to myself, do I care, do I really care for the person and do I feel the person cares for me? That's number one and number two…and as for whether or not do I trust them, I would hafta tell myself…just like I'm tryin to make this thing work. The proof of the pudding will go along with itself, you know, because if the man is halfway right, I'm gonna be knowin' it. Believe me, I'm gonna

know it, you know, it ain't gonna take long for me to know it
either. You see….that's the way I would look at it. See cause
what I'm saying. babe is I…I've had all kinds of shit happen to
me, good and bad. I can honestly say that…good and bad. But
I found out that when the bad shit happens to me, you know,
what's important for me is to keep from gettin' an attitude
about it, you know? Now am I gonna allow this to be Fu-----
with me, or what am I gonna do? Now that's just the way I
feel. But I think in a relationship like I was tellin' you about
you and me, you know, I genuinely know what I feel for you
and to tell you the truth, I may be in the wrong myself, to show
you what kinda fool I am. I really think you care for me. You
just can't figure out how to deal with it. I think you care for
me just like I care for you, Marci."

I said, "Ray, I don't wanna be treated the way I've been
treated, ever again."

He yelled, "I don't…I ain't talkin bout what used to be.
Can't you get your mind offa that??? Alright, babe. I'm gonna
leave…I'm gonna let you go. baby."

"Ray!!! You just want me to say, 'Okay.'"

"No, I don…you can't tell me what I want you to
do, Marci."

"Yeah, Ray…I can hear you tellin' me that. I can hear you
saying it."

"Yeah, but that's in your mind, babe. Why don't you let
yourself go, Marci, you know? I promise not to kill you, you
know. Believe me. I promise I won't kill you."

"No…I…I just can'…." I said. "I'd rather wait and if you
want me then you come and lay the cards on the table to me,
when you want me. When you really want me, you let me
know. I told you that all along, Ray."

"O….Okay, Marci. Very good. I got it. Alright, babe."

"When you decide you want me, you tell me."

"Okay, honey. Okay, babe."

This was in 1988. We were still trying to make something
work that was never going to work. But we did get back

together again as usual, and all went as well as could be expected between a woman who could never trust, and a man who could never make her trust him.

Ray tried for nearly thirty years to mold me into a mouse, but I've always been a cat. Sometimes I purr and sometimes I scratch.

As he found out, I'm not a very forgiving person and I certainly don't forget. So after the bad experience in 1969 (*I know – get over it Marci – but I never could*) anything he did would cause me to erupt and then stubbornly not budge. That, in turn, sent him into flurries of frustration. Then he would just sadly give up, but not for long. Within days or sometimes weeks, he would try to soothe me and calm me. Ray knew his craft and he knew it well. He knew when to pause and let me settle down.

I read this chapter to Mary Ann, as I did every chapter, and she asked why I wasn't more descriptive about what I wanted our relationship to be when Ray asked me.

I did say I wanted security, and I wanted us to be together more, but knowing Ray the way I did, I didn't have any hope of either. So rather than getting my heart broken even more, I didn't allow myself to expect much.

After twenty years, I thought he should know what I would like. I knew that he didn't like me seeing other men, and I didn't have men beating my door down. I knew he was trying to lock me in by my commitment to him, and that's what all of this discussion was about.

So he continued to run in and out of here. But I wasn't as easy to control as I once was.

The one thing that I stayed absolutely firm about was using protection when we had sex. I was deathly afraid of Aids so I stopped all unprotected love making. Ray hated that. In that, he would never control me.

40
Palimony

Sometime before we went to L.A., I ran into a prominent St. Louis attorney in a local restaurant. I joined him at his table, and during our conversation, I told him about my long and on-going relationship with Ray Charles, and I told him that I was very frustrated because Ray didn't follow through with any of his promises to me. I also mentioned to him that I had a lot of taped phone conversations of Ray. The attorney, Charles Shaw, said, "Why don't you bring them to my office? I'd like to hear them. You might have a palimony case."

He called me a few times to tell me his thoughts and each time I talked to him, he was more convinced that he could make a case for me. He asked me to come to his office to finalize our discussions, sign papers, and so on.

But when I got there, I decided not to go through with it. I couldn't do that to Ray. As frustrated as I was with him, I loved him too much. I also just didn't want to go through the ordeal of a legal confrontation with him. In fact, that was actually one of the reasons I had the abortion–to avoid a huge legal mess with Ray. And suing him for palimony would not only have shocked and hurt him–it would have really angered him.

I'm glad I didn't go through with it, although in my estimation he deserved it. In spite of everything, I still had a need to talk to him and see him. Had I sued him, it would have been like death and I wasn't ready for that finality.

In 1991, three months after she won the "Smirinoff Makes You a Star" contest, Lisa moved to Huntington Beach, California, a half hours' drive south of Los Angeles. The next contest was the big one and the winner would get a large cash prize. I flew out for the big event (and to participate with Lisa in the perks she won!). I hadn't seen Lisa's condo. It was so nice—two stories, three bedrooms, two baths, but best of all, just seconds from the beach. I loved it.

Mitzi and her boyfriend had gone earlier so the three of them picked me up at LAX. I hadn't seen my Lisa for three or four months, the longest we had ever been apart, and it felt so good just to touch and hold her. We all cried. (That's a family trait. We cry about everything...even Henry was a crier.)

We went to Patrick's again for breakfast. We ate, chatted with Patrick and really enjoyed ourselves. Then we went to Venice Beach where we shopped and I bought all of us an outfit. Lisa and Mitzi roller bladed on the boardwalk and everyone thought Lisa was Cher.

The next morning Mitzi and her boyfriend went jet skiing at Dana Point and Lisa and I went to the mall, then to the Rusty Pelican for a nice ocean-side lunch. We had already packed for our two night stay at J.W. Marriott, so after lunch we took the 405 up the coast to L.A.

The J.W. Marriott hotel was located on Avenue of the Stars. It was a luxurious hotel and Lisa was awarded every amenity imaginable. All of our meals and drinks were complimentary. Lisa didn't drink, but Mitzi and I made up for it! The mini fridge was full and restocked every time we took anything out.

Lisa and Mitzi enjoyed frolicking in the beautiful pool and sauna. They looked so cute in their fluffy white robes with their hair in French braids.

A limo was provided for us and Mitzi and I used it to go to the Mall to get movie-star-Lisa something to hold her short, tight dress down. We got this thing that looked like a garter belt which hooked to her dress hem and to her thigh-high hose —typical Cher style.

Then Lisa had dress rehearsal and was chauffeured to Studio 21. Mitzi and I hung out in the lobby and when Lisa returned we took a picture of her with Morton Downey, Jr. He had a television show called "Bigmouth." We also saw Jerry Lewis there which was fun.

Then we went to watch Lisa perform. She was great, but the Liza Minelli look-alike won. Lisa was spotted by a Ron Smith, a look-a-like scout, and the next day we went to Hollywood to their office and Lisa was signed to an exclusive contract with their agency.

It was a very good and lucrative move for her.

The Ron Smith Agency got her gigs on *The Carol Burnett Show, Vicki Lawrence Show, Sisters, Family Feud* (for the whole week), *Entertainment Tonight* and she was Cher's double on her Equal commercial.

Cher, her sister and her friend Paulette were on the set, but not one of them said a word to Lisa. (Cher obviously isn't as nice as she tries to appear on talk shows.)

Lisa was told the rules before she went on the set—no asking for autographs. No asking for anything period!

She said Carol Burnett and Vicki Lawrence were so pleasant—nice and relaxed—and so was Swoozy Kurtz on the set of *Sisters*.

I have such fun memories of that time in our lives—hanging out with Mitzi on the beach while Lisa was at work, riding bikes with Lisa, walking on the boardwalk in Newport Beach, going to the Breadcrumb in Huntington Beach for breakfast. All too soon it was time to go home. I hated leaving Lisa, but she was very happy. I don't blame her—what a great place to live.

One day Lisa called to tell me that Ray was doing a show in Anaheim, California and she would like to go and take her roommates, Sherry and Yvette. She asked if I would call Ray and make the arrangements.

I left a message and a few days later he hadn't called Lisa, so I left another message asking why he hadn't called her.

Here is the message he left me—verbatim.

"Well, I just wanna tell you, you're raising so much hell. You forgot to give me Lisa's phone number. I don't have her number. You want me to call her. Why don't you put her last name on it? You say Lisa and then her last name. Is it Soto or not?

"Well anyway, yeah put her name and phone number on my machine, dear, pleassssee darlin'. I love you, baby. You little Devil you – you're a hellcat. I know that."

I thought I had given Ray Lisa's number when she first moved to California. And I don't know why he was questioning her last name unless he thought she got married–if she had, he would certainly have known about it. It made no sense to me. And about my "hell raising," well as usual, he took too long and my message said, "Why in the hell haven't you called Lisa, Ray?" Then I got an immediate response. Sometimes I had to be a little hellcatish to get him going.

So he called Lisa, and one of her roommates answered the phone. Ray said, "Yeah…this is Ray Charles. Is Lisa in?" Her roommate said, "Yes" and excitedly ran to get her, saying, "Oh My God!! Ray Charles is actually calling our number. Lisa! Lisa! Ray Charles wants to talk to you. Oh My God!!"

Ray said, "Lisa, of course baby, you can come to the show. How many will there be?" She said, "Sherry, Yvette and me."

"Okay, sweetheart. Somebody will be at the gate to greet you and bring you to your seats and when the shows over, he'll come and bring you and your friends to the bus."

Lisa was thrilled. She had no idea that they would be invited on the bus. Her friends told her that Ray was in rare form that night and his performance exceeded excellence. When it was over, a crew member came and escorted them to the big black elegant bus.

Once on the bus, they headed for the back where Ray was waiting for them. They had a great time with Ray and his band members, laughing, talking, playing chess and getting their pictures taken. A half hour later, it was time to say goodbye.

Lisa kissed Ray's cheek, hugged him and thanked him for inviting them to the show and especially for staying around after the show to spend time with her, something he rarely did. Ray was usually out of there immediately after his show.

I called Lisa to ask how her evening had turned out.

"Phenomenal" was all she said. She said her girlfriends were so impressed that they got to meet "The Ray Charles," a once in a lifetime experience for them. But of course, Lisa would see him again.

While Lisa lived in California, Mitzi and I kept the airways hot visiting her. We missed her something awful. We both loved being in California so every penny we made we spent going to see her.

In 1992, my mother died. Lisa was in Scotland for two months doing her Cher performance, so we waited for her to return to the States to have a memorial service for Mom.

During that time, Ray was here supporting me. He stayed with me for three or four days when he had off-time. He liked my mom a lot.

Mitzi was a Godsend. She was with me throughout mom's illness (cancer). Every time mom would have a setback, she was right with me getting her to the hospital.

After Lisa came home, we went to Lutesville, Missouri, my hometown, for mom's memorial. Lisa was here for a week, then went back to L.A., and took her cat, Missy, with her. I had been Missy's "foster parent" until Lisa could take her, and I missed her when she was gone.

Sometime during this time, Ray asked me to go to Louisville, Kentucky for a couple of days. It was during some sort of holiday–I don't remember which one–but I would be off from work and was able to be away.

I agreed to meet him, but with the stipulation that there would be no unprotected sex. I hadn't been able to do that since the Norma thing. He hated wearing a condom–he said it ruined it for him so he might as well not even do it. I just said, "Okay. That's fine. We don't have to do it."

He said, "Okay, honey. I'll make flight arrangements for you, and we'll work on the other problem when you arrive."

At the St. Louis Airport I saw Lyle Wagoner. He was with some actor named Anderson, but I've forgotten his first name.

They were no longer in demand by then, and they were going to Louisville for a golf tournament.

When I boarded the plane, my seat was next to a nice young man who said he would be in Louisville all spring. He was so nice to me. When I went to collect my luggage, it was not there. We were in line (for some reason, I don't remember why), but he held my place while I searched for my lost luggage. I never found it.

When I got to the hotel, I couldn't get into Ray's room. He was asleep and didn't hear me knocking. Finally, after about ten minutes, his valet, who was in a room just across the hall, came to my rescue and called Ray.

Ray answered the door in his boxers and undershirt, all disheveled and unkempt looking–I was pissed. I started complaining. "Damn, Ray. Couldn't you at least be awake, showered and in a robe? God!!" I couldn't shut up. "And maybe have a bottle of wine chilling?"

He got right on the phone and ordered a bottle of wine.

After we had a glass of wine and I calmed down, I told him about the airline losing my luggage and about the nice young man I sat next to.

"What was his name," Ray asked.

"Jose Quansetto,'" I answered.

"Are you sure it's not Conseco?" Ray questioned. "He's probably down here for Spring training. He's a well known baseball player. Didn't you recognize him, honey?"

"No," I said. "I'm not a sports person, Ray. You know that. I don't know any sports players."

"I know that, honey. You're just my little soft sweet baby."

"I don't know how sweet I am, but I know that I can't go to the concert tonight. I don't have anything to wear."

The hotel had a boutique, but there was nothing there for me. Ray said I looked fine and that I could wear what I had on. It was his show, I was his woman and he wanted me with him. At least I had my carry-on with all of my grooming essentials in it, so I was able to brush my teeth, freshen my makeup and style my hair. When we were about ready to leave, the desk clerk called to inform us that our limo had arrived.

Ray and I walked to the elevator then, through the beautiful lobby. Him in his tuxedo, and me in my black and white polka dotted leggings, black spaghetti-strapped casual top and–cowboy boots. Oh My God!! I *hated* Delta Airlines for losing my luggage!!

There were so many people with cameras–I guess they were fans. Some of them appeared to be the press waiting for Ray to exit the hotel and get into the limousine. I asked if he wanted to talk to them and he said no, just keep on going and get us into the car. He said he had already had a press conference that morning.

When we got to the Symphony Hall (Skitch Henderson was also a guest performer with the Louisville Symphony that evening), and into the dressing room, Ray asked one of the band members to escort me to my seat. I sat next to an elderly lady who asked if I was with the band. I said, "No, ma'am." Then she asked if I was a wife, and I told her I was Ray Charles' girlfriend. I thought she must be wondering why I was dressed the way I was, but I didn't explain.She was all dressed up in her evening attire. Thank God it was fairly dark in the auditorium.

Just before the performance ended, someone came and took me to Ray's dressing room. Very soon, Joe Adams escorted Ray off the stage to meet me. People were oohing and aahhing over Ray while I talked with Joe and got my picture taken with him. (I did explain to him that my clothes were lost and that was why I was dressed like I was).

Soon Ray was calling my name and I went to get him. We waded through the crowd to the waiting limo and were driven to our hotel. There were some fans there too, but it didn't take long till we were in our room, undressing and getting comfortable. We ordered dessert and coffee. When we finished eating, we lounged in bed.

I reminded Ray about using a condom. He refused, so I refused his sexual advances. He would get very handsy and then he'd say, "Oh, Oh, I'm sorry!!" That went on for some time. Finally I got perplexed and slept on the couch in my clothes. I told him I was leaving the next morning–and I did.

He said over and over, "I can't believe you're doin' this, Marci. You came all this way. You know I'll be here tomorrow and you're leavin'."

I said, "I told you what I would and wouldn't do before I left St. Louis, so you knew."

"Okay, I'll behave myself."

"No, I'm going" I said. And I left.

He knew that if I said it, I would do it and he had pushed me too far. After that "Norma thing," I was not going to expose myself to unprotected sex with him. Period. Knowing what I now know about Ray, he probably had me replaced within minutes!

He continued to want to be with me, however, despite my refusal to comply with his unprotected sexual desires.

I said, "Ray, aren't you afraid of AIDS?" His answer was, "Yeah, babe. I'm afraid of AIDS, but I'm not afraid of you." In 2005, I found out how many of us he wasn't afraid of.

Sometime in the 90's I got a call on my answering machine. Ray was in Osaka, Japan.

"Yeah, Marci. You sound so sweet, baby. I know every time I talk to you I'm always out of the country, right? Well, I think I told you I was...I was gonna be leavin'. I'm in Japan right now. In Osako (Ray always pronounced it that way.) Well I sure miss you, baby. I hafta tell you I...I don't know...I had a dream about you. That's why I'm callin' you...just dreaming and dreaming.

"Okay, babe. I'll try to call...you sound good on that machine, dear. I must say. I'll call you back, honey. I love you, baby."

I saved the message. It's about twenty years old now. I still listen to it (and the one about Lisa wanting to go to his show).

So many things happened in the early to mid 90's. Lisa came home for a visit just in time to help Mitzi, my brother, my nephew and I clean Dad's house after a major flood seriously damaged it. It was awful. The water and silt were four feet high on the walls. It was a horrible flood, and there would be more to come in 1993.

Dad refused to move, so we cleaned and sanitized as best we could. He lived there until he died in May 1993, at the age 81. Once again, Lisa came home for a memorial, this time, her grandpa's.

Ray was in and out of my life, but nothing was progressing between us. Same old, same old. I loved Ray, but still felt the need to continue with my life. I went to Key West with a girl-friend and met a man who I was attracted to. Unfortunately, he lived in Philadelphia.

Ray was upset when I told him, but he didn't have to worry. The relationship didn't work out. The guy was too far away and we eventually lost contact, making Ray Charles a happy man.

41
Bringing Lisa Home

୬ଡ଼ଡ଼ଡ଼

In August of 1993 Lisa decided to come home for good. I flew to L.A. to help bring all her things home, but first we decided to have some fun.

We went all over Orange County and L.A. We went to the famous Spago restaurant for dinner, and hit some other favorite places. We went to Palm Springs, had lunch and drove around the city. I had never been there, but Lisa had done a Cher look-a-like gig there a few months before. Ironically, we checked out Sonny Bono's restaurant.

Then we went back to Redondo Beach where Lisa was living. We rested for a night, then took the freeway to San Francisco. We drove everywhere–across the Golden Gate Bridge, to Fisherman's Wharf and to China Town. Lisa drove her Nisson stick shift auto up the steepest hill in San Francisco. I was scared to death! I thought the car would tip over backwards, but she got us to the top and then down the crookedest street in the world–Lombard Street. Then we drove to Salsalido, a quaint town with lots of houses built on the water, a mini Venice, Italy. We loved it.

We drove back to L.A. via Pacific Coast Highway 101, which is a beautiful drive, but so scary. The edge of the highway was right there, dropping off hundreds of feet into the Pacific Ocean. The cliffs were so precipitous that when Lisa pulled over to a look-out area, I hit the floor, terrified that the brakes would give out. I felt like I had electric currents running through my body I was so paralyzed with fear.

Finally, after Lisa got her crazy mother settled down, I was able to get out of the car and take in the awesome beauty.

The jagged faces of the rocks jutted out in different shades of black, brown and gray all the way down to the undisturbed vast blue ocean. With the fog rolling in, it was an ethereal experience. It was worth the fear just to view the lovely secluded sight with Lisa.

Simultaneously, we said, "I wish Mitzi were here."

Then she said, "Look, mom, that's where we have to go."

I said, "Oh, God! I can't do that." It was a bridge with nothing but space under it for what, in my mind, looked like miles–then another steep twist even higher than where we had been.

I said, "I can't go over that bridge, Lisa!"

She said, "Hit the floor, mom. I'll get us there." And she did.

We spent the night in Monterey, then another night in Santa Barbara and Big Sur.

Everyone should take that coastal drive. It's so beautiful. It's a vision that I will cherish always, especially us sitting on the rocks by the ocean in the midst of otters, sea lions and tiny ground squirrels.

When we got to Los Angeles, we went straight to the U-Haul place. The first thing Lisa did was head to an empty lot, check the brakes on the trailor, etc. Then she practiced backing up. She drove it like a Teamster! I knew she could. She had to drive her roommates big U-Haul truck a few months earlier.

We had breakfast at Redondo Pier and watched the pelicans (my favorite) search for sand crabs. Then we went to her apartment and started the daunting task of loading the U-Haul. Oh! My God! So much stuff!

We slept, went to the Breadcrumb for breakfast, which was my favorite breakfast place. Lisa said a sad goodbye to Christine, her roommate and best friend. Then we left, pulling a U-Haul that was packed to the brim, and sharing the car with Lisa's two cats, Jake and Missy. Lisa had rescued Jake from the street on Balboa Island. An exhausted mom and daughter began the long drive home to St. Louis.

It was dusk when we headed into the Mojave Desert. We didn't see the "Last Chance for Gas" sign. Honestly, we didn't even realize we were in the desert until suddenly there were no buildings. We saw nothing but headlights.

And yes, of course, we ran out of gas. It was pitch black and so dangerous. Big trucks were whizzing by nearly side swiping us every five minutes. I quickly loaded my "trusty" .38 and followed Lisa to the call box. I was afraid of kidnappers and night-crawling rattlers.

The trooper who answered the phone was disgusted with us for being careless. (Did he think we meant to do it?) Gas was there within a half hour. I cracked the window just enough to pay him, thanked him and off we went. We made it to Needles, Arizona and stopped for the night. The cats made themselves at home and we all slept.

I was awakened with a loud hysterical sounding, "Mom!!" I yelled, "What?" and sat straight up. Lisa said, "Mom, I thought you were dead. Your eyes were half open." We got tickled and Lisa said, "Oh, my God, Mom! I thought I was going to have to prop you up next to me and drive us home."

We stopped just outside of Albuquerque, slept, then went on to Santa Fe. What a quaint city. We strolled around and watched the Indians, who were sitting on the sidewalks next to the buildings, selling their wares. We had lunch, then hurried back to the car and let the cats out for some air and exercise.

I neglected to elaborate on how splendidly beautiful and absolutely awesome the Red Rock Mountains were through Arizona and New Mexico. It was more desert-like, than Northern California, but had the same jutting cliffs and jagged edged mountains–and was just as breathtaking.

On the way to Kansas, we nearly ran out of gas again! Oh! God! Here we were, singing and laughing, and our tank was on empty! Luckily, there was a service station nearby. We made it to the top of the hill and coasted down to the station.

We spent one more night in a motel, then we kept driving till we got to St. Louis. Mitzi and Terry, a best friend, were here to greet us, and I treated everyone to dinner.

Wow! Fourteen days of fun–and another fabulous memory

for me. Lisa, Missy, and Jake lived with me when she first came home. One night, she went to visit her sister. They were just going to chill out and watch "Friends" on television.

They both had brand new cars parked side by side. Rain was coming down like the Victoria Falls in Africa, but my girls were comfy and cozy without a worry in the world–so happy to be together again.

They were engrossed in their television program, when they were startled by the sound of a car horn. Mitzi looked out the window, but at first, was afraid to go down. She thought her car was being broken in to. When she did go down, she saw water up to the floorboards of their cars, and before Lisa got down the stairs and out to their cars, the water had risen to the seats. They tried to start their cars but no luck. They tried to push them out of the water but couldn't. Mitzi ran through the apartment complex alerting tenants.

Both cars were declared totaled by their insurance companies and they were towed to the salvage lot. What a disaster! My girls were just sick. It took some time and inconvenience, but they both bought new Preludes with their insurance settlements.

That was "the great flood of '93" and it was a freak of nature that that particular area flooded. There was a small stream beside Mitzi's apartment, but something blocked it further down stream and that caused the water to back up and flood.

Me and my little Fiero got a workout for about a week, either driving them to work or lending my car to whichever one needed it.

It was just one more hurdle to jump in the saga of the Soto threesome! Hurdles might have slowed us down, but they never stopped us.

Ray called and offered his condolescences. *Big Woo!*

The first time I ever had an answering machine was when I went to get Lisa. I got it because of my housecleaning business. I had employees and they had to check in every day to see if any clients cancelled or see whatever else might have happened.

Starting a business was one of the hardest and most discouraging things I've ever done. I started it in 1975. I damned near starved to death trying to get it going and I worked like a slave–long days for very little money. I gave up my own clients to my employees and took a small, very small, percentage. I kept running ads in newspapers to get new clients, which was very costly. It was a long and arduous task. I would get a new client and an employee would steal them from me or the client would steal my employee. It took awhile to get to where I made a decent living.

Thank God I knew how to live frugally and had the determination to keep going and make a success of my business.

Did Ray Charles help me? Only when he gave me two or three hundred dollars occasionally. He certainly didn't take care of me. But every little bit helped.

I always had some money because I saved every cent that I didn't need to take care of my children. By the late eighties or nineties, I was doing all right. When Lisa came home, she worked in a hair salon until 1995, then she started helping me. She was such an attribute. We named our company "All About Cleaning." I worked with her until 2004.

I no longer work in the business. Lisa is the sole proprietor. It's still hard, but at least now we have resources to help protect our business–an attorney, an accountant, etc, so it isn't so easy for people to steal from us.

In 1995, Don Eaker had open-heart surgery. We were all worried, including Ray. When I told him he said, "Oh, honey. I must call Don and Colleen," and he did immediately.

Colleen said, "He just happened to catch me at home. I was going back and forth to the hospital so much I was rarely there."

Don interjected, "Ray always said, "Colleen uh...uh this is Ray Charles."

Colleen laughed and said, "Like I didn't know."

She said to Ray, "Well, I know exactly who you are."

Ray said that he was concerned about Don and just wanted to call. Don said when she told him, he was thrilled and thought it was so nice of Ray to call.

Then I called and told Ray how much it meant to them. He said he talked to her for a while, asked questions about Don, their business, etc.

సౌ

1995 really was a busy year for the Soto girls. The Rolanda television show was doing a segment on botched plastic surgery. I applied and was invited to appear on her show, all expenses paid, for two nights.

Lisa and I went, but Mitzi couldn't get off from work.

We extended our time one day and made a three day vacation out of it. We were all over New York City. We hit lots of famous restaurants for lunch and dinner and did lots of sightseeing. Rolanda was so nice. We liked her immediately. I have a tape of the show. One woman sort of hogged it, but I was okay. I got on, and Lisa and I had a fabulous time for free.

We loved New Yorkers. They didn't live up to their unfriendly reputation. We found them to be captivating and eager to help with directions, etc.

The next big event in our lives was going to Italy. What a spectacular time. Rome, Florence, Tuscany and Venice. Another wonderful memory for my mental archives. Well...one memory wasn't so pleasant...

We took a bus to Florence, a train to Venice and a boat to St. Marks Square. All went well but we didn't know that we should buy a berth ticket on the train back to Rome. There were no seats–only tiny little round stools along the corridor of the passenger compartment. Oh Lord! I was sick with a cold and kept falling asleep and nearly falling off my little stool. When one of the nice passengers came to her stop, she tapped me on the shoulder and gave me her seat. People everywhere were so nice to us. I was grateful because we had a long ride ahead of us back to Rome.

In November of 1995, we moved Mitzi into her newly acquired condo. She had to work so Lisa and I did most of the moving. That wasn't the first or last time we moved her, but she was always there for us too.

Ray was here right before that and spent two days and nights. I told him that "The Geraldo Rivera" show was going to air a segment on women who were involved romantically with a celebrity and that I had written a letter about him and me and that the show invited me to appear on a certain date, and that I was going to do it.

I asked what he thought about it.

He said, "Well, babe. If that's what you wanna do."

I knew he didn't approve, and ironically two days before Lisa and I were scheduled to be in New York, someone from the shows staff called and cancelled me.

I've always thought that Ray had something to do with that. When I asked him, he said, "No, why would I do that?" But I know why. He didn't have control of that situation and had no idea what I would say.

I thought it was okay because he had been divorced for years, so who would it hurt? Little did I know he had a menagerie of women that he wanted to keep it from.

I regretted that I told him because I most certainly would have gotten on that show and exposed him. I would not have bad mouthed him, just simply told the truth about us.

I'm guessing Joe Adams nipped that in the bud. I don't blame him. He was just doing his job–if he did it.

Sometime during the nineties, Ray played Riverport–an outdoor theatre here in St. Louis. I invited my friend and she brought another friend. The show was great as always and our seats were close to the stage. After the show, I took them backstage to meet Ray. I disappeared into the facilities and Ray started calling me, "Marci? Marci? Where are you? Where's Marci?"

My friend said to me, "It must make you feel good to have Ray Charles calling your name."

342

I said, "Yes, it does. I'm used to him calling my name after so many years, but it's nice to hear. After all, he was Ray Charles."

My friend had suggested to her friend that they buy Ray a rose, but her friend didn't want to. I appreciated the thought, and told Ray later when he came to my house. He said, "Awww, that's sweet."

I thought it was nice and definitely appropriate. After all, they did have complimentary tickets and got to meet him. But some folks aren't as gracious as others.

My girls and I made a few trips to Mexican Resort cities. It was easy and safe to get there during this era.

Ray said, "You're never home anymore." But I was. I just wasn't here when he was available I guess. I certainly didn't go out much. I didn't go to Kansas City anymore because Mary Ann had long since moved back to Arkansas where she was from.

Lisa, Mitzi and I drove down to see her once. I flew down once and she came to St. Louis twice and those are the only times we've seen each other in all these years. We do talk on the phone at least twice a week, though. I would feel like a part of me were missing if I couldn't communicate with Mary Ann on a regular basis.

My house was paid for, thanks to Brother Ray–and every cent I earned after setting aside money for utilities and food, I saved toward travelling. So when an inexpensive deal was advertised in the newspaper, we would go.

I did see Ray fairly often, and I was not trying to ignore him, but at this time in my life, I was more independent. I had not had children to take care of for years and I was moving on with my life. I didn't wait on Ray to call. I was not living with that unreality anymore. *About time huh?*

I have a picture of Ray sitting on a tall stool at my kitchen counter. This was the only picture I had of him in the kitchen since I had taken out half a wall and made the table a counter. He said he liked it better. It felt more roomy.

We had our coffee there in our Frank Oma cups that Don and Colleen had given us so many years ago. We talked for a while – then we went to the bedroom and made love. He had to wear a condom and hated it, but I was still adamant about that. Then he put his bedroom slippers on and headed for the bathroom to take care of after-loving ablutions. I followed when he finished.

He relaxed on the couch and read his Playboy magazine. Ray really *did* get it for the articles! He spent a couple of days with me and then he was gone again.

I loved him just as much as I always had. I just coped better with his absences. I occupied my mind with things other than him.

By this time, I was beginning to landscape my patio. I planted vines so that they would grow on my wood fence, giving me the privacy that I loved. My goal was to have a tropical looking courtyard which was very quiet and secluded.

I had a volcanic rock fountain that I had gotten when Lisa lived in L.A. and I had it shipped to me. It was actually too small, but the tinkling water sounded so pretty. Ray loved that sound as much as I did.

We both enjoyed the quiet, no sound at all, sometimes just the whirling sound of the breeze blowing with the windows open. Later when I replaced the window with sliding glass doors, we could hear the little waterfall outside and listen to the humming birds and feel the breeze. I loved those times with Ray. Just the absolute ordinariness of it was what he said was so precious to him.

My relationship with Ray was an oxymoron. It was simultaneously as gentle as the balmy sea and as stormy as a raging hurricane. But mostly, when we were together, it was gentle and sweet.

He was always a gentleman, never crude or mean, just soothing and calm, unless I upset him.

He said I could upset his whole system so much that he couldn't perform well. During the first six or seven years after we met, he didn't want me to travel with him because of it.

That was during the time when I wanted to be with him every minute. I complained a lot, but that changed after I took a four and a half year hiatus from him. Then he wanted to be with me, but I became more distant. I did agonize over him–he just didn't know it. I kept it inside.

Ray was complicated, yet simple–or in his words, common. That was a word that he was partial to and what he considered himself to be. How absurd of him to ever think of himself as common. He was the least common man I've ever known or will ever know.

42
The Ecstacy and The Agony
৩৩

In March of 1997, Ray invited Lisa, Mitzi, their dates and me to the Variety Club "Dinner with the Stars" Gala–$300.00 a plate. He was going to be the guest performer and our tickets and dinner were complimentary. He really wanted us to go. He hadn't seen my girls in a while.

I said I didn't have a dress to wear to that sort of occasion, and he said, "That's no excuse. I'll buy you a dress." So I accepted his invitation.

Lisa and Mitzi were thrilled. Lisa invited Tom O'Brien, her steady beau. Mitzi took a date and I, of course, had my date.

I was a little nervous about going. Not only did I not have proper attire, but I had gained a couple of pounds since I had last seen Ray. Everyone knew about Ray and how he felt about people being overweight. He didn't like it.

He called when he got to the Adams Mark Hotel (it closed its doors in 2008 and became the Hyatt Regency) and wanted me to get there as soon as possible. I did and we had a good time talking, laughing, loving and, yes–he had to use protection. He complained about it but it didn't stop him.

I asked him if I had gained too much weight. His answer was, 'No, baby, you're fine, but you can't gain another pound." I weighed 127 pounds which was two pounds more than I wanted to weigh. I weighed 105 when we first met, but that was long gone. I didn't even want to weigh that anymore.

When we woke up the next morning, we ordered breakfast. Then in the afternoon, Mitzi and I shopped for a dress for me to wear to the event. We were gone a few hours and Ray complained that he wasn't getting to spend enough time with me, but I reminded him that we still had the whole night together. The show wasn't until the next evening.

Ray and I lounged, slept, loved and talked about trying to get a firm relationship established again. I asked what he expected, and he said, "You're my woman and I'm your man. No question about it. I love you and I think you feel the same way about me."

Of course I did, but I was still apprehensive. That conversation sounded like a broken record to me. I wanted desperately to believe him, and millions of hopeful thoughts raced through my mind. Millions of doubtful thoughts loomed in the back of my mind, however, and memories of our past kept rearing their ugly heads.

I didn't talk to Ray about my doubts. He didn't want to relive the past, not even a portion of it. Just bringing up one thing would ignite volcanic emotions from him and he would shout, "Can't you get that offa your mind?"

But I couldn't, even though Ray said, "The past, for all intents and purposes, is dead." But the "past" appeared in my head like a lurking ghost ready to squash any positive thoughts I might have had.

On the third day, I left in the afternoon to go home and get ready for the show. I was more comfortable getting ready at home since my curling iron, makeup, and all my essentials were there. Mitzi had taken my new dress home with her the day before.

That dress set Ray back $500.00...and I didn't even like it. I just couldn't find a dress that I loved, so it had to do. I'm wearing it in the picture of me and my girls with Ray, backstage at the Adams Mark hotel. It was the last picture I would ever have of my sweetheart, my girls and I together.

Ray asked me to hurry up so I could come back to the hotel room and be with him while he got ready, then walk down with him. So I got ready and called to tell him I was on my way.

Even though I had already been to the Adams Mark Hotel the day before, I absent mindedly missed my highway exit and was on my way across the damned river to Illinois! Oh My God!!

I panicked and started whimpering then gave way to full blown crying. I wound up down in the old stockyard area of East St. Louis–all alone and not a light or a street sign in sight. This was a very dangerous area in East St. Louis with a lot of serious crime occurring every day. I was hysterical.

Thank goodness I had a car phone. I called Ray, crying my eyes out.

"What's wrong, honey?" Ray asked, shocked to hear me so upset.

"Oh, Ray! I'm lost and scared." Then I told him where I was.

"Call the kids, baby," he said. "I don't know how to get you here. Calm down and call Lisa or Mitzi."

I was scared to death. Everything was pitch black. I could hardly see to dial the phone and I was afraid to turn the inside light on. Finally I reached Lisa who immediately put her boyfriend Tom on the phone.

Tom was my lifesaver and hero. God knows, I don't know how he did it, but he somehow got me out of that hell hole and back on the bridge to St. Louis.

When I got to Ray's room, I was absolutely exhausted. Ray consoled me, but I was still so upset, I didn't even want to go downstairs. I felt like I had been through the wringer, but Ray convinced me to go down, have dinner and watch the show.

Our table was not the most desirable. It was all the way in the back, far from the stage, and I had had better food at a fast food restaurant. Of course, me being vegan and Lisa and Mitzi being vegetarian, our plates were not what was being offered that evening so we just picked at our food. We impatiently waited through the speakers' accolades to one another for Ray to come on stage.

While we were waiting for Ray, Mitzi asked me how things had been between Ray and me the past few days. I gave her a progress report and told her that Ray really wanted us to be permanently together.

I said, "He has been sooo sweet–from champagne on ice, to rubbing lotion all over me. (I think he liked that more than I did.) He was very attentive and romantic, repeating over and over how much he loved me and had for nearly thirty years.

I told Mitzi that I believed him and was going to give us another chance. I also told her that I was going to prove to him how much I loved him by not insisting that he wear a condom, and giving myself to him completely.

Mitzi was thirty years old and had been with Ray and me since she was three years old, so it was perfectly normal for me to discuss my thoughts with her. She and Lisa had always been my little buddies, but after they grew up they became my best friends.

Mitzi said, "Go for it, mom! Give him another chance. You've always loved him."

When the show was over, we made our way backstage. There were a lot of people trying to talk to Ray. I rescued him from the crowds, and he latched on to Lisa and Mitzi and clung for dear life. Even Chuck Berry didn't get much more than a couple of words from Ray.

We took a few pictures. Ray chatted for a bit with my kids. Then Lisa and Mitzi kissed him goodbye and left. That was the last time they would ever see him.

Ray and I were in the VIP suite which consisted of a living room, guest bathroom and our bedroom and private bath. It was spacious and very nice.

I ordered coffee which arrived within minutes and there was champagne left from earlier, so we relaxed and talked about what was going to be different this time around.

Ray said he would be here a lot more if I let him and would accept more responsibility. He certainly was saying the right things and I wanted desperately for us to work it out this time. We were both older. I was 58 and Ray was 66, so I thought maybe now we had a chance.

I let myself go willingly under Ray's captivating spell that night. We made passionate love. Ray was so happy. He said,

"Oh, baby! Now I have you back like it's supposed to be," (because I didn't insist on him wearing protection.) I gave myself to him completely, trusting him, loving him and believing him when he expressed over and over his love for me.

We slept very little. We were both ecstatic.

The next morning, he had to leave at some ungodly hour, 5:30 in the morning or so. We ordered coffee, talked some more and before long, we were once again engaged in some very sensual love making. Right in the middle of it, Ray abruptly stopped. He got out of bed and went to the bathroom.

I asked what was wrong.

"Nothing's wrong, baby. I just want to get this packing and stuff off my mind so I can be as close to you as possible with no thoughts of anything else."

He came back to bed, held me, kissed me and made love to me like never before. I knew I would remember this moment forever.

Ray said, "This is the last thing I want on my mind when I have to leave you. I told you once, I don't take this lightly. I treat each time I'm with you as if it were the last. Marci, you're my missing link. Without you, I'm not complete."

I said, "Ray, I love you. Don't let it be the last time. Let it be a new beginning for us."

As we held one another, he said, "I'll definitely call you next week and I'll try to be back by then."

"Oh, good," I said. I was so happy. My hopes were up again–maybe there was just a slight hint of fear and doubt lurking in my mind. But as Ray had so diligently tried to teach me to do over the years, I hurriedly changed that "doubt and fear" channel back to the happy one.

And then, once more, the valet came and picked up Ray's luggage. Ray gave me a quick kiss and he was out the door and gone. Although I didn't know it then, he was gone forever. I would never see him again.

I stayed in bed, stretching, yawning and lazily contemplating what I had just experienced with the love of my life.

I relived every moment with him, and although I never thought of Ray as a Don Juan or the best lover in the world, I loved him completely. Much more than just the physical aspect of Ray, I loved his inner being. I loved his soul, the sweet sincerity of him, his touch, his voice. There was so much more to him than the physical part–at least there was to me.

After I showered and collected my things, I went to the restaurant for breakfast. Whatever I wanted was complimentary. All I had to do was sign Ray's name and put our room number on the bill. I always signed his name, with his permission of course. There was nothing unusual about that. He had told me before he left to order room service or go to the restaurant.

I chose a table by the window overlooking the sculpture garden. Beyond that, the Mississippi river was lazily rolling along, It was a soothing view. As I gazed at the sky, I visualized Ray flying along with a Mona-Lisa-smile on his face, reminiscing about us. (Given what I know now, he could very well have been contemplating his next encounter–not a happy thought for me.)

I finished my coffee and breakfast roll and headed for the hotel garage. I started to pay and the attendant said, "It's been taken care of–courtesy of Mr. Ray Charles." When you're with a super star, you're treated like one, but when I left, I was just Marci on her way back to Kirkwood, with a happy heart and a head full of dreams...again.

When I got home, I called my kids, who wanted to know all the details of my time with Ray. I told them what Ray and I had discussed, and that I was excited about finally, "going to make something of ourselves," as Ray had called it. Now all I had to do was wait for him to call.

I whistled a happy tune at work every day the first week, eagerly looking forward to mine and Ray's future together as he had promised. By the end of the week, I had not heard from him. Seeds of doubt were sprouting in my mind like a fresh spring garden.

I was overcome with negative thoughts and they were inundating my mind. Through the second week, I was getting angry at myself for believing Ray and angry at him for lying to me. I managed to work with Lisa's help. She was helping me run my business at that time.

And I cried, what felt like an ocean of tears. I was either consumed by heartbreaking misery or raging anger. Disappointment followed me like a shadow...and still, no phone call from Ray.

My poor kids were sad for me and mad at Ray.

In the middle of the third week, I answered the phone and heard, "Yeah...Marci...I...I had to fly to...I was in Europe, baby."

I yelled, "You asshole Ray! It's been three weeks! I've been to Europe. They have phones there. You're doing the same old shit!!!"

'Honey, listen...uh...," he tried to say.

"No! You listen, you lying sack of shit!!! I trusted you again! I made love with you without protection and I don't know where in the hell you've been or who you've been with. I'm a damned fool, Ray, and I've been sick inside for three long weeks!"

"Honey, I can explain," he tried again.

"No you can't, Ray, and that stupid article about the hen house and the rooster was in the newspaper when I read your review. How fu$%ing embarrassing is that!"

"Marci, I can't help what they put in the papers," he said.

Again I yelled, "No, I guess you can't. Maybe you shouldn't have said something that Goddamned stupid in the first place. What the hell were you doing–bragging? Mr. Super Cock!"

Ray had never, in his nearly thirty years with me, heard me rant and rave like I did that day. He quietly listened to my scathing outbursts of expletives. Finally, he said, "Listen, babe, if you're gonna keep yelling, I'll talk to you later."

"No you won't, you son of a bitch! Don't you ever call me as long as you fu$%ing live. I never wanna hear your Goddamned voice again as long as I live!" and I slammed the phone down.

I've never meant anything in my life as much as I meant that–at that moment and, really, for the next seven years. (However, I did want the comfort of knowing he was there).

I did hear from him in 1999. He left me a message that said, "Yeah, Marci. I miss you, honey," but I didn't return his call. I really was through. A few weeks after Ray left that message, my personal number became my business number, so our greeting was in Lisa's voice and said, "You've reached All About Cleaning."

Even if Ray would have tried to reach me, which I doubt, that greeting would have made him think it was someone else's number. I don't think he ever knew the name of our business.

Towards the end of 1999, Lisa, Mitzi and I went to France. We had a wonderful time. Sandra, Henry's wife, met us in Paris (Yes, I was good friends with Henry's wife). We were there for a week or so, then we flew to Nice, rented a car and drove to Cannes, Monte Carlo, Antibes and San Tropex.

Mitzi had been to Monaco the year before and stayed at the Lowes Monte Carlo, one of the fabulous hotels that jutted out of the hillside overlooking the Mediterranean Sea, so she sort of knew her way around. We had the greatest time...except for a couple of little incidents.

The very morning we were leaving for the airport for our flight to France, I got off my kitchen stool and my knee made a terrible cracking sound. I couldn't walk on it, so I had to be wheelchaired to our gate.

I flew all the way to Paris with an icebag on my leg and I had to keep it elevated. It got better, but flared up from time to time. My kids had to wheelchair me through the Louvre and Geverny, Monet's garden.

The other incident was that Lisa was newly pregnant with twins, but we didn't know that yet. We thought it was only one baby. She would have occasional bouts of sickness, but then it would subside and she would be okay again. We had planned our trip months before Lisa became pregnant.

In April of 1999, Lisa and her husband, Tom O'Brien, welcomed their baby boy, Tristin and baby girl, Peyton into the world.

Of course, Mitzi and I were at the hospital. Mitzi grabbed a baby and disappeared into a corner. She was mesmerized.

I regretted for a moment that I couldn't be sharing this news with Ray, but the occasion was so exciting that the thought was not lingering. I was caught up in the moment. I was too mesmerized–my first grandchildren and they were twins! Ecstatic was an understatement.

In the year 2000, Ray performed at the Veiled Prophet Fair on the Riverfront, but I didn't see or hear from him. I didn't even know he was in St. Louis. I was told by my friend Barbara Manse who went with her husband Arthur to see him.

Ray once said to me, "The only way I'll stop trying to see you, Marci, is if I can't find you and no one knows where you are."

He couldn't call me because my number had been changed, but he did know where I lived. Knowing Ray the way I did, I knew he would never just appear at my door for fear of finding out I was married or with someone. He would have preferred not to know.

During 2000 and 2001, my kids and I did more traveling –Southbeach –Cancun–Playa del Carmen, etc.

In 2002 Chase Foster, Mitzi's first child, was welcomed into our family. I watched him being born. Oh my God! What a mix of supreme emotions–the wonder at seeing my grandson born and the agony of seeing my precious daughter in so much pain. Twelve months later, Mia, my granddaughter (Mitzi's second child) entered our world.

When Mitzi was six months pregnant with Mia, she and I went to Playa del Carmen, Mexico.

We rented a jet ski and she took me for a fast ride in the ocean. My girls are daring. I'm not. Sometimes I wonder whose kids they are. They are nothing like me when it comes to sports. They do all sorts of things–ski, jet ski, roller blade, ice skate. My grandchildren are in all sorts of sports activities, too.

I don't do any of that–none–never did. If it looks like it could hurt me, no thank you. The only thing I ever did that exerted any exercise or possibly could have hurt me was ride my horse. And don't ever throw a ball to me and expect me to catch it. I will most certainly dodge it. I'm the one lying on the beach, or by the pool, or in bed, or sitting in my garden reading, writing or sketching.

I do my share of gardening. I love the results. Getting a picture of my garden along with a nice write-up in a local St. Louis magazine was affirmation that I am a pretty good gardener.

I love the Tropics. In spring and summer, I set about making my surroundings as tropical as possible, given the fact that I live in the Midwest. My garden looks like a mini rainforest and the inside of my house looks like a beach cottage. My garden is a secret garden –no one knows it's there. It's a pleasant surprise when someone sees it.

This is a happy place for me. It's a wildlife refuge, also. I feed every animal who stops by. Watching my 23 species of birds, including three woodpeckers, keeps me glued to my window for hours.

Then there are the chipmunks who fight, locking together and rolling from the middle of my small bridge to the sidewalk with their cheeks stuffed full of nuts. I watch as a squirrel works feverishly gathering its nuts and furiously digs a hole where it deposits an acorn, its' little rear up high, wiggling from side to side, as it shoves the acorn even further. Then he meticulously covers the spot, patting and raking the blades of grass to hide it, and ultimately leaving it to look just as it did before this excavation process began.

Then there's my little raccoon family. Mom is a small little lady who I named Roxie. She would come within touching distance of me, but I didn't even try to touch her. Dad is a large guy and their five rambunctious babies fight and grumble incessantly.

Hummingbirds show up in late August and early September, eating often, preparing for their long journey to Costa Rica. Bees pollinate my flowers.

And best of all is my snow-white opossum with black ears, nose and feet. Tristin, my grandson, named him Casper. Peyton, my granddaughter, named her Sugar. I personally thought it was a she so I called her Sugar.

I could sit on my steps with her food at my feet and she would come, but I couldn't touch her or she would amble off. I did get to rub her back once when she was slowly (opossums are very slow) climbing the 20 year old cedar fence that I love (because it has weathered to just the right patina for me).

I even have a brown snake who stretches leisurely across the path that Buster, my rescued Pit Bull and I once stepped over without realizing. As much as that startled me, it didn't take away the serenity that I felt and still feel in my garden. I love it there. It is my sanctuary.

43
Animal Rescue 911

I mentioned that Buster, my Pit Bull, was a rescued dog, but the truth is, he is a *stolen* dog. *I* stole him, along with several others and some cats. Here's how it happened and why.

I went to a health clinic across the street from where these poor dogs were tied on a short, heavy, tow truck chain. Their collars were cutting into their necks and their ears were eaten by flies. They were full of fleas. The poor things had miserable lives and I couldn't sleep at night because I knew it.

With the exception of Buster, all of the dogs were pretty vicious, but I didn't care. I would be vicious too if I lived in those horrible conditions! I knew in order to help them, I had to make them trust me, so I carefully and strategically started feeding and watering them every day.

I would put their food in a paper bag and throw it in to them at first. While they were eating I would hurry and pour water into their buckets and carry them just to the end of their chains, where they couldn't attack me. And yes, they tried.

After weeks of this, I would go sit down close to them and, very soon, they would nuzzle my neck. (Please be very careful befriending strays. I feel that I have a very special connection with animals–they know I am on their side. Not everyone has that special connection, and it could be very dangerous).

I couldn't rescue all of the dogs at the same time, but all of them were rescued after midnight when the cruel caretaker was gone.

All in all, I rescued a red Chow, two German Shepherd mixed breeds, two Rottweilers, a beautiful black Collie and a Pit Bull–all from the same awful place.

I was pretty good at stealing neglected dogs in the wee hours of the morning. I only had a couple of setbacks. One was Buster, but that wasn't his name then. He was probably called Brutus or Killer or some inappropriate name they thought befitting a Pit Bull, but now that he's *my* eighty-five pound sweetie, he's 'Buster'.

Buster was tied in the mud in front of a dog house that had no floor and was barely held together. He was cold and wet, to say the least, and he shivered and batted his paws at flies.

I tried to loosen his collar by letting it out a notch but he shook his huge head and got loose! Panic is an understatement.

I frantically started calling "Come here, puppy. Come. Come." And being the sweetheart that he is, he came. And he let me tie him back up in that muddy hell hole.

I had to do it because I had to wait for the right opportunity to get both Buster and the Shepherd mix away from that awful hell. The Shepherd's ears were nearly eaten through by flies. It was very painful for him and it made me sick to look at them.

At midnight, a few nights later, I decided to get both dogs.

The Shepherd was hooked to a metal stake about two feet tall, so I thought I could just slip the chain up and over the stake, but the top was frayed from hammering it into the ground, so the chain wouldn't come off.

I neglected to add that this all happened in the dead of winter. Not only was I cold but I was in an unsafe area and nervous as hell.

I went home and got a hammer, screwdriver, pliers and my daughter Lisa. She was the get-away driver. I didn't usually let my kids participate, but this time I had to.

I pounded and pried and finally got the Shepherd loose from the stake and into the car. We quickly took him to Lisa's backyard and hurried back to rescue Buster. Once we got Buster in the car, Lisa took off like Mario Andretti and we put Buster in my garage.

I found homes for all seven dogs with the exception of Buster. I decided to keep him because I was afraid someone might use him for dog fighting. Now he is happy and treated like a king. His days of being tortured and neglected are over. He has anything he wants, including much love and affection.

I've also rescued a few cats. One day I decided to drive down a street for no reason in particular, and I saw a beautiful, but sickly looking cat sitting on a porch. I drove home and got some cat food and went back and started to feed her. She was so hungry that she gobbled it like a dog.

I said, "Come on. You're out of here," and I brought her home. She was in bad shape. She had millions of fleas and was extremely malnourished.

After I got her home and cared for her, she was feeling much better. She lived the rest of her life with me, sleeping in her basket on a fluffy pillow. I named her Zoe.

There are four stray cats I have had spayed and neutered, and bought houses for. They are currently living in an industrial area not far from my house, and I feed and water them twice a day, rain or shine, summer or winter.

I'm not writing about them to get approval. As a matter of fact I get a lot of disapproval. I'm doing it because I love them.

Lisa and Mitzi both lost their cats–they just disappeared– just evaporated. We searched everywhere, including all of the shelters, but to no avail.

We set a humane trap to try to catch them, but Mitzi actually caught two other cats and returned them to their rightful caretakers. Unfortunately, there was no Bella or Emmie. We're very sad about it.

I know first hand how awful it is to lose a cat. I lost my little three legged cat, Topi. Lisa had found her under a car in the pouring rain. Her front leg was dragging, and she was soaked. She was so tiny.

I took her to the vet, and he said her leg would never recover–that it had no feeling and needed to be amputated. We had a family pow-wow, agreed with his diagnosis, and soon she was our little three-legged cat.

She was always with me. When I did the dishes, she would sit beside me on a bar stool. She could jump all the way up to the basement window ledge on three legs. She was amazing. Six years later she was gone–her organs were too small to accommodate her body. She died three months before my Mom.

I regret leaving the rest of my animals out of this story, but there were too many and all of them were with me until they died.

Writing about all of my animals has brought back so many memories as far back as when I was a little girl.

Maybe I should write a children's book about my lifetime with animals. Maybe I should start it in Cancun.

In Cancun, there were these caged tropical birds who had spoiled fruit for food and murky water to drink. They were so stressed that they had pulled their feathers out. Lisa and I gave them fresh fruit, bread and clean water twice daily, but we had to leave eventually. So we went to the hotel manager and brought the matter to his attention.

When we returned to St. Louis we wrote letters to everyone we could think of complaining about that hotel neglecting the birds. They should leave the exotic birds in the jungle where they belong so they could live their lives free and happy.

44

The Last Good-bye

❦

Everyone knows what happened in 2004. It was the shock of my life losing the love of my life, Ray Charles. I had no idea that he was ill, much less as ill as he was. I hadn't read or heard anything about him being sick.

In March, 2004 Lisa called and said "Mom turn on the NAACP awards. Ray's on." She stayed on the phone. When I saw him I gasped and said, "Oh my God, Lisa. He's very sick. He's so thin. Look how his suit is just hanging on him." He was a shockingly deteriorated ghost of the man I was with in 1997.

Lisa was very emotional and said, "Mom, you have to call him."

I agreed, but when I called the number I used to call, it had been disconnected. So I waited and worried. I called R.P.M. Studios the next morning and left a message.

Ray didn't call me back for a week and a half. I knew he would call me if he got my message and he did. His receptionist said, "I have Ray Charles on the line for Marci."

I said "This is Marci."

His voice was so weak, it was barely audible. He sounded so unlike himself, so frail. He said my name and I said, "Hello, Ray."

He said, "Marci I haven't heard from you in a long, long time."

"Yes," I said "It's been almost seven years."

Again he repeated, "A long, long time."

"Ray, you sound so weak," I said, sounding almost as weak as he did. I was so emotional I could hardly talk.

He responded, "Well, babe, when you're sick, you're just sick. Ain't nuthin' you can do." He said he had liver disease.

Then I began to softly cry and tell him how sorry I was. Someone had told me that he had had hip surgery and I asked if that had caused any of this.

He said in his typical fashion, "Ain't got nuthin to do with it." His next question was, "How are Lisa and Mitzi?"

I told him that Lisa said I should call him.

He said, "Good ol' Lisa. She's lookin' out for me."

I told him that she had five year old twins, a boy and girl, and they loved "Hit the Road Jack."

He was surprised about Lisa having twins and said, "Kids seem to like that song."

He asked if Mitzi had kids I said yes, a little boy age two and a one year old little girl.

I was barely able to contain myself, I was so sad.

I asked, "Who's taking care of you, Ray?"

He told me he had five nurses around the clock. He didn't mention anyone else. I was relieved that he didn't mention any women. I don't know why–I hadn't even spoken to him in seven years. The truth would hit me later–and it would hit me hard.

I was having hip surgery in a couple of days. I told Ray and he said he would call to check on me. He asked for my number. I had left it at his office but he punched it in. I guess he wanted it in his book.

His voice was getting weaker, and I couldn't talk without crying, so I said, "I'm so sorry, Ray" over and over throughout our conversation.

His voice sank to a whisper.

Finally, after a period of silence, I said, "Bye, Ray. I didn't say, "I love you, I always have and I always will."

Misery washed over me like a London fog. Fear of the inevitable pierced my heart. *Dear God, there were more things I needed to say and didn't. Maybe I won't get another chance.*

Time dragged on and my heart felt like concrete. I can't

begin to put into words the depth of sorrow that came over me. Every now and then I found myself weeping uncontrollably, trying desperately to navigate an emotional terrain that was broken and maybe could never be fixed. I wanted to find out more about Ray's illness, so I called R.P.M. Studios and asked the receptionist who I could talk to. She connected me with his daughter Evelyn who refused to tell me anything.

I told her I had spoken to Ray. She said "Well, you spoke to my father. If he wanted you to know anything, he would have told you."

"I've known him for thirty-four years and I'm sad," I said "and I just want to…"

"Well," she interrupted, "I've known him well over fifty years. He's fine, so dry your eyes."

I just said thank you and hung up. I didn't get the opportunity to tell her I didn't want to keep her father on the phone because he was struggling to hard to push any sound from his voice.

I was so very worried about Ray. I had my surgery (another unnecessary surgery) and I hadn't heard from him. I didn't want to call the number he gave me. I knew he was too weak to talk to me.

I called R.P.M. Studios again and got the nice receptionist who I had spoken with before. She still had my number and repeated it to me. I asked her how Ray was really doing. She said, "He's doing…" she hesitated then she said, "just okay."

I thanked her, but I knew the truth, that he most certainly was not okay. I knew that before I made those phone calls. I was just hoping that someone could tell me something optimistic–but it didn't happen.

Ray didn't call after my surgery like he said he would. *What's new?* But at least this time he had a reason. I knew how sick he was.

Shortly after my surgery, I was back in the hospital–this time for a cat bite–by my own cat! She was twenty-years-old and heading out the door, and I grabbed her around her tummy.

She turned and bit my thumb. In her mind, she was protecting herself from an attacker. My thumb hurt badly for a couple of hours but I thought it would get better. Then I saw the red streaks going up my arm.

I drove myself to the hospital emergency room where I was immediately given a room and hooked onto an I.V. with antibiotics. I was there for four days and nights–hurting like hell.

"Did I keep Pebbles, my cat?" Of course, and I'll always remember her. I have my screwed up thumb as a reminder (giggle).

So now I had a thumb hurting like crazy, a hip that wasn't heeled yet, and a heart that was breaking more every day, waiting for the inevitable news about Ray. I was a mess.

I saw a picture of Ray in the Enquirer looking really sick, so I called them and actually was connected with the writer of that story. He asked me some questions: "How do you know Ray Charles?" "How long have you known him?" etc. etc. I answered him as briefly as I could, because *I* wanted to ask *him* questions–which I did. My question to him was, "How ill do you think Ray is?"

His answer was more truthful than I was prepared for. He said "Ray Charles' death is eminent." Then he asked if he could write my story–that he wanted to publish it before Ray's death. I wasn't expecting that request. It really upset me. I told him, "No thank you."

On April 30th, my birthday, I watched on television as Ray's building - R.P.M. Studios at 2701 west Washington Blvd. Los Angeles, California, 90018–was dedicated as an historical landmark.

I sat glued to the television as Joe Adams made the announcement, and I watched, wiping away tears, as Ray was led to the microphone and then, even more saddened as he uttered, "I'm weak, but I'm getting stronger," in a voice so weak he could hardly be heard. I knew he would never be stronger. I wanted to put my arms around him and just hold him.

I was happy to see his friend, Clint Eastwood, standing beside him. Ray told me one time that Clint said that he was nervous about singing a duet with him in the movie "Any

Which Way You Can." I said, "I can't imagine Clint Eastwood being nervous about anything."

Ray said "Yeah, babe, he said he was...but honestly he's very talented and a super nice guy."

In my opinion, Clint Eastwood is a genius too. It's no wonder they liked each other so much.

Ray's building becoming a historical monument must have made him proud. It was his home for so many years, and now to know that it would be forever safe from demolition had to be a comforting thought for him.

I'm sure it was appropriate for Ray to be flanked by "stars," but I wondered why Joe Adams or his sons, Ray Jr., Bob or David were not there to celebrate that huge event. As I watched Ray struggle just to be present on that so-very-special-day, there were no words to describe the degree of despair I felt. There was nothing left for me to do, except wait for the inevitable. I spent those days of May and June gardening and contemplating my life with Ray, despair spreading thru me like a fever.

Would I have changed anything? Maybe my own temperament. Perhaps we could have been more at peace with one another had I been a calmer person. I talked to Mary Ann about that feeling. She said, "Marci, you could never change the way you are. Try to accept this as being a part of your life and don't allow regrets to cloud your mind and heart. You know how you valued every moment you spent with Ray. Be grateful that you had that time with him."

Obviously, I couldn't have changed my temperament even if I wanted to. Proof of that was what I did right after talking to Mary Ann.

I bought a tabloid with Ray's picture on it and the article mentioned his long-time partner, Norma. It made me furious. As sick as I knew Ray was, I still called the last number he gave me and left a scathing message about him lying to me about her for nearly thirty years and I asked if she knew about me. I said, "Well, she damn sure will now." I called him a lying asshole. And no, I don't feel bad about that. To me, if you've been a liar for thirty years, you don't stop just because you're sick. The title still fits.

I never knew if he heard that message or not. He might have been too sick, but I certainly meant for him to hear it. It was true. If he did hear it, he probably smiled at my hot temper.

As I sat in my garden listening to the tinkling of the water in my small pond, mesmerized by the soft, undulating movement of the water, I could visualize Ray sitting in the white comfy wicker chair on the patio, reading his Playboy magazine or Readers' Digest. That picture in my mind gave me a moment's relief from the reality of Ray's condition.

On June 10th, 2004, mid-morning, I was at Mitzi's house, sitting on a stool at her island in the kitchen. I answered my cell phone and the man from the Enquirer asked, "Have you heard the news?" after he had identified himself.

"No, I haven't," I answered.

He said, "Ray Charles died this morning."

"Oh no!" I cried, breaking down. I said, "Thank you for letting me know," and hung up.

I cried, shoulder-shaking sobs. Mitzi did too. Lisa's twins were there and Mitzi's two kids. We were all crying.

I couldn't get control of myself and I wanted to go home, but Mitzi wanted me to stay until I could stop crying so much. I waited and finally I left.

When I got home, I went through all the rooms where I could feel Ray's presence. Memories flooded my mind as tears flooded my face.

I lost the love of my life today.

I couldn't stop crying. I was despondent–just beside myself, feeling that awful dull ache in my heart. Ray had crippled my heart all through the years. Now it was completely broken.

I had left him so many times before. Now for the first time he left me–and this time, it was forever!

I regret that I didn't tell him how I loved him and missed him, but I was too stubborn to call. How I wished I could have touched him, held him, just one more time.

I watched his funeral on television, quietly grieving and crying all alone, because that's how I grieve when I'm so sad.

I thought Joe Adams organized a wonderful ceremony for the ending of Ray's life. Just like he had always done, he took good care of Ray. Joe is another genius in my estimation.

Ray must have been proud of his son Reverend Robert Robertson. It was impressive seeing the young Bobby that I knew, leading the celebration of his father's life–at the end of his life.

From June through October of 2004, I stayed to myself, except to function with everyday life. I only communicated with Lisa, Mitzi and Mary Ann. They were always there for me.

I spent my time grieving, crying and listening to my taped conversations between Ray and me. That helped me. It seemed as if he was here talking to me. I'm so glad I have those precious tapes. I used to listen to them just to relive our conversations, never realizing how important they would ultimately be to me.

I was consumed with thoughts of Ray and our life together, right here in this house where so many memories surround me daily.

He permeates my soul and pervades my being. He flows through me like liquid. He was, and is, my true love–and is a lingering part of me throughout eternity–my other half.

I can hear him say, "Marci, you're my missing link," and he is mine. I can feel his presence.

As the months dragged on I was more able to talk about my feelings. Then when I watched the Academy Awards that year, at the end, they gave the list of ones who had passed away and Ray was one of them. My heart fell again. I was sick inside. It was as if that sealed the fact that Ray was absolutely gone.

Jamie Foxx did a wonderful job portraying Ray in the movie, *Ray*, although that part of his life was before me. The Ray I knew was more gentle and easy-mannered, not so harsh. I'm glad I had the part of him that I had.

I'm content now. I've achieved my goals. All I'm missing is my sweetheart.

There's no sound from Ray anymore, but his echo in my head is always with me.

Do you ever cross my mind?

Yes, sweetheart–you do–endlessly.

Ray & Me

Random Thoughts and Memories

When I would refuse to see him, Ray would always say, sadly, "Okay, babe, if that's what you want." Then the phone calls would start. He'd tell me he missed me, but I would just sit there and not say anything. He would tell me he was just dreaming and dreaming about me. He said I was always "running round in his head" and begged me just to let him hold me.

I loved Ray so much, but after awhile, I just couldn't stand the emotional roller coaster. He would tell me that we could work it out–that we were a part of one another. "Listen Marci. I have to have you," he'd say. "You're like food and water. You're something I can't live without." But he did, for six and a half years.

ℰ

He always told me I was runnin' around in his head. The first time I heard it was in 1968 when my brother took us to the airport and I was all cuddled up with him in the back seat. I asked him, "What are you thinking," and he said, "Nothing'. Just you runnn' round in my head." He would always have this contented smile on his face and say, "Hmmmmmm."

ℰ

After reading Michael Lydon's book, I was shocked. I didn't know *that* Ray, thank God. His behavior then reminds me of an un-neutered dog, just sniffing and feeling his way around.

ℰ

I'm so thankful now that I didn't remain in Los angeles when I went to Ray. I would have been so miserable. I can see now that I would not have stayed there–there's no way in hell I would have knowingly competed with all of those women, nor would I have tolerated that partying existence. I could not have stood that. ...And him hitting one of those women...I can't imagine him doing that. He seemed so gentle to me. He was lucky it wasn't me. I hit back. I've never been a believer in turning the other cheek.

❧

In 1997 when I ended our relationship, I had been getting tired of it for a long time, probably 15 years. I did go on with my own day to day life, and I even had dates that he wasn't aware of, but I always felt him tugging at me and being so awfully sad that I could never really break it off with him. But in 1997, I had gotten to the point of no return.

❧

Just one little thing would set me off and my last attack on the phone with him was vicious and to the point, adamant and final. "M_F_, do not call me again!" He knew then that the last straw had been broken. When he died, I had not heard from him for six and half years, nor had I called him except for that last time...March 10...before he died in June. I was so sad. I cried and cried for him.

❧

Then when I found out in *The Inquirer* that Norma had existed all along, I went berserk one last time leaving him an explicit message about being a lying asshole throughout our relationship and what a goddamned low down jerk I thought he was. I told him that if I ever have another encounter with him in the hereafter, I'll slap the hell out of him (guess that threat will keep me out of heaven–giggle).

❧

I've done a lot of thinking now that I know so much about him. Things I didn't have a clue about that awful day in Los Angeles in 1969 when he slammed the phone down and left me standing at a pay phone completely bewildered. Did I unknowingly interrupt a rendezvous with one of his many other ladies? Did I irritate him like Margie did in the movie and cause him to hang up on me? Or did he become wary and scared after being threatened during his show at the coconut Grove by my husband and his private investigator? I'll never know. But I'm finding that he was capable of detached and uncaring behavior. That one time was the only time I ever experienced it. That was enough. I left. I guess we both learned a lesson–you be nice and I won't leave you.

A talented person is a truly gifted person. Genius, however, is when that gifted person becomes totally consumed like Ray was. I feel that he had to get away from himself and just relax his mind and soul. I'm not sure that he ever did, even when he was here with my warm and loving family and friends. We still had him at the piano playing and singing occasionally, but we were considerate of his feelings.

He was always at our disposal. If we wanted his time when he was here. He was very generous with that aspect of himself.

What he wasn't generous with was his money. He handed it out in small increments. I don't think he ever knew that I was as desperate as I really was. There were many times when I had to tighten the budget and my girls and I lived very frugally, but they didn't know it either. No one did. I was overloaded with independence and pride. Ray was aware, of course, that I was able to financially get myself to Los Angeles. He didn't offer to help me and I didn't ask. He was also aware that I was able to leave Los Angeles, and soon I had an apartment. Within two years, I had my own house, so he might have thought I was doing okay in the money department.

I believe he truly loved my ability to be so independent. I know he loved that I could be so (as he put it) heavenly sweet, but he also loved the firey part of me. That seemed to excite him and keep him wondering if he was going to be allowed back.

I was off-limits to Ray from about 1974 until 1978-1979. From reading Lydon's book, I learned that Ray was having a difficult time finding a label. I, of course, was not aware of it. I was ony aware of the sad, lonely phone calls pleading with me. "Marci, please baby, I miss you." Of course, he was back to having to hang up if a man answered, just like in New Orleans when I was married. He didn't like it, but according to Lydon's book, he was having no trouble making babies in France during that time (which I learned in 2005).

I'm sad that there was a period when Ray's music was not in demand. I had no idea that Quincy attempted to rescue him, and all the while, Ray maintained so much pride. When they roasted him at the Coconut Grove in 1978 and not many showed up, it broke my heart. I guess it was payback for all the mean things he did to people. Again, I was here and knew nothing of his struggles. He didn't complain to me. What I do remember is him saying, "Well, babe, I'll never see the bread say a Wayne Newton gets." I was shocked by that. I said, "Come on, Ray, Wayne Newton?" He said, "That's right, babe." I don't mean to diminish Wayne Newton, but God! This was Ray Charles. I was truly shocked and saddened. Ray was sad about that too. He said it about Sinatra. That didn't surprise me–certainly not because I thought Sinatra was better, but because of the publicity that always surrounded Sinatra. In my mind, Ray surpassed everyone.

Delores, my brother's ex-wife, said, "I couldn't believe Ray in the movie. The times when I was around him, he was so sweet and such a laid back gentleman." This was on December 20, 2005. She met Ray more than once and liked him so much. He really was shy, sweet and charming. Thank God she wasn't available–Ray would have fallen in love with her. She was beautiful and had long, thick hair.

৵৶

Do I ever regret having the abortion? No. I would have loved that child also, but I wouldn't have wanted to go through the heartbreak that would have come with it. I had a fairly hard time raising my two children, and I know it would have been even more difficult with another baby. I don't think Ray would have made life any easier for me.

৵৶

I told him that my girlfriend and I were discussing furniture, and she said that in the bedroom, the bed should be dominant. She said it should be the first thing you see when you enter the room and should be facing the door. "Well, honey, you can see yourself that's not possible," Ray said. Then he went all around the room making his point. "See, nothing can go here but the chest. Here's the window–only the dresser can fit here. The bed can't go against this window, then you wouldn't have one night stand let alone two. No, I'm sorry, babe. She's wrong. You have it the only way it can be, period."

৵৶

God knows Ray had more than one little boy's share of misery and so did his mama and his little brother, George. I can see how he became so strong and determined and believe me, he was. It was unfair that he had to live through it, but he always said, "Nothin's fair. You got to make it fair. Ain't nothing fair." On the other hand, he said, "Marci, God's no respector of persons and that is fair."

৵৶

A lot of Ray's songs sounded like he was mourning. You waited for him to weep the song out.

☙❧

I was strong sometimes, but I had a real weakness for Ray. Just the look on his face or the crackling in his voice if he was sad made me sad. Just remembering makes me weep now.

☙❧

I'm sure that when Ray started with drugs, he thought it would give him some relief from the flashbacks, but of course it made him even more sad. But the drugs loosened him up and released his soul through his music for the world to absorb, and I believe we all absorbed him whether we knew him or not. I know I soaked him up all the way into my soul, the total depth of my being. Even now I can feel him, hear him and see his face. He's so planted into my inner vision, I'll never be free of him nor would I want to be.

☙❧

I'm grateful that I didn't know Ray before 1968. I feel that I got the sweetest and most gentle part of him.

☙❧

After I found out he was married, it was too late for me. I was already into him too deeply. I couldn't resist his charm. And of course, we didn't discuss it much. He did call me as soon as he was divorced, but I had started seeing another man by then. Ray was trying to get me back, enticing me with statements like, "I'm free like the birds now, babe," and it wasn't long before I was back in his web.

☙❧

There are a thousand memories running through my head: Him standing in the bathroom shaving; holding each other and swaying to one of his new albums; shifting the gears in my V. W.; telling me how much he dreamed about me; playing chess (he would guide me and let me win); going through the plane to greet him; walking through the airport together; people gathering and calling his name; I would tell him that everyone was looking. He'd always say, "They're looking at you babe 'cause you're looking so good. Come on, Marci. You know that."

ৼৣ৵

I picture him coming in the patio door with his luggage and hanging up his coat. Then his aroma, Cannon cologne, would permeate the air. When he would leave, Mitzi would open the closet door and say, "Mom, it smells like Ray. Come here." And it did. My little babies always knew how much I loved Ray and still do.

ৼৣ৵

I think about him sleeping in my bed, maybe with one of my kids lying on the other side watching T.V. I remember playing our old upright piano downstairs and singing and harmonizing. We were so happy. I can picture him pouring himself some coffee (no gin). I only saw him have gin and coffee before he went on stage. He said it cleared his throat and vocal cords.

ৼৣ৵

I look where my couch used to be and see him lying there, bedroom slippers on, glasses off, just relaxing, sometimes wrinkling his forehead when he talked to me. His conversations always started with, "Well, babe, it's like this."

ৼৣ৵

I remember early in our relationship sitting on my steps in Sunset Hills thinking, "Well, we're at least under the same moon and sky." I would think of the sky as a big blanket covering both of us. I really was always lonely.

ৼৣ৵

I remember how it was taking him to the airport; getting him on the plane; never wanting to leave him; watching the plane till it disappeared into the clouds; crying all the way home and for days, feeling so lonely.

❧

Ray was always leaving me to go to work for weeks at a time. In March of 1997, it was for good. This was the last time I would ever see him, ever feel him, hold him, smell his aroma. Had I known, I wouldn't have been so stubborn. I would have called him and I'm sure things would have resumed where we left off. But I didn't and he didn't and now it's too late. Even though I was lonely and miserable a lot of the time, I'm so glad we had the time we had. I truly wish that in March of 2004 I would have told Ray how much I loved him and would love him until I stopped breathing. He surely knew it.

❧

I'll say it one more time. I didn't like his music. I loved his music. I hear it in my head over and over, along with his professions of love for me.

❧

October 19, 2005–today is my mom's birthday. She would be ninety-six years old. I miss her. I miss Ray, too, and some-times I talk to him. I tell him how much I loved him–and still do–and that sometimes I feel so lost and sad.

I have to be a strong woman for my girls but I'm not, really. I somehow still need Ray to guide me and soothe my jagged edges, and at times, I feel him right here with me. I know better, but I feel him trying to comfort me, feeling sad for me because I'm crying and yearning for him as I always have.

I see his face with so much character in it...the structure, the sensuous mouth, the sadness, the smell of him. I can still smell his wonderful aroma and it gives me the warm fuzzies.. There was nowhere I would rather be than snuggled into his body knowing that he wanted me so close to him. "You're mine, Marci, from the top of your head to the tip of your toes."

377

And he was right. I was and still am—and always will be.

I have to survive without him, and even after all these years, it's still hard. I remember when he said, "Mama ain't comin' back" and I know "Ray ain't comin' back." That part of this stage play is over. Gone forever—with nothing left but haunting memories.

৽ৎ

One thing's for sure. Ray couldn't be blackmailed because he simply didn't care. He did get furious at an ex-employee, however, when he thought he told me some things that Ray didn't want me to know. But he was wrong. The employee didn't tell me—Ray's son did.

৽ৎ

When I listen to Willie Nelson sing, I hear a mournful sound on some of his songs, and I see a sadness about him—a gentleness similar to Ray. I'm not surprised that Willie thought of Ray as his soulmate.

৽ৎ

Ray was so weight conscious. Every boyfriend I've ever had, including Ray, told me their weight never changed. Well that may be so, but it's certainly shifted. I noticed the belly. (Sorry Ray.)

৽ৎ

Ray didn't ever drink water. He was used to pure water from his childhood and couldn't stand the added chemicals. I also had well water as a child. It is much softer and better water.

৽ৎ

He smoked KOOL cigarettes and quit for awhile, but resumed after his plane, fondly known by his band as "The Buzzard," ran off the runway because of brake failure.

৽ৎ

Ray once told me a story about he and some guys going

down to Mexico (Tijuana, I think), and they were going to a prostitution house. He stayed in the car, drinking, and got sick. He said he was really cold and tired and had no idea where the guys went, so he was stuck. That experience from his younger years soured him on alcohol, he said.

భా

As I reminisce, I sometimes wish I would have not argued and stressed so much and just gone along for the quiet ride. I know things between us would have been better. I left Ray a lot and I know it made him insecure about me, too. Mary Ann tells me, "Marci, stop dwelling on that. You couldn't have been any different anyway–it's not your nature."

భా

"You should have USDA stamped on you, honey. You're so good." I asked, "Who would do it? You can't." He said, "Well, you know I can feel my way around pretty well when it comes to you, babe. But instead of USDA, I had his initials tattooed on my tummy, at the very end of a stem on my red rose tattoo, and it's very discreet. If you didn't know it was RC, you couldn't tell. I called Ray and told him. "Who did that, Marci?" "Don Eaker," I said. "Well, it's OK if Don did it. Where is it?" "On my tummy." "Oh, I see." But he was excited. "Babe, that's nice. Does it mean my label is on you?" "Yes, sweetheart, but your label has always been on me." This was about 1983. The next time he was here, he wanted to know where the tattoo was. I took his hand and placed it on my tummy, but you can't feel a tattoo. He loved that RC was tattooed on me for life.

భా

In 1984, I drove him to the Barn Theater to perform. My kids, their friends and a friend of mine went. I introduced my friend to the road manager and they had a long relationship.

❧

Later in our relationship, probably in '88 or '89, when he would come, I wouldn't have him stay at my house. I wanted him to take care of me. I wanted to be in a nice hotel, ordering food and drinks (non-alcoholic). I didn't like the way things were going and wanted him to be a little more responsible for my happiness. He still stayed here when I was OK with it. He liked being here, but he knew that I wasn't really OK with things.

❧

One time, his son, Bob, stuck a hairpin into an electric socket and had to be rushed to the hospital. He told me that early on and warned me about covering electric outlets. I listened. Most of the time, I paid attention to what he said. Another time, David, the middle son, was riding in the car with them and Ray was reprimanding him for something. David pinched or hit him, and whichever it was, Ray did it back. He said, "Babe, the first thing I do with kids is establish the fact that I'm the adult and you're the kid, period!" Ray also told me that his son, Ray Jr., had a great impact on his stopping the use of drugs. I happen to think getting busted on his plane had a great impact, also.

❧

Ray didn't tell me he went into a hospital to withdraw from heroin. He told me, "I started it by myself and I ended it myself." He never did say he regretted doing drugs, just that he didn't do it any more, and I know from 1968 on he didn't because I never found anything suspicious when I was with him. He smoked pot and asked if I minded and I just said, "No," but I wouldn't do it. Once I said, "I need some cocaine. I'm too fat." I wasn't serious, of course. "Oh, babe, don't even joke about something so serious–that's tragic. Never, never ever do anything even related to that." Of course I wouldn't. I've never touched drugs. I just told him that and he went over the edge.

❧

Mitzi used to sing along with Van Cliburn. Ray heard her and said, "Listen to Mitzi, honey. Maybe we'll have a classical singer." Well, she isn't a classical singer, but she's a wonderful daughter who has given me a great son-in-law and my little grandchildren.

❧

When Ray and I awakened in the mornings, of course we snuggled, then I opened the blinds and made coffee. He would jump in the shower, then we would both go back to bed, having our coffee in our mugs from Frank Oma Pottery. He would smoke a KOOL cigarette, and we would snuggle some more, talking about everything–music, politics, my girls, Mary Ann or Don and Colleen, my folks, my barnyard stories, horse riding, just everything. Then I would shower, go back to bed to lounge. In the summer, I would open doors so Ray could listen to the patio waterfall and the birds singing. He loved that. We would have lunch and then Ray would move to the couch and either read his Braille magazine or watch TV (always the news, and if a ballgame was on, definitely). Then the kids would be coming home from school, so we would have to behave. Sometimes we went out to dinner, but most of the time we had dinner in. After dinner, we'd watch more TV, either in the living room with the kids or in the bedroom. Sometimes the kids would have their friends over, we'd go downstairs, Ray would play and we would sing or just listen to him sing.

❧

Once he left his kit here and I didn't know where to send it. He called and I FedExed it to him.

❧

He would leave a jumpsuit or robe here and wear it the next time he came.

❧❦

He never went barefoot. He always wore his bedroom slippers.

❧❦

Much later, after I remodeled the bedroom and added sliding glass doors, he would go out on the patio, sit in a chair and read and listen to the windchimes. I think that was very peaceful for him.

❧❦

In the 70's and 80's, I burned incense. He'd say, "Whatcha' doin' burnin' incense?" as if he thought I burned it to camouflage something. But I just liked it. In the 90's, I switched to candles and rarely burned incense any more. I still love candles. I love serenity and ambience.

❧❦

When Mitzi was a little girl, she said she really didn't think Ray was blind and would wave her hands back and forth in front of him. I wish I would have known that. I would have had him say, "BOO."

❧❦

When I first heard the news of Ray's death, I was at my daughter's house and was called on my cell phone by *The Inquirer Magazine*. I had been talking to them about a possible story. The man on the phone said, "Did you know Ray Charles died?" I just broke out crying and crumbled. Mitzi was crying too, trying to help me. Obviously, I didn't know until then about his death. I stayed with my daughter until I could get my bearings, then and throughout the funeral. It was so hard. It took me from June 10th until the last of October, four months, to get back to normal. I was so depressed.

৵ঙ

It made my stomach knot when they played the "Deceased Ones" on the Grammy's and this time Ray was one of them. I cried again. I called my best friend, Mary Ann and she was crying.

৵ঙ

When I saw Ray on the NAACP awards, I realized how ill he was, but I must have gone into denial. Somewhere deep inside of me, I thought he would be okay. "He has money," I told myself. He has the best doctors." But he wasn't okay. I spiraled into the depths of despair–such heartache, gloom, doom and misery. I would function mechanically in public, but when I got home I would face that agonizing emptiness and despondency that I thought I couldn't bear. Years later, I still felt that lump when I thought about him being gone forever. I still feel the lump....

৵ঙ

Ray called me one night and sounded down. He said, "I wish I could see you, babe." I said, "You can see me." "No," he said, "You don't understand–I mean *really see* you." "Oh, I wish you could, too, sweetheart. I wish you could see everything!" I said.

৵ঙ

He would say things like that when things were not going the way he wanted them to.

৵ঙ

One time when he was here, we were in bed just talking and talking. He said, "What shade would you say your skin is, honey?" "Well, I'm not real white," I replied. Then I started trying to think of something he might remember. "Oh! You just called me 'honey.' I'm two or three shades lighter than honey." "Oh, that's sweet, babe," he said.

When Lisa was 8 or 9 and Mitzi was 6 or 7, I said, "Ray, it seems like you talk more to Lisa–why?" "Well, babe, I can relate to Lisa better because she is older." But later, he directed as much attention to Mitzi as to Lisa, especially when they started playing the piano. He really liked to hear them pound those keys.

Lisa and Mitzi would bring friends in the house and say, "Shhhhh, Ray's sleeping," It was so cute. He would hear them and tell me now cute it was.

Mitzi asked why Ray put his fingers in his food. "Well, honey, because he can't see. He couldn't get his food on the spoon or fork if he didn't. He needs to feel everything, remember?" She said, "Is that why you cut everything up for him?" "Yes, it is." "That looks yucky, mom–well, it would be if you or I did it. But not for Ray." She soon adjusted to his way of eating and nothing more was ever said.

I asked my kids if any of their friends asked about Ray. They said, "No, mom, they got used to him. Besides, when you're a kid, he's not as important." I guess that's true. That's how it seemed.

I didn't read "Brother Ray" until about 1980. I was in another relationship and couldn't have Ray's book laying around. But when I opened it, I came right to the part about the hen house and one rooster and the lions den and one lion. I certainly had never thought of him as a super cock-a-doodle-do or King of the jungle. I never did get over that quote and it angered me every time I saw it in print, which was a couple of times. I thought it was an egotistical and dumb remark.

Ray was always calling himself "ya stupid" when he did something mistakenly. Well, in my estimation, that was one of the times when he was "ya stupid."

I truly believe that had I called him at any time during the six and one-half years that we were estranged, he would have been here within two days to a week. He always was.

1-213-###-####–that phone number will always be implanted into my brain until eternity. I know for sure it was Ray's number from 1968 until 1997. Maybe the area code changed before 1997, but the number was the same. I don't know when he got his new number. I didn't get it until he called me in '04. I didn't try. He just gave it to me. I used it once to leave a mean message about Norma.

I questioned him about why I couldn't come to his house, "You can come to mine," I reasoned. "Because I'm never there," he said. "Where do you live, Ray?" He told me the number on San Vicente. "You can go there, but I will be at my studio." I didn't ask about it any more until I found out about Norma. He said, "That's a g–damned lie. I don't live with no Norma."

Everyone's going to wonder why I put a book out now after so many years and with Ray gone. Well, I felt it would be therapeutic for me. I thought maybe it would help me vent some of the feelings of resentment I feel. I also wrote it to express the great love I've always had for him and still do. After all, he was the love of my life, just after my kids. And to share with everyone just how simple he liked things to be. The things we did were so ordinary.

෨෨

People also probably wonder why I kept putting up with his behavior. My answer is that I was an emotional cripple for years and years and Ray Charles was very convincing, manipulative, persistent and persuasive. He could be irresistable. I somehow was finally able to stay away from him for long periods of time. He told me that he would never stop trying to be with me. The only way would be if he couldn't find me anywhere.

෨෨

Since my two girls have grown into the wonderful caring persons they are, I have become much stronger. I have my best friends and I'm not so frightened all the time. I have at least achieved that much. Now I have the best support group ever. My girls are grown. They are my two best friends. I don't feel so helpless. I also feel less lonely than ever. I see my daughters and grandchildren every day. I am so lucky.

෨෨

I feel like I made some wrong choices, but on the other hand, I don't know that I had so many choices or that I was in an emotional or knowledgeable enough state to make wise choices. Now I am, but a lot of years have passed since then.

෨෨

Back then, I was just surviving and nothing more. Now I know myself better and I realize that I am strong, smart and determined and will live my life the way I feel is best for me. I don't live what would be considered a conventional life style. I have firm beliefs. I'm a vegetarian (mostly Vegan). I keep cruelty out of my life as best I can. I remove myself from situations that interfere with the flow of my inner peace. I need quiet time–time for contemplation and studying everything (ie. life, people, nature and religions).

❧

I've never found a religion that fits my profile better or even as well as my own way of life.

❧

I think Jamie Fox portrayed Ray better than anyone else could have–other than Ray himself. I knew Ray really well and I was drawn into Jamie's performance. I saw no white woman in the movie "Ray" which featured Ray's life until 1979. I'm here to tell you that he met one who was in his life until 1997 - Me!

❧

My kids suffered the sting of racism in grade school, but being half Mexican, they got a worse blow from a neighbor who said, "Go to your end of the street you little Mexican Nigger Lovers." That was said by a little girl's family and that girl used to ride to and from school every day with me.

❧

I see so much self indulgence in people. People think nothing of killing an innocent animal so they can eat their flesh or, the worse self indulgency, wear their skin. They tell me about God...please! To not care about the pain or discomfort of any creature is beyond me. I simply can't comprehend it and never could! I never will.

❧

Ray said in Rolling Stone magazine "I hurt some musicians. Tell them Brother Ray loves them." Ray also hurt a lot of women and I didn't see that mentioned. As for me, he always was saying he was sorry, but I could never, ever get past that 1969 trip to Los Angeles and nearly thirty years later, as kind, sweet and gentle as he was to me, I never got over it and he never got it fixed. When I allow myself to think about that part of my life, tears still sting my eyes.

۶∽ى

I wanted a conventional relationship. Ray couldn't give it to me. My relationship with him was truly *The Agony and The Ecstasy.* I was surrounded by the rapture of being with Ray only to be dropped into an emotional anguish that seemed unbearable. The way I survived it was to do what he taught me to do–"When things bother you, babe, change the channel. Turn it off." He came to regret telling me that, because that's exactly what I did.

۶∽ى

When he would leave me, I felt his aura all around me. I felt as though a cloud surrounded me with his aroma and feather-like touches. Ray had more self control than anyone I have ever known–about everything. His eating, drinking, smoking–even his lovemaking–he could stop making love in mid stream if he wanted to prolong a magical moment, whispering "Let's make it last, baby. Let's savor every moment." I would whisper, "Okay, sweetheart."

Mitzi and Lisa's Thoughts

(Lisa) Sitting on the bed watching TV while Ray was sleeping in his white muscle shirt and boxer shorts.

(Mitzi) Standing in front of the TV waving my arms around, checking if he could see me.

(Lisa and Mitzi) Him calling and saying, "Who's this, Lisa or Mitzi?" and we'd say, "Hi, Ray."

(Lisa) Mom calling Ray when I lived in California to see if my roommates and I could come to his show. Ray called me back and one of my roommates answered and was freaked out that Ray Charles had called our condo.

(Lisa) Going to the concert as Ray's guest and being so proud and feeling so special.

(Lisa) Being invited onto the bus so that my friends could meet him. It was so sweet of Ray to do that for me. And again, my friends were so knocked out that they got to meet Ray Charles. We were in our mid twenties. It was 1992.

(Mitzi) Playing piano for Ray and him loving it and being so proud of us when we were young.

(Lisa and Mitzi) Singing Christmas songs and other songs with all our friends around while Ray played the piano.

꿍

(Lisa) Going to Red Lobster for dinner with Don, Colleen, Mitzi, Mom and Ray. I ordered oysters rockefeller and I gagged. I could not eat that. So Ray let me order something else. (Mitzi got popcorn shrimp.)

꿍

(Mitzi) At the Chinese restaurant, the four of us having dinner when a lady came over and asked, "Are you Ray Charles?" She left and came back with her little girl and asked if she could have Ray's autograph. Mom said, "No, he doesn't sign autographs." The lady asked some more questions and finally Ray said, "Look 'ma'am. We're just trying to have our dinner."

꿍

(Lisa and Mitzi) When we would be telling him what we did in school and he'd say, "Ahh, that's sweet."

꿍

(Lisa) When mom called Ray and he didn't understand my number. Mom called him upset because he hadn't returned my call. Ray called her and said, "Marci, you called out here raisin' hell. I didn't understand Lisa's number when you called. I was going to call you and get it, but you didn't give me time. Mom apologized and he called me.

꿍

(Lisa and Mitzi)
Picking him up at the airport.
Always kissing him hello and goodbye.
The smell of his cologne.
Him shifting the gears in the VW while mom drove.
Mom yelling at Ray on the phone.
Mom being sad.

Postscript

This book is my gift to you–my precious Lisa and Mitzi. I'm sitting in my cozy little house in Kirkwood, Missouri, where I have lived for the past thirty-eight years, where you two spent your childhoods and teenaged years, and where you are still frequent visitors along with my grandchildren, and where Ray spent twenty-six of his nearly thirty years with us.

I wander through my small house and everywhere I look, I see and hear wonderful memories that are filed in my mental archives forever. No amount of money can buy those precious thoughts.

I hear the tinkling of piano keys and the laughter of you, Lisa and Mitzi, and your friends, surrounding Ray downstairs at the old upright piano.

I hear the laughter of you and your friends and the splashing of water from our above-ground pool in the backyard.

I see Ray coming in the back door with his garment bag and hanging it in the closet, then putting his "kit" in the bathroom.

I hear the crash of the car into the garage when you Lisa, at age 16, let your 14-year-old sister drive.

So many memories...

I know this is the only place on Earth that I could have written this book. It's titled *Ray and Me*, but it is really *Ray and Us*. There are so many reminders of our lives together.

Writing this book has helped me get through the sadness of Ray's death–and it has opened my heart to treasure troves of future exciting adventures with you two, Peyton, Tristin, Chase, Mia, Josh and Tom, my wonderful family.

I Love You All,
Mom